Bare Hand Crafting

Two Hands - No Needles!
Crochet * 3D Knitting * Embroidery

Bare Hand Knitting Book II

Bare Hand Crafting

Two Hands - No Needles!
Crochet * 3D Knitting * Embroidery

Bare Hand Knitting Book II

by
Aleshanee Akin

Illustrations by Elizabeth Auer

Printed with support from the Waldorf Curriculum Fund

Published by:
Waldorf Publications at the
Research Institute for Waldorf Education
351 Fairview Avenue, Suite 625
Hudson, NY 12534

Title: *Bare Hand Crafting: Two Hands – No Needles!*
   Bare Hand Knitting Book II
Author: Aleshanee Akin
Illustrator: Elizabeth Auer
Copy editor: Patrice O'Neill Maynard
Proofreader: Ruth Riegel
Layout: Ann Erwin

Copyright © 2020 Waldorf Publications
ISBN # 978-1-943582-28-0

Table of Contents

Introduction 7

chapter 1
Barehand Crafting Curriculum Year by Year 9

Order for Introducing Techniques
Stitch Stories

chapter 2
From Sheep to Skein 19

An Overview of Spinning
Cleaning the Wool
Carding the Wool
Spinning
Plying

chapter 3
Nature-friendly Dyeing 37

Mordants
Solar Dyeing Project
Preparing the Dyestuff
Cultures and Their Colors

chapter 4
Getting Started with Intermediate Barehand Knitting 47

Geography of the Hand
Pinches
Measurements
Yarn
Geography of the Work
Choosing Our Materials
Techniques
Terms

Chapter Review

chapter 5
Finger Crochet 55

The Tail-tugger Slipknot
Crochet without a Hook
Creating an Autumn Scarf
Circular Crochet
Crocheting a Hat

Vocabulary Review

Crochet Polystitches

Projects
Making a Doll Blanket
Making a Trivet
Making a Light Shoulder Bag

Table of Contents

chapter 6
Rooted Stitches 85

- Casting On and Casting Off for Barehand Knitting
- Casting on
- Casting off
- Keywords Reminder
- Variations

Chapter Review

chapter 7
Tunnel Knitting 99

- Creating a Scrunchy with Two-digit Tunnel
- Ending the Work
- A Project with a Tunnel
- Four-digit Tunnel: Creating a Recorder Case
- Variations

Chapter Review

chapter 8
The Switchback 131

- About Barehand Switchback
- Creating a Wide Winter Scarf
- Keywords Reminder for the Switchback Cast-on
- Keywords Reminder for the Switchback Cast-off
- Full Block and Let Dry
- Setting Your Work Aside
- Resuming Work
- Practice Project: Doll's Vest

Chapter Review

chapter 9
Tapering 153

- Widen and Narrow the Fabric
- Creating a Gnome Hat
- Expanding the Width of the Fabric
- Narrowing the Width of the Fabric
- Pattern for Making Barehand Indoor Ball

Chapter Review

chapter 10
Spruce. 169

- Sprucing It Up!
- Keywords Reminder
- Prepare for Stitching
- Sewing Your Viking Pouch
- Grafting Variations

Chapter Review

chapter 11
Barehand Embroidery 187

- Decorative Stitching
- Floater Stitch
- Cling Stitch
- Continue Stitching
- Castle Stitch

Chapter Review

Looking Ahead 198

Acknowledgments 199

Introduction

To say that learning barehand knitting gives us tools might be an oxymoron; yet this skill gives us not external but internal tools that help us cope with our increasingly alienating technology-driven world. Our ancestors, for untold millennia, used their hands to carve and shape and spin and weave and craft their daily survival, and it is now understood through recent scientific brain research that it is, in fact, the use of the hands that drives the development of the brain, more than the other way around. These proclivities are still there, waiting in the very architecture of our minds, to be used again, and to be used to their fullest. In their use we find satisfaction, relaxation, and creative expression—especially as the productive results are a physical expression of our love for, and bonding with, our families. When we engage in hand crafts we are walking the well-worn paths laid down by our ancestors, just as indigenous people do every day in ancient cultures all around the world.

Amaterasu is the Japanese archetype goddess of the sun, who weaves or knits the rays of sunlight together, bringing light from out of darkness. The mythology revolves around the theme of transformation. There was a "terrible violation in her secret weaving hall," when her weaving companion is "pierced through by the Shuttle of a Loom and killed." Only after a prolonged isolation in a cave does the figure of Amaterasu crack open the door only to discover the reflection of her own rays. With her very being she penetrates the darkness to "weave the rays of sunlight together," returning joy to a world that had been cast into darkness.

In the Japanese language the word for *knitting* and *weaving* are one and the same. I love to imagine that Amaterasu was doing some hand knitting

yubiami while in her dark and isolated cave, transforming this into a time of healing.

The rebirth or resurrection theme that echoes in this mythology correlates with difficult journeys that may be encountered in life.

When my older daughter was trapped in the snares of the mental health industry, knitting with her hands was as medicine to the mind. It is faith that has sustained us through the darkest of times.

When we relax at home, snug in front of a fire, and knit our dreams from natural wool with our bare hands, we are walking the paths of our ancestors. It is a good place to walk.

chapter one

Barehand Crafting
Curriculum Year by Year

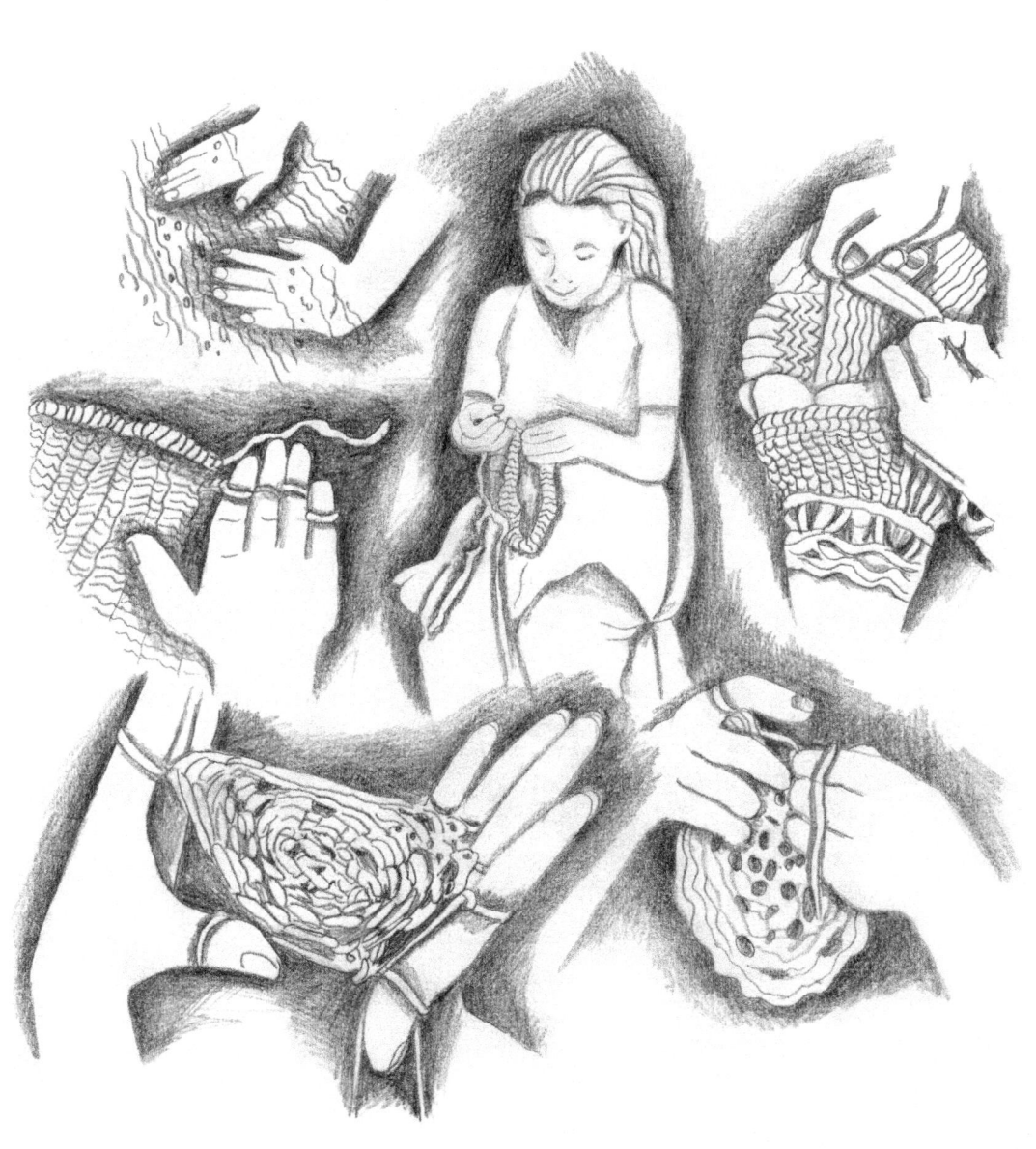

chapter one

Order for Introducing Techniques

For children, important developmental milestones have been taken into consideration for the age-appropriate introduction of techniques. These recommendations are outlined below. You might think of this as a guide map to a whole new exciting world that has, all along, been hiding in plain sight—literally, at our fingertips.

For all ages it is recommended to first learn a new technique with your dominant hand in the active role, before applying it to two hands. Much of what is learned can be accomplished while sitting, standing, or even during a walk in nature. Calming music also has the potential to enhance the therapeutic value of this art form.

Age recommendations

Techniques for children up to the age of 7 and above are the main focus of *Bare Hand Knitting* Book I. The book you are holding now is designed for children in the elementary grades and beyond.

For ages 9 and up:
Tail-tugger slipknot
Barehand crochet
Rooted stitches
Casting on and casting off

For ages 10 and up:
Spruce knitting
Barehand embroidery
Barehand fiber grafting
The Tunnel technique

Barehand combinations

Once barehand techniques are learned, they become second nature. The practice projects in this book are generally on the smaller side for learning purposes. However, these methods can be applied to projects of any size. The various techniques can also be combined to create more elaborate and interesting patterns.

Childhood development and handwork

The advanced barehand curriculum has been designed to broaden the spectrum of traditional handwork for the grades. In certain situations a barehand method may be helpful as a preparation for a specific tool-based method. It may also serve as a happy alternative for those with challenges that make the use of needles problematic. These methods are not intended to be substitutes for traditional methods but, on the contrary, an enhancement. I myself came to love all traditional handwork through this portal of discovery.

Barehand Crafting Curriculum Year by Year

From the perspective of childhood development, the young mind needs far more handwork and crafts early on. This need is especially clear in light of the challenges of modern life. Even in Waldorf schools, where handwork classes are generally brought in for two periods a week, additional classes could be added to focus solely on methods that bring the hands into direct contact with the medium. Yarn and wool, as well as clay and wood, can be sculpted using very few basic tools. The development of the opposition pinch of the Thumb and Index fingers, as well as the precision pinches of the Thumb and the other fingers—all of which are used for barehand knitting—is intrinsic to awakening the capacity for human thought. Such work develops the mind and, with the introduction of this curriculum, this process will unfold in new and transformative ways, nurturing the inner architect.

Contemporary brain research has illuminated the reality that the full myelination of the neurons in the brain, another way of saying completely developed brain maturity, is stimulated by manipulation of the hands and crossing the midline with hands and arms. This myelination allows for smooth communication among all parts of the brain, fostering clear and quick formation of judgments.

An overview of handwork lessons as they relate to the period of early childhood was given in *Bare Hand Knitting* Book I. That book goes up to the time of the nine-year-old change; with this book we pick up at this same significant moment in a child's development.

Eight going on nine

The departure from early childhood carries with it some predictable challenges. Rudolf Steiner, who developed the curriculum for the first Waldorf School, referred to this time as the nine-year-old change. A key to supporting this transition is to bring activities that foster a sense of security and belonging in the world. Giving children basic tools and fundamental skills for life helps them to feel empowered and competent, making the adjustment to their new consciousness at this age less difficult. Skills engender enthusiasm for projects.

chapter one

A full third-grade curriculum might include farming, cooking, and traditional artisan crafts including fiber arts. In the Waldorf curriculum, hands-on projects involving native structures and shelter-building skills are part of the year.

The timing of this has to do with a relationship between the evolutionary development of human consciousness and the stages of child development that recapitulate this ancient journey in mysterious ways. To relive an experience of past epochs through the mythologies, handcrafts, and music of age-old cultures is to walk the stepping-stones toward the future evolution of humanity. Such a foundation supports a child along his or her own path of unfolding as an individual, and the acquisition of such skills assists as they cross great milestones along this passage into adulthood.

Barehand knitting component

To begin this journey, a foundation in handwork skills is paramount. The age-old activities of wet-felting, spinning, weaving, sewing, and plant-dyeing make up an important part of a curriculum that boldly meets a student through the ninth year of life.

Very basic methods for cleaning, combing, and spinning wool (Chapter 2), along with some tips for environmentally friendly plant-dyeing techniques (Chapter 4) are part of the curriculum laid out here. You do not need expensive tools or processed chemicals to have these experiences. These earliest technologies are efficient and are still in use in many cultural pockets. Many are even making a comeback among professional artisans in search of certain artistic achievements.

The basic barehand knitting and whip-stitching techniques introduced in *Bare Hand Knitting* Book I are expanded with the technique for the rooted cast-on and cast-off stitches (Chapter 6). The *tail-tugger slipknot* (Chapter 5) is recommended for this age group in preparation for barehand crochet toward the end of the ninth year.

Nine going on ten

Once the ninth birthday passes and the tenth year of life has begun, there begins for the child a time of striving for a sense of belonging and to gain a sense of where he or she stands within the larger scheme of things. Connecting with one's locality, both geographically and culturally, is an important part of this process.

By age 10, dominance—right- or left-handedness—should already be well established and there will not likely be a question as to whether a child is one or the other. At this point, students are internally ready to take on more complicated handcrafts. A developmentally appropriate curriculum will include traditional embroidery and cross-stitch, which develop fine-motor skills. The small yet focused movements of the hand and eye repeatedly cross through the vertical midline, helping to break down the midline barrier between the left and right hemispheres of the brain and prompting the all-important myelination. It is for this

reason that a special-lesson teacher, working with hemisphere-integrating therapies, is sometimes needed as a support for children at this stage of development.

For this age group, it is very relevant for the teacher to bring into the classroom traditional crafts from the historical and existing cultures of the local area. Some examples would be very basic basket weaving and beading. This is also a time when it might be necessary to emphasize slowing down to do careful and meticulous work, removing one's own mistakes and redoing the work when called for.

Medium motor skills development

The barehand techniques develop *medium motor skills*. The stretch to doing fine needlework, such as traditional embroidery recommended for this age, can be a big one for some late bloomers. Barehand techniques for this age group are beneficial for children who need a safe and sturdy bridge to help them cross over from gross to fine motor skill development. Gross motor skills bring the *will forces* into the limbs and body, whereas fine motor skills bring the will forces right in through the fingertips from where the will then moves into the *head realm*. Medium motor skills development is midway between gross and fine motor skills, and hands-on felting and sculpting projects support this development.

Barehand component

Barehand skills have the potential to connect the will to the region of the heart. What this world needs today are more heart forces, and through handwork we find a direct path for getting us there!

The Spruce technique (Chapter 10), tunnel knitting on one hand (Chapter 7), and barehand embroidery (which is not the same as traditional embroidery but develops many similar skills) (Chapter 11) are unique in that they develop medium motor movements.

You may also have already noticed that children in their tenth year of life love puzzles, magic tricks, riddles, treasure hunts, and the like. Handwork methods for this age group, and especially with the barehand methods recommended here, involve many elements that meet this stage of development.

Ten going on eleven

This is an age that is widely known as the golden age of youth, or the heart of childhood. This moment in time, which carries inner balance through the harmonizing of the rhythmic system, is also outwardly expressed in the body as well. During the twelfth year of life the bodily proportions are that of a full-grown adult. This is a fleeting moment of harmony and balance when the breathing and heartbeat attain the proportions of adulthood. This harmonious quality is reflected in artistic accomplishments of the students. Exposure early in life to works of art and to the harmonies of music, as well as beauty of nature, develops an esthetic sense that now begins to surface.

As the inner artist unfolds, it is important to continue to create opportunities for children to explore various artistic media, including the fiber arts. If you have ever witnessed a classroom full of 11-year-olds engaged in an art project, you may have sensed the quiet enthusiasm or experienced the harmonious quality reflected in the work that marks this "golden age" of childhood.

A child-development-sensitive handwork curriculum for this age group will include more complicated and time-consuming projects such as knitting socks. This involves circular rows and requires the use of five knitting needles. In addition to socks, students of this age are often taught to knit hats. The work is no longer just flat and two-dimensional. The child's thinking begins to open up and to take in something of the periphery and the surrounding world.

Presenting a variety of color choices can stimulate quality-related assessments by the students, who must then exercise discernment to develop esthetics. Some handwork teachers feel that, for this age group, such lessons should for this reason include an opportunity for choosing from both plant-dyed and acrylic-dyed fibers.

Barehand knitting component

The Switchback (Chapter 8) and the Tunnel (Chapter 7) are appropriate for this age group. Tapering (Chapter 9) allows the students to knit a perfect ball at a time when human development recapitulates the consciousness of the Ancient Greeks, who were able to perceive the Earth as a Sphere.

Bilateral techniques (techniques for two hands) and small group Social Knitting are more advanced and can begin to be introduced to this age group toward the end of this year. However, these techniques, among others that are more advanced and are suitable for those aged twelve years and up, can be affirmed through a periodic journal for "Barehand Knitting for Enthusiasts."

Projects for the above-mentioned techniques are necessarily more involved and time consuming than previous ones. As the complexity of the barehand methods increases, so can the teacher's growing awareness of its potential therapeutic value.

A teacher's aid

In the next chapter you will learn steps for the practical art of processing wool and spinning it into yard, but here we take a little detour for handwork teachers to recall one of the best classroom tools of all: the power of imagination.

Stitch Stories

Stitch Stories were created to help knitters remember the sequence for a given set of instructions. The visual images they invoke and the rhythmic component of rhyme can be a real support to the learning process for children and adults alike. Indigenous cultures rely heavily upon such learning aids. Like nursery rhymes of old, they are both useful for enhancing the learning process and adding to the joy of the learning process.

While the Stitch Stories do have a childlike feel to them, they are derived from the actual movements of our fingers and the yarn and are meant to be more useful than entertaining. As a fourth grade teacher I found it helpful to tie all of the little stories together and give them context and meaning in a larger story.

As you make your way through the chapters, you will find more condensed rhymes derived from these stories for helping to learn the various techniques.

Like the techniques themselves, the Stitch Stories found here are the original work of this author. Some of the rhymes were based on my stories and were composed by my father.

The Land of Hand

The Mysterious Land of Hand is filled with as honest and hardworking folks as you might ever hope to find. It is filled with Nature's glory, including many animals of the Americas such as sea animals and rare and exotic birds like the oropendola. If you are lucky, you might meet a gnome or a fairy or even catch a glimpse of a mermaid.

Below you will find examples of the background stories from which the Stitch Stories have been distilled. Against the backdrop of The Land of Hand, all of the *Bare Hand Knitting* stories brought by a teacher of hand crafts—whether from this book or drawn up from your own image correlations—can be strung together into a longer continuous story that is built upon from one year to the next. In this same way, the skills for barehand methods build one upon the other, over time. Stitch Stories can be introduced in early childhood, perhaps with puppet shows, just to plant seeds that can be replaced later in the grades with age-appropriate instructions.

The Oropendola's Nest

(Story for the Tail-Tugger Slipknot)

Along both shores of the large strip of open sea, between Loomland and Shuttleland, are where the turtles live and lay their eggs. Beyond that is a wet, subtropical forest, home to many exotic birds, not the least fascinating of which are the oropendolas.

There is a mama bird, an oropendola, and her long oval nest hangs down from a tall tree. Baby Bird is hungry for his next meal. It sticks out its beak and lets out a loud chirp until its mother hears it and swoops down from the sky.

Mama Oropendola spots a worm and soars down to get it. Poking her beak up into what appears to be a hollow tree, she pulls the worm till it slides from a twig. But something pulls back so Mama Bird has to realize that the hollow tree is actually an old crocodile and the hole is, in fact, its mouth. Well, Mr. Crocodile is not about to part with his tongue so he pulls right back and Mama Bird flies away to find a real lunch for her young.

For the rhyme about the Oropendola, see Chapter 5, page 56, on Finger Crochet.

The Cozy Woodchucks

(Story for Rooted Cast-on and Leaping Cast-off)

On the grassy meadows of Palm, where the buffalo grass grows, lives a family of woodchucks. When the winter weather comes, they put on a winter coat allowing the young woodchuck pups to play outdoors as long as possible before they must withdraw deep into their holes to wait out the coldest frosts.

For casting on

One chilly autumn day, Mother Woodchuck feels that winter is drawing near. Her children have emerged from the nursery chamber ready to go out to frolic and snack on buffalo grass. Mother puts on her sweater and pokes her head up out of

chapter one

their hole, feeling a chilly wind against her neck. She reaches down to get her scarf and pulls it on. Just then, Brother Woodchuck pushes up through the same burrow without any winter wear. He is hoping to get out of having to dress warmly. Just then, a cold wind blows past him from behind. He ducks down for his sweater and pulls it on. But he still feels a chilly wind blowing around his neck. He ducks back again to retrieve his scarf and pulls it down over his head.

Sister pushes up through the same burrow that brother is looking out from. She too feels a cold wind blowing from behind. She reaches to retrieve her sweater and pulls it down over her head. She ducks to retrieve her warm scarf and pulls it down over her head also.

Baby Woodchuck follows after her siblings. She pushes up through the same burrow that her big sister is looking out from. She does not want to put on winter clothing, but then she too feels a cold wind blowing from behind. Now she allows herself to be dressed in a sweater and a scarf. And so, the woodchuck family is now dressed in their winter wear, and so go out to feed on buffalo grass and play.

For the rhyme about the Cozy Woodchucks, see Chapter 6, page 86, on Rooted Stitches.

Squirrelly Cast-off

Up in the trees, not so far from the woodchuck-filled meadows, that same chilly autumn wind that inspired the woodchuck family to put on their winter layers was letting the flying squirrels know that it is time to get very busy packing away nuts for the winter.

The chilly wind wakes the flying squirrel. He rouses himself to go in search of nuts for storing, and to spread the word that autumn is in the air.

Leaping up over the top of the tree and landing on the back side, he called out, "Autumn is here!"

The next flying squirrel hears him and hurries to the top of the tree, with the same good intentions of finding nuts and spreading the news to his neighbor. He hurls himself, flying into the air, limbs fully spread, air-pockets full, to land on the neighboring tree.

But, "Oops!" In his excitement he landed right upon a neighboring squirrel.

The neighboring squirrel was startled and slipped out from underneath him and scrambled to the back side of the tree.

Meanwhile, that chilly autumn wind blows past again, reminding the squirrel of his duty to find nuts and spread the news.

Leaping up over the top of the tree, and, landing on the back side, he called out, "Autumn is here !"

The next flying squirrel hears him and hurried to the top of the tree, with the same good intentions of finding nuts and spreading the news to his neighbor. He hurls himself, flying into the air, limbs fully spread, air-pockets full.

But, "Oops!" He lands on the neighboring tree, right upon a resting squirrel. The neighboring squirrel is startled and slips out from underneath him and scrambles to the back side of the tree.

Meanwhile, the chilly autumn wind begins to blow past again, reminding the squirrel of his duty to find nuts and spread the news. Now that the whole neighborhood has been alerted, the little gossips are able to take a rest before a busy day of nut gathering ahead.

For the rhyme about The Flying Squirrels, for this technique, see Chapter 6, page 91, on Rooted Stitches.

Coyote Comes to Fox's Aid

(Story for the Switchback method)

It is now evening and the neighboring sheep are just leaping the fence to safety for the night. Fox is at it again. The chicken eggs are nice, but oh how he would love to get one of the farmer's nice big duck eggs. But Farmer Anthony is no fool. He has installed a heavier hatch door, with a double rope handle, on the Duck's nest boxes. Fox waits till it's dark and tugs on the rope handle, but the trap door closes before he can slip in. He tries several times and nearly gives it up when he hatches a whole new plan. He decides to let old brother Coyote in on his little thieving venture. Old Fox was tired of doing all the lifting work, anyway. Fox whispers his plan into Coyote's ear, and clever Coyote agrees.

Knitting rows

The two schemers slip past the front of the henhouse and right up to the thick hatch door. Coyote takes the double rope handle in his wide strong jaw and tugs up and back. Ever so quietly, Fox brings an egg back up. Like clockwork, Coyote lets the trap door close down again, and the first egg goes to Fox. They move over to the next hatch door and continue their thievery.

And the story goes on: Coyote and Fox are very pleased with themselves. Fox smoothes out his long fluffy tail, Coyote licks his lips, and each evening when the sun has set the two resume business together.

So far, all has gone well for both the Fox and the Coyote, but if you do business for too long with the fox or the coyote you are liable to be tricked out of something, or outfoxed, as Farmer Anthony has been.

Casting off the knitting

Although Fox and Coyote are quite careful to take only one egg from each egg-box, every night, eventually Farmer Anthony is on to them and puts an end to their scheme by installing a latch lock. *And so the story goes…*

For the rhyme about this technique, see Chapter 8, page 132, on the Switchback method.

chapter one

Take creative license

While not every background story is shared here, stories can be derived from the rhymes in each chapter. Some of the poems are longer than others and need not be memorized. The hope is that the imagery gives the student an imaginative picture to help remember the process while learning a technique.

If poetry is not the way you want to bring the story, keep in mind that there are other approaches. For example, I recently brought a story for finger knitting a chain to an early childhood classroom. It was first depicted in a puppet show. On the very next day, when the technique was introduced, it was picked up so quickly it seemed as if the children already knew it. You may find it interesting to derive a background story from the imagery in the poem. Otherwise, you are encouraged to come up with themes that work well for you and your group. If one is working with the same group of children from one year to the next, it can be nice to have a single background story with which to tie all the stories together.

chapter two
From Sheep to Skein

chapter two

An Overview of Spinning

The original ancient activities of twining and spinning fibers to produce cordage and yarn are still with us today. From the untraceable moments when the first drop spindles were created, nothing has really changed for drop-spinners save for the beautiful enhancements found in later spindles of carved wood, clay and metal.

A drop spindle is held suspended in the air by the twisting fibers that follow the motion of the spindle. The spindle's spinning action increases the tension already imparted by gravity. The thin group of fibers, rather than breaking, increase in strength as they are twisted into yarn. Untwisted fibers can be broken one-by-one, but when twisted together, their strength is combined. It is no wonder that the act of spinning is considered by ancient cultures to be a spiritualizing activity for the world. Through the spiraling movement, rhythm and form are born into the materials. Both the process and the product are beautiful. The art does take some practice to master but, with good guidance, can be accomplished with surprisingly little training. A true respect for the ancient art of spinning is reflected in the craftsmanship that can be seen in so many of the drop spindles found in museums and in the mythological archetypes attributed to the art of spinning in ancient civilizations. What is profoundly striking is how little the technology needed to change over the course of many thousands of years. The first and most dramatic alteration to spinning technique did not take place until a very recent moment in history in Western cultures: the sixteenth century with the introduction of the spinning wheel.

Flax has been cultivated for its remarkable fiber for at least five millennia. The fabric it makes is linen. The spinning and weaving of linen is depicted on wall paintings of ancient Egypt. It was processed, spun, dyed, woven, and sewn by hand. As early as 3000 BC, linen was processed into fine white fabric (540 threads to the inch—finer than anything woven today).

Artistic depictions of cheerful women walking together, drop spindles in hand, happily socializing amidst the beauty of nature, date all the way back to Ancient Greece. Drop spindles have the advantage of being small and light and can be brought along anywhere. At the California Wool and Fiber Festival held in Boonville, California, each fall, there is a Spinning Competition, and women come from far and wide with their vast experience and fancy spinning wheels. But every year that I attended, the winner was a Navajo elder who used a traditional wooden floor spindle. She would draft the wool with her hands while simultaneously spinning her long wooden stick off from her thigh as the bottom of it spun against the bare floor. No one could beat her speed and the quality of the yarn she produced.

I myself am still a student of spinning and have been blessed with some extraordinary teachers over the years at the Fiber Craft Studio in Spring Valley, New York. The approach I share here comes mainly from their teachings; it is out of my love for accessible hands-on methods that I have chosen this particular approach.

As we come to appreciate the beauty of the processes involved in sustainable and child-friendly methods of cloth-making, alongside the beauty of the product, we will be capable of fully appreciating the work of our ancestors. Below is a basic description of how to spin. This step-by-step process, if followed and practiced, can lead you right through the door from cloth-consumer to weaver and artisan.

In this chapter, you will learn how to create wool yarn from a raw fleece using a rock and stick.

Cleaning the Wool

In ancient times, sheep would molt each spring, with clumps of wool snagging on bushes, where the first fiber-crafters gathered it up. Few breeds of molting sheep remain. Today, most sheep—whether raised for wool or meat—must be shorn. Much of this wool is not considered to be worth the trouble of processing and is simply discarded. If you contact farmers who raise sheep, they will often give the fleece away for free or for very little. Alternatively, you can buy wool roving, which is wool that is ready for spinning—but it can sometimes be fairly costly. Contact your local Fiber Shed for helpful information. A farm trip for fleece, should there be one in your area, can be a great educational outing for children.

To begin with, you will need to obtain a raw fleece. The fleece of a Jacob sheep is nice because the wool comes in several colors and is a good length for spinning. If it is possible to obtain an entire fleece, one might notice how, within a single fleece there are areas of fleece with varying degrees of coarseness or fineness, long or short fibers, matted or clean fibers. The fibers may have more or less lanolin, which is the rich, naturally occurring oil in sheep's wool, and also more or less dirt incorporated into the fleece, depending on the type of terrain where the sheep live and whether or not they had been dressed in a protective fabric coat.

The Navajo, who have been left with few resources, spin their wool in the raw (in the unwashed form) and later let the river take away the dirt from the skeins that are submerged in it. For our purposes, we will use the common practice of washing the wool prior to spinning it, included in the steps of our instructions.

Process the wool

Before we start twisting the fibers, we will pre-draft them. This is done prior to washing the wool.

Making wool clouds

Amazingly, it turns out to be quite efficient to process raw fleece one little handful at a time. Take up a small clump of fleece and open it up into a cloud form. Get the feel of the sticky lanolin on your fingers. (When rubbed in, it will make your fingers soft.) Remove any leaves, grasses, or twigs from your fibers in preparation for soaking and washing. These tell the story of where the sheep lives and roams. Loosen the tips that are stuck together.

chapter two

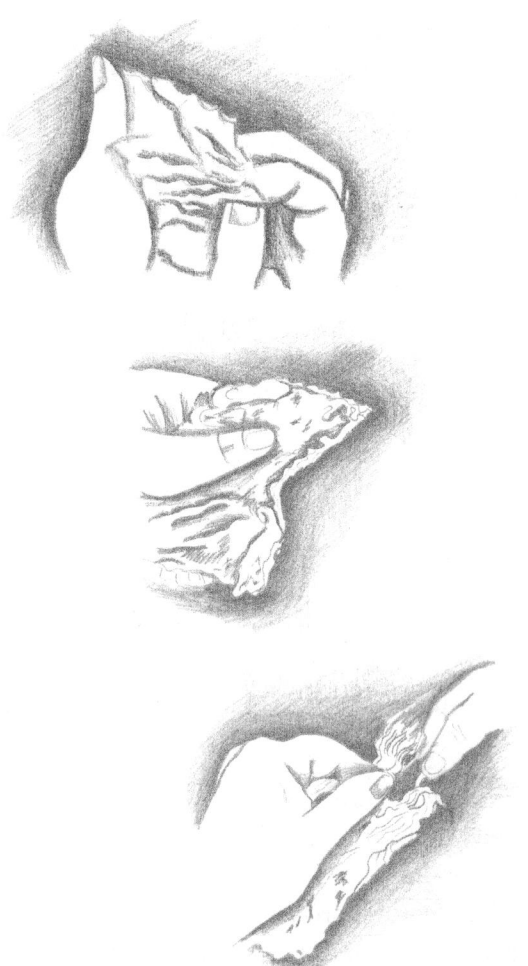

You may want to place a towel on your lap to catch any debris. This process of separating the fibers is called pre-drafting as it gets the fleece a step closer to actual drafting, or spreading and thinning the roving (fleece) with the fingertips as you spin.

Continue until you have a good-sized pile of wool—at least half-a-bucket—for washing.

Classroom tip

Relaxing activities such as storytelling and singing can accompany this process. An old folk song called "Clouds" is a nice accompaniment (referring to white puffy clouds in a blue sky).

The approach laid out below is child-friendly and hands-on and is practiced with success by spinners and knitters.

Clouds

Christina Rossetti (1830–1894)   Folk Song

White sheep, white sheep, on a blue hill, When the wind stops you all stand still. When the wind blows you walk a-way slow. White sheep, white sheep, where do you go?

Washing the wool by hand

Preparing the wash water

Prepare four buckets of equal size—at least a few gallons each—and provide each with some sort of cover for keeping in the heat. Place them in a row and mostly fill each with hot water from the tap—about the temperature of a good hot bath, but not so hot it could scald. In the first and third buckets, add some regular bath soap. The second and last buckets are for rinsing. As you work, the water will slowly cool, but the idea is that they should all cool at the same rate, so that the wool will not be shocked going from one to the other.

Have a nice large towel or a drying screen ready near the last container of water.

Submerge the wool in the first bucket

Remove the lid from the first bucket, drop in the prepared wool-clouds, one handful at a time. You might need to push the fluffy clouds down into the water to submerge them, but do not stir or agitate. Your movements should be slow, deliberate, and sparing.

In *Bare Hand Knitting* Book I, the dynamics of felting were introduced. The same facts of the matter apply here. Remember that the very things that cause wool to felt are moisture, agitation, and temperature changes. Since it is necessary to clean the wool, exposing it to water is inevitable, but you want to avoid the other two felting factors, temperature change and movement, as much as possible so that we end up with fluffy clean roving rather than matted globs of felted fiber. Replace the lid and let the wool soak for 20 minutes.

Move to the second bucket

After 20 minutes, remove the lid from the now-dirty water of the first bucket and carefully lift out the wet fibers, one handful at a time, gently squeezing out the excess water, and dropping them into the second bucket. Replace the cover and let them soak for another 20 minutes.

Tease-out remaining dirty tips

By now any dirty tips of wool that were still stubbornly stuck together with lanolin, sweat, and dirt should have softened and can be gently separated out by your fingers as you transfer the fibers from the first to the second soaking tub.

Move to the third bucket

When the 20 minutes have passed, move the fibers to the third (again, soapy) bucket, gently squeezing them first so that the dirty water drains back into the second bucket. and let them soak for another 20 minutes. Do not agitate the wool.

Move to the last bucket

Finally, when the 20 minutes have passed, scoop up the fibers, gently squeeze out the liquid, and then drop them into the final rinse bucket. Soak in the fourth bucket a final 20 minutes. Alternatively, you can just take a handful of fibers from the third bucket and carefully dip it into the final rinse before you gently squeeze the water out and set the wool on a towel to dry. With each succeeding bucket, the water should get clearer.

Having a bit of soap residue left on the wool won't hurt it, and a final rinse with a dash of vinegar in it can just as easily be done once the wool has been spun into yarn. If the plan is to first dye the wool, just know that a bit of normal soap will not affect your dyeing process, at least not negatively.

Place onto drying towel

One handful at a time, and ever so gently, squeeze out the fibers and place them onto a towel or another clean surface for drying. Turn the fibers over once or twice during the next couple of hours and let dry overnight. The wool will now be clean and dry and ready for hand-carding.

To continue the process of transforming a raw fleece into wool roving, the fleece must now be carded. Altogether, the cleaning, washing, and rinsing of the prepared wool-clouds should take less than two hours, but the washed wool will need to dry overnight. Some fleeces are dirtier than others and may require an extra soaking cycle. Also, if you are planning on dyeing the wool, then the lanolin must be thoroughly removed. Fisherman's wool, on the other hand, is undyed and left lanolin-rich to protect against harsh weather. If you are washing wool with your students and cannot complete the process in one class, it is also okay to leave the fleece soaking in the water overnight. However, you will want to consider doing a cooler washing process or even-out the temperature between wash buckets when you start up again.

chapter two

Carding the Wool

Once washed and dried, next the wool will be carded. Some readers will be familiar with "carding boards," a pair of paddles embedded with a bristly surface of short, sharp needles. (They can be dangerously sharp for children.) As the wool is drawn between the carding boards, the fibers become aligned. Below we will learn an ingenious tool-free method that is actually preferred by some artisan spinners, as it gives them better control over the results and can be easier on the wrists than carding boards. Hand-carding is ergonomic and strengthens the wrists against carpal tunnel, which carding boards are known to exacerbate.

The hand-carding method

Take up a handful of washed-and-dried wool in the Loom Hand (non-dominant hand). The amount might be the size of an orange, or a croissant. Use your Shuttle Hand (dominant hand) to grasp a bit of wool near the end and tug it, then walk your fingers in toward the middle and tug again. Keep doing this with the object of pulling the fibers away from each other's tight embrace and straightening them. Finally, as you reach the middle, let the tuft in your Shuttle Hand pull

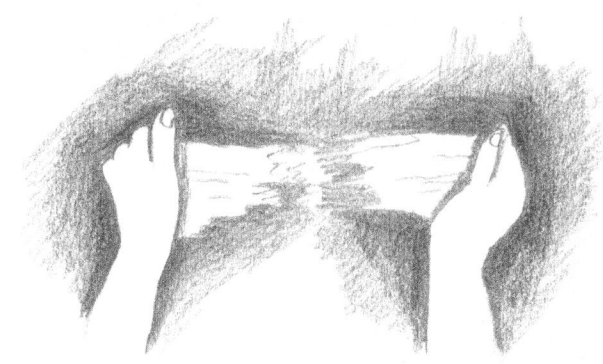

completely away from the other bunch. Then lay one tuft upon the other, keeping the fibers lined up in the same direction, and repeat the process. Do this roughly thirty times, always in the same direction. This handful of wool has now been hand-carded and thereby transformed into a "mini-batt" of wool.

The goal is to have the fibers in alignment with each other, so try to place them in the same direction each time you layer them up.

You are thus straightening, separating, and elongating the fibers so that they will end up lying smoothly in the same direction.

Creating a rolag

A *rolag* is the fluffy rolled-up spiral blanket of wool that is pulled from a carding board. It is from a rolag that a spinner pulls the fibers to be spun. Here's how to create rolags with our bare hands: Holding your hand-carded mini-batt in your Loom fist, pull at the fibers again with your Shuttle Hand in the same way the fibers were carded, only, instead of pulling the clump completely apart, just

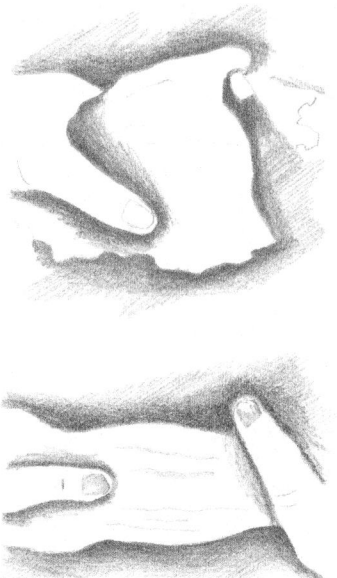

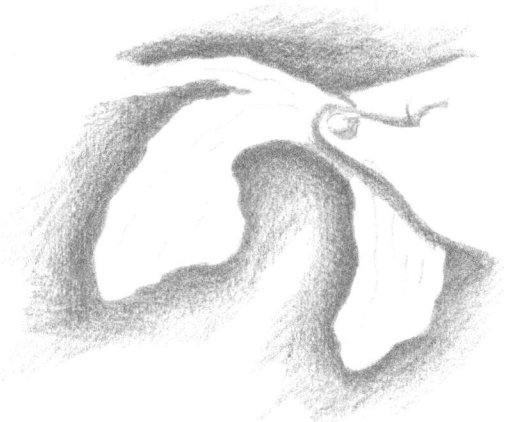

tease it out into a long strip (called roving) about three feet long. Roll it up and smooth any loose fibers into the rolag.

✱ You have now created a rolag for hand spinning.

Create rolags of all of your cleaned roving and place them in a basket. Your fibers are now ready for hand spinning.

Spinning

Dominance

For this segment we will sometimes use the designation dominant and non-dominant instead of applying the usual barehand knitting terms Shuttle and Loom for the right (dominant) and left (non-dominant) hands because spinning can be done using either hand but is very different from weaving or knitting work. The terms "clockwise" and "counterclockwise" also come in here because these directions must be to standard. The terms "right" and "left," meaning "dominant" and "non-dominant," will be used where needed.

Spinning: the stick method

We will warm up to the drop spindle by starting first with an even simpler technique, called stick spinning.

Find a stick

Find a nice straight stick with a twig coming off near one end for the hook. Sticks from a butterfly bush are great, as are those from an apple tree, but you can use any branch with a fairly straight tendency and at least one good crook from a twig

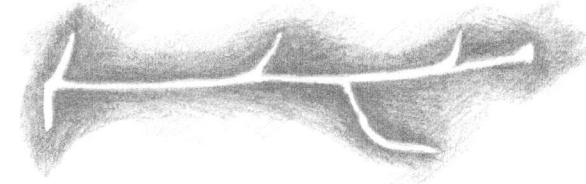

still attached near one nd. Remove any extra twigs and break off any extra unneeded length from the stick so that it begins with the hook and extends a foot or so from the point.

Roll and draft

Take up one of the rolags from your basket and hook the stick into a bit of fibers at the center tip at one end.

Hold the rolag in your non-dominant hand and roll the stick toward you from your knee to your upper thigh. (This way you will impart a normal Z-twist to the fibers. More on that below.)

As your dominant hand rolls toward you, twisting tensions into the fibers, the other hand supports the process by holding the rolag. Rather than grip the rolag in your fist, let most of it fall behind your hand while your Palm and Thumb cup into a loose passageway through which the fibers are channeled.

And as you release the fibers from the rolag little by little into the forming yarn, you will find it necessary to pause frequently to free-up the hand that is rolling the stick for helping with an important job: drafting the fibers. This entails opening, thinning and stretching the fibers in readiness for smooth spinning with the stick.

Identify the drafting triangle

The drafting area is the flattish triangular area, or delta, just under your fingers where the fibers are taut but not yet twisted into the yarn.

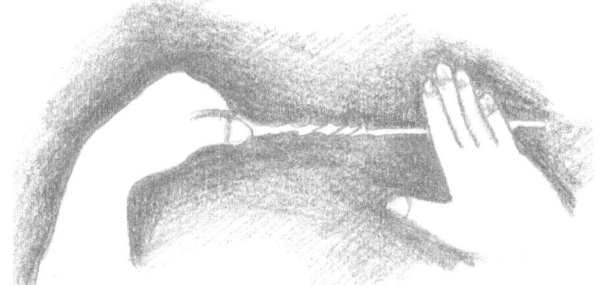

The action with your non-dominant hand is a little like making the universal hand-sign for money: your Thumb rubbing against Pointer and Middler, with the fiber *delta* passing between them, being rubbed. In this way the fibers are smoothed and flattened and lumps are worked out. Every once in a while you will need to use the bird-pinch of the hand with which you are rolling the stick to grip the apex of the delta to stop the twist from traveling into the fan of the delta, as your left hand stretches and thins the fibers feeding into it.

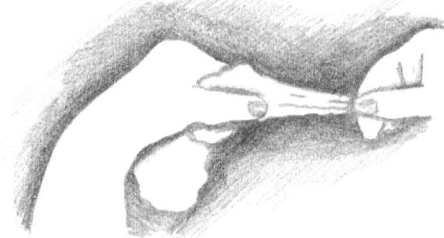

This action forms an elongated triangle, and as your right bird-pinch slowly releases its grip, the tension will feed right into the delta. Let go with your dominant hand and resume rolling the stick.

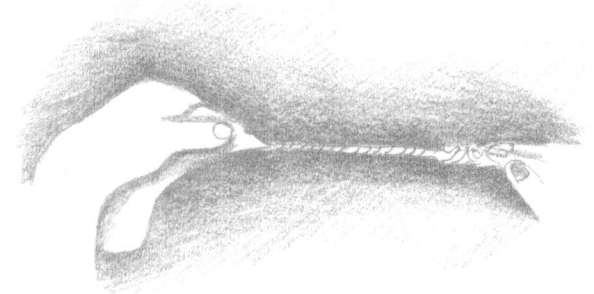

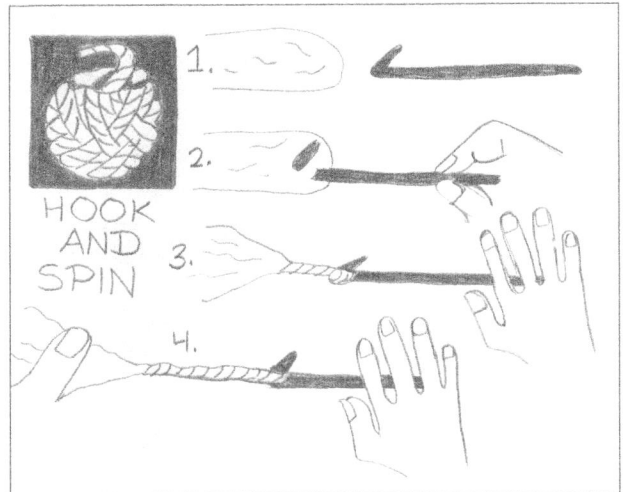

Feel the twist

Feel for when the tensions have reached your left-hand fingertips again. Then release by sliding that hand slowly back away from the point of the elongating triangle and watch as the twist feeds into the delta. When the drafted roving runs out, stop the tensions at the point of the delta with your dominant hand, bird-pinch again, and gradually slide back with the left hand, teasing out the wool feeding into the wide end of the delta.

It's rhythmic

Eventually you will find that there is a rhythmic pattern to the tensions building and releasing through the delta.

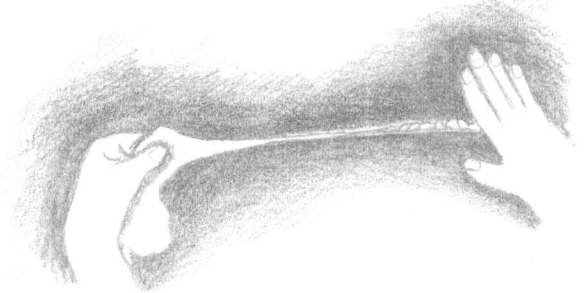

Wrap the yarn on the stick

As the yarn grows in length, wrap it around the stick itself, angling the yarn first toward the free end of the stitch, then angling it back toward the crook end.

Once the yarn only (not any of the loose roving) is wrapped around the stick, remove the previous yarn from the hook.

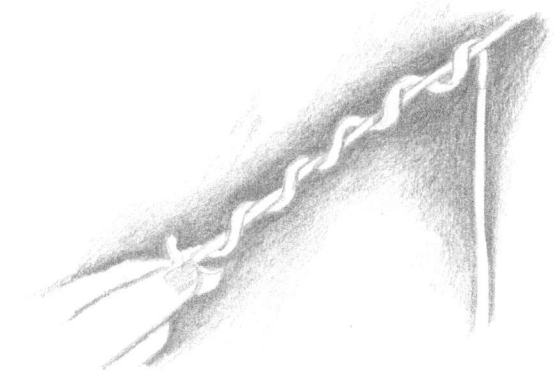

Re-hook the crook around the growing yarn to continue.

This is a temporary holding place for the yarn, while you spin.

chapter two

Roll with it

Continue to repeat the process of twisting, drafting and wrapping as needed until you have transformed an entire rolag or two into yarn. As time goes by, you will find that your fingers become wiser about the work than your head is. When you run out of space on the stick, unwind it and coil it loosely into a skein.

Note: If you need to join two rolags, wait till the first one is nearly all spun-up, then overlap the final little tuft to a new tuft of fibers teased out of the end of the fresh rolag, and draft the fibers out together.

Finishing

Quick-ply

Fold the single yarn at the mid-point, doubling it, then smooth two strands together. As the strands are pressed together between your fingers, the loose fibers become entangled and they will stick together sufficiently well for many purposes. For example, you might join the ends of your newly spun and quick-plied yarn into a necklace.

Wet-setting single yarn

If you do not want to ply, that is, double up the yarn but use it as a single at its original length and thickness, you can wrap it into a loose hank and drop it into very hot water—water that is slightly too hot to touch—for 20 minutes, then take out and let dry. This will "set" the twist.

You will want to practice spinning several rolags in this way before moving on to the weighted drop spindle described next. Set aside a few yards of stick-spun yarn to use in making your drop spindle.

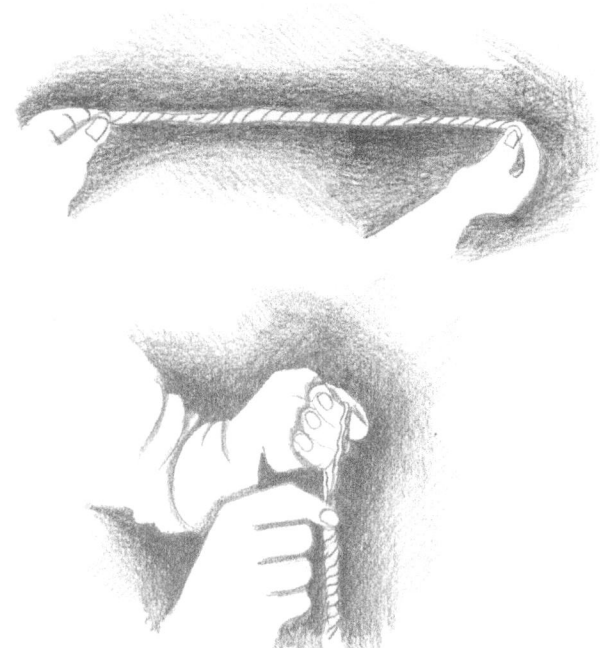

Drafting is the key

As you move on to use a drop spindle or even if you later choose to go on to a spinning wheel, you will find that the key to spinning is in the drafting: how your nimble fingers draw the fibers out of the rolag and feed them into the delta to be twisted into yarn. This skill can only be mastered through practice. The uniformity you are aiming for depends a great deal on how well you've performed the carding in advance. So keep practicing each of the basic elements. As you do better with each, you approach mastery of the whole.

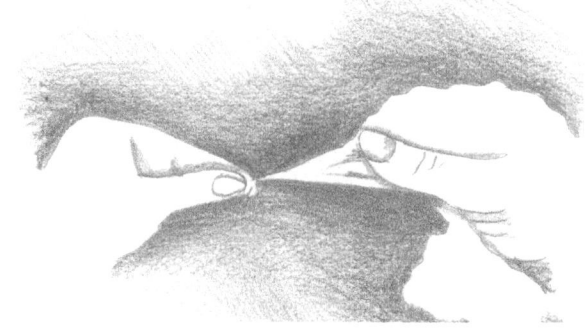

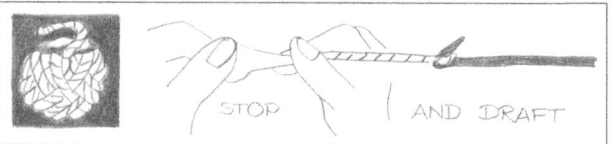

Let's do the twist

All strands that have a twist to them can only spiral in one of two directions, sometimes labeled as "right" and "left," or "clockwise" and "counterclockwise." In science, this property is called "chirality." The word comes from the Greek χειρ (kheir), meaning "hand," as in right and left hand or as in mirror image.

No matter how you turn it around and look at it, the chirality of a twisted strand doesn't change. But describing and labeling these twists can be confusing. That's because the concept of "clockwise" does reverse when you look at it from the opposite direction. If you watch a bicyclist riding down the road going from your left to your right, the wheels are, as you look at, turning clockwise. But to someone across the street, the same wheels are turning counterclockwise.

Spinners have a practical way to identify the two kinds of twists that avoids all confusion: When you hold up a twisted strand, if the lines tend to slant from the upper left down to the lower right, it is called an "S-twist," because the middle part of the letter S slopes that way. The opposite twist, from the upper right to the lower left, slopes like the middle part of the letter Z, and so is called a "Z-twist."

S Twist   Z Twist

If you turn this book upside-down, you'll see that the twist-angles do not change—just as the letters S and Z themselves do not change!

When using a drop spindle, if the spindle spins clockwise, as seen from above, it will impart a Z-twist to the fibers. Counterclockwise spinning creates an S-twist. This is important because completed yarn is normally both spun and plied. Plying, you now know, is when two or more strands of spun fibers are then twisted together. And yarn is always plied with a twist that is opposite to how it was spun. If spun with a Z-twist, it must be plied with an S-twist. If spun with an S-twist, it is plied with a Z-twist. Most conventional yarn is Z-spun and S-plied.

Yarn that is only spun but not plied—called "single" yarn—will want to unspin, to kink-up and twist back on it self. While such yarn might work for weaving, where the warp threads are kept taut, it is unsatisfactory for knitting and crochet. Plying the strands in the opposite direction enables the forces to balance out, giving a material that is stable and workable.

Spinning on the rock

"Spinning on the rock" is a phrase that means using a drop spindle of any kind. It derives from the earliest drop spindles that were, indeed, rocks. Save yourself a trip to the store and find all the tools you need already waiting for you in your own backyard.

Making your spindle

You will want a rock that is about the size of a lime but slightly flattened; perhaps shaped more like a biscuit or a bar of soap. Find a stick that is fairly straight and smooth and about two or three times longer than the length of your rock. You will also need a small twig or straight hairpin.

chapter two

Lay the stick on the flat part of the rock, horizontally so that the stick is aligned with the longest dimension of the rock. Take the few feet of the stick-spun yarn you had set aside, and holding it with your Thumb against the stick and rock a few inches from the end of the yarn, wrap it tightly around the stick and rock, binding them together. Next, do a few figure-eight turns that cinch-up between the rock and stick, finishing with a twist of the final loop, creating a half-hitch. Now, cut the yarn about 6 inches from where it emerges from your rock drop spindle. This length of yarn is called the "leader," and it is where you first attach the fibers of your rolag.

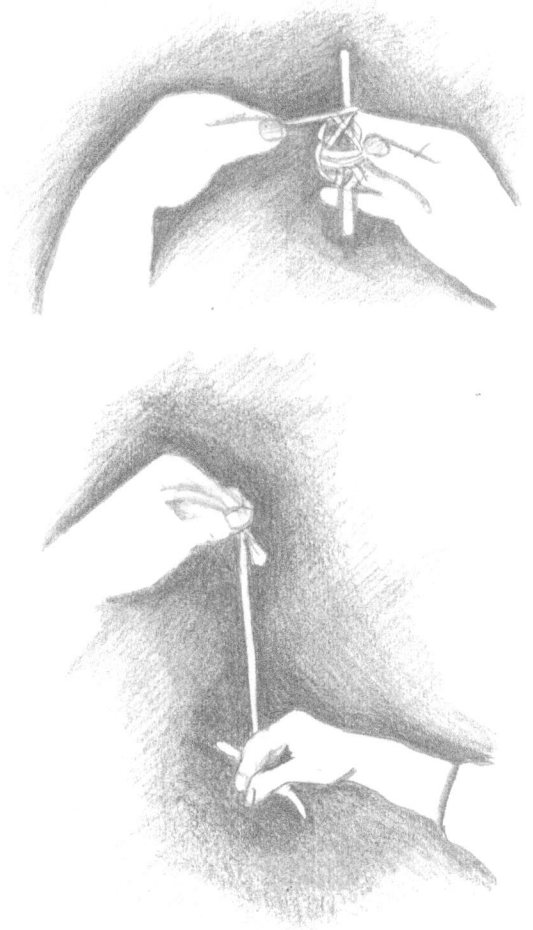

When you hold the end of the leader, suspending your drop spindle, the spindle will likely lean at a slight angle. That is perfectly fine.

Attaching to the leader

Sit with your new spindle resting in your lap. Tease a tuft of fibers out of one end of your rolag and stretch it until it sticks out a few inches. Overlap these fibers onto the leader and pinch them in place with your non-dominant hand bird-pinch. Next, with your dominant hand, begin twisting your spindle clockwise, just as you would tighten the lid on a jar. Soon you will feel the twist move up between your pinched fingers, and you can loosen the pinch slightly, as you keep twisting. Once the twist reaches the rolag, the join is complete.

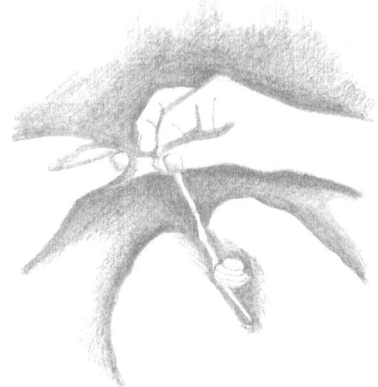

Rock and roll

Now, let the rolag hang over the back of your non-dominant hand to have it out of the way as you feed it down through the portal formed by Thumb and Pointer. Draft (or pull) a section of the rolag and hand-twist the rock clockwise. Keep doing this, hand-twisting and drafting, until, eventually, you take courage and lift the rock into the air and flick the stick, spinning it clockwise. As the

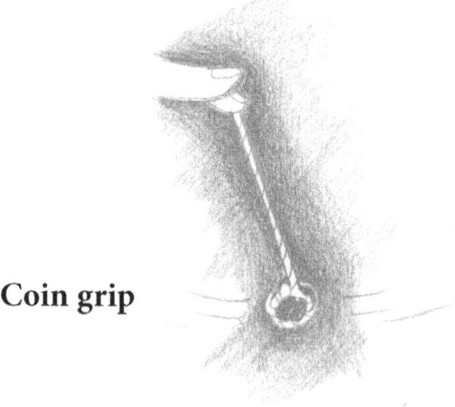

Coin grip

30

spinning slows to a stop, let the rock down into your lap again; bird-pinch the apex of the delta with your dominant hand—the one you were spinning with—to keep the twist from creeping into the delta, and gently slide your non-dominant hand coin-pinch back (that is, sliding back without letting go entirely, holding to retain some control) to elongating the delta. Now, again, lift the rock and resume its spinning. You will find that the yarn has lengthened to the point you need to hold the rock over the floor, away from your lap, to continue.

Wrap the yarn as you go

When the rock reaches the floor, you need to take up the yarn and wind it out of the way. Wrap the yarn, figure-eight style, around the rock and the stick until you have but six or so inches of twisted yarn left.

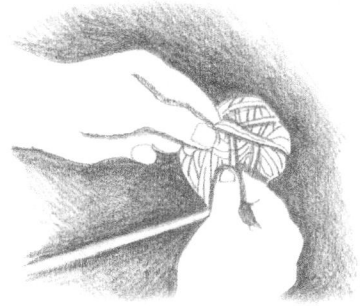

Push a bight (a loop) of yarn under a clump of strands on the top of the mounting pile of wound-up yarn and place a twig or hairpin through it to prevent it from slipping out. Remove the twig when you are ready to wind more yarn around the rock. This trick makes it possible to spin a skein of an impressive size on your little rock spindle.

When you are done with one rolag, just leave enough dangling yarn to connect a new tuft of

roving. Pick up any rolag from your basket and pull out a tip from one end of it. Hold the new tuft so that it overlaps with the previous end and allow the twisting action to join the two together.

Draft as you spin

Sooner or later, you will again be overwhelmed by a rash impulse, and you'll start using both hands for drafting while the rock spins in air. Sometimes the spinning will stop and then the rock will even begin to unwind, turning in the opposite direction, but if you catch it quickly, no work will be undone. At this point you can rest the rock spindle in your lap again while you get the drafting sorted out or, if you are ready, just continue spinning clockwise.

Go easy on yourself

At first your yarn may be bumpy and lumpy and uneven, but do not mind this! Don't expect to create perfectly smooth and fine yarn from the get-go. Continue spinning. If you get at all discouraged just remind yourself that everything worthwhile takes practice, and you can most certainly learn to do this well. Eventually, once you have learned to make amazingly smooth-flowing and thinner yarns, you may want to try making the bumpy "artisanal" type, as it is considered to be quite beautiful and actually the most difficult type to master. So just consider it a bit of beginner's luck that your yarn is bumpy now and move on.

Congratulations! You are now engaged in one of the most ancient rituals of our kind: the gathering of fiber from nature and magically transforming it into the substance of clothing, infusing it with the spirit of love so that it might adorn us with beauty and protect our loved ones, embracing them with warmth.

chapter two

Hank or center-pull?

If you intend to use your new-spun yarn as un-plied single yarn, then wrap it into a regular hank, as will be described, and drop it into hot water to wet-set it. If you intend to ply it with another strand, then you will want to make a center-pull skein, unwinding it directly off the spindle as you do so, as will be described shortly.

Making a hank for single yarn

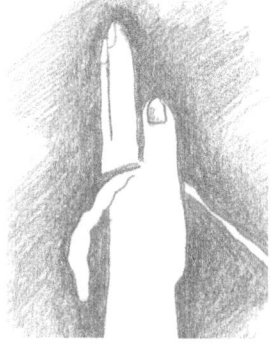

Let the end of your newly spun single yarn hang through your Thumb Notch to the back side of your hand and begin wrapping it around your elbow and back again through the Thumb Notch, unwinding it from your spindle as you go. Then the two ends are each tied separately with an overhand knot around the nearest arm of the bundle, to keep it neat.

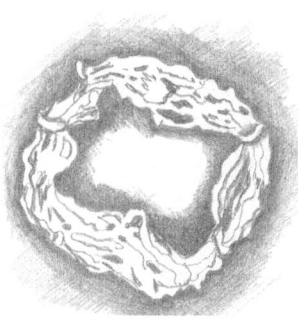

Smooth it together and set it aside. Later, you can drop this hank into hot water to wet-set it, as we have described. Smooth it together for storage.

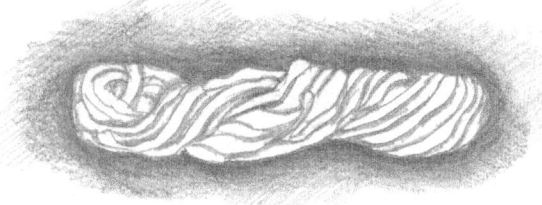

Winding a center-pull skein for plying

You may be familiar with the skill of rolling a regular ball of yarn for knitting. Here we will learn to make a center-pull skein for plying. In fact, we will need two center-pull skeins that we will make from two batches of yarn so they may be plied together.

Once you have filled your drop spindle with all the yarn it can hold, you will then form a center-pull ball as you unwind directly from the spindle. Take the loose, most recently spun end of your yarn and wrap it a few times around your left Pinky to secure it. Next, bring it forward through Pinky gap across the Palm and behind the Thumb.

Next, do three figure eights around Thumb and Pointer.

Slip the loop off Pointer and flip it over onto Thumb, so it sits on top of the loop already there.

Now, continue to unwind from your spindle as you wrap the yarn around the ball building up on your Thumb, like Little Jack Horner's plum.

Wrap clockwise in a diagonal orbit so that the yarn passes first over, and then under, the "plum." Introduce some precession into your windings by rotating the plum slightly around the Thumb, counterclockwise. This way, the yarn will cross at different points along the equator and not build up at one point.

Do not wind the yarn so tight as to squeeze the growing ball out of shape or stretch the fibers. Try to keep all sides of the skein even in size.

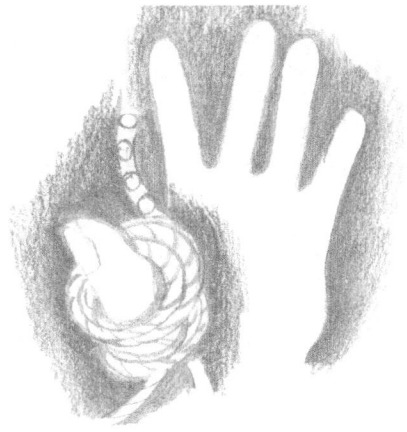

When you have wound up all of your yarn from your spindle, tuck the last few inches under a few strands of your skein to hold it in place. Pull your "plum" off your Thumb and turn it over, and behold, a little round, hollow, basket-shaped ball of yarn! Now, unwrap the tail end of the yarn from your Pinky and poke it into the middle of your little skein—but not so far in that you will have trouble finding it again. This is the end of the working yarn, or leed, for a future project.

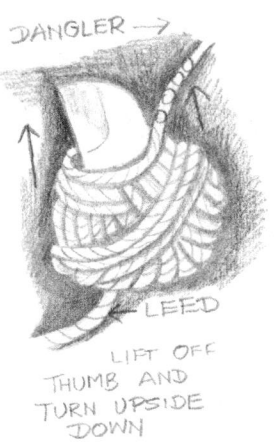

LIFT OFF THUMB AND TURN UPSIDE DOWN

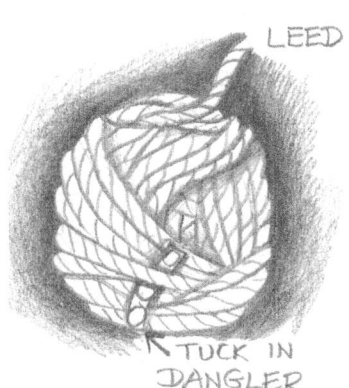

TUCK IN DANGLER

The dangler you can just tuck into the ball under some strands and out of the way. When you work with the yarn you will be pulling it out from the center.

Now, spin another spindle-full, and use it to make your second center-pull skein.

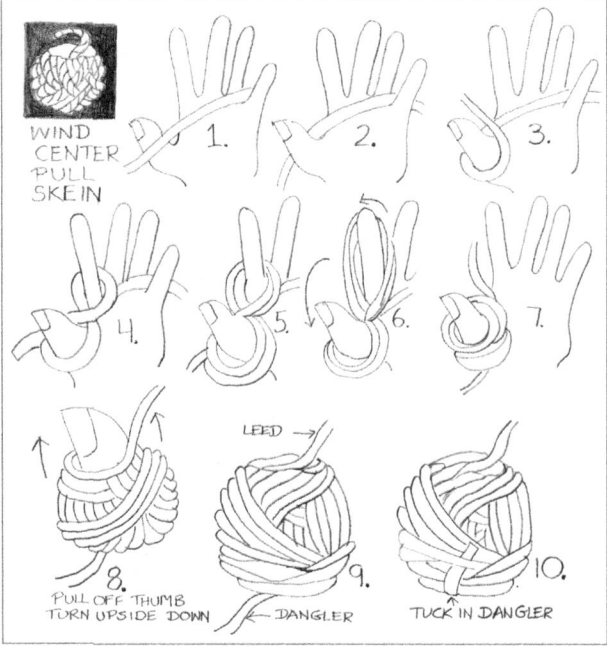

Plying

Plied Yarn is thicker so you might need more room on your spindle to hold it. You could make another spindle with a larger rock and stick, or you could even obtain a different kind of spindle that holds more yarn.

The center-pull skein works well for spinning because it does not roll away from you as you work. Lift out the end from the middle of each skein.

You can work sitting or standing, but I've found it convenient in either case to set my center-pull skeins behind me, on the floor or in a basket, so that the singles cross over each other and feed in over my two shoulders. The two strands then pass through my left-hand coin-pinch. It's much easier than it sounds.

Holding your spindle in your right hand, bring the ends of the two singles together and overlap your leader just as before. Begin hand-twisting your spindle, but this time in a counterclockwise direction as seen from above (as if unscrewing the lid of a jar). This is because we created the singles with a clockwise Z-twist, so now we need a counterclockwise S-twist for the plied yarn to be balanced. Continue hand-twisting until the yarn is safely attached to the leader, then you can drop-spin, keeping in mind to keep the spindle spinning counterclockwise.

As the spindle reaches the floor, wind the newly plied yarn onto the stick as before, securing it with a half-hitch (or wrap around the hook if you are using the fancier type).

Plying will proceed much quicker than spinning, as we don't have to deal with the fuss of drafting. Gently allow the fibers to pass through your coin-pinch as tensions build and release into the

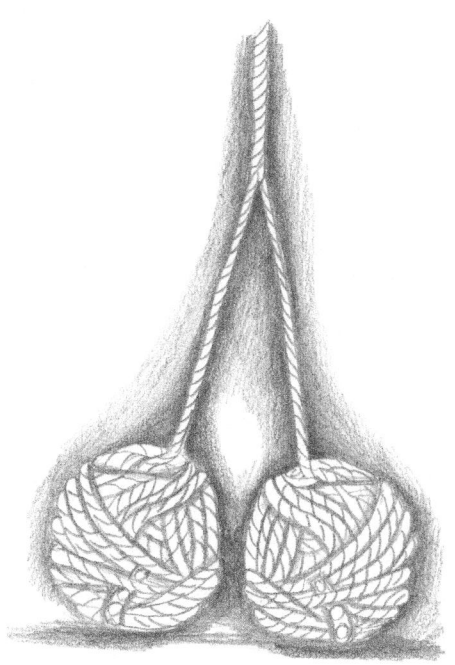

twirling strands of yarn. As a result of the tensions working in opposite directions, the two lengths of yarn should now cling together as one two-ply strand.

Once you have plied all your yarn, if you don't need to use your spindle again right away, it is better to leave the yarn in place for a while—perhaps overnight. This helps the strands to bond together and set. When you are ready, simply unwind it and form it into a hank, as described before.

You will find that spinning is very meditative. It has its own internal rhythms, its own music. The work flows the way water flows. Individual fibers are joined simply by way of close proximity into forming strong bonds. There is a kind of magic to it, such as we can all use in our lives.

chapter three
Nature-friendly Dyeing

chapter three

When you have put such care into your natural, hand-crafted creations, you will no doubt find yourself wanting to have them be natural, through and through: colored, not with manufactured chemical dyes, but with flowers, roots, leaves, moss, and bark that you can find growing in your area. Although there are many kinds of plant materials that will color fibers when first applied, only certain of these can be called dye-plants—that is, the pigments will survive washing or exposure to sunlight without fading.

When it comes to dyeing, we generally need to divide all fibers into two broad categories: protein fibers and cellulose fibers. Wool and silk, being animal-derived, are called protein fibers. Cotton, hemp, linen, etc., are plant-derived cellulose fibers. Protein fibers take to dyes more readily, but as far as wool goes, it all must be thoroughly washed before dyeing, to remove the lanolin. Silk takes up dyes most easily.

Once raw wool has been cleaned and carded, it can be dyed. Alternatively, you can spin it first, and then dye it, or even knit it into a garment and dye it afterward.

Mordants

A *mordant* is a fixative that helps a dye stick to the fibers. Mordant comes from the Latin *mordere*, which means to bite—it was thought to help the dye bite into the fiber and hold on. When a mordant is used to treat the fibers beforehand, we call it a *pre-mordant*. One common mordant is tannic acid—found in tea—which is safely derived from various leaves, husks or barks, making it amenable for use with younger students. Salt, vinegar, and cream of tartar—an edible byproduct of wine-making—are also used as mordants. The Navajo have a tradition of using minerals from rocks to enhance their dyes as well. Some natural dyes do not need added mordants because they

contain their own mordants. Other common mordants include metallic salts such as alum. But for the child-friendly purposes of this book, harsh or reactive chemicals are avoided.

Words to a young weaver
by Noel Bennet

Noel Bennet spent much of her life learning traditional fiber arts from the Navajo, who also refer to themselves as the *Diné*—meaning "the people" in Navajo.

We are the Diné, my child
With the Earth we live
With the Sky we live
    With the Plants we live
    We know their ways.
Heed well the Plants, my child.
Learn the ways of each, my child.
Some you must ask for gently,
    Pick their tips
    Heat them softly
    And they give.

Some you must demand of strongly
>   Dig through the rocks
>   Pound hard the roots
>   You will tire
>   And they will give.
Give to each as it requires
>   It will give to you, my child,
>   It will give to you.
We are the Diné,
With the Earth we live
With the Sky we live
>   With the Plants we live
>   We know their ways
Nature comes as it comes
>   Gives as it gives
We do not plan Nature.
We do not control Nature.
>   It is so in dyeing wool.
Receive your colors as they come.
Learn the ways of each.
Some Plants dye strong enough alone.
Some take strength from other things.
>   The Ashes of the Juniper
>   The Minerals of the Soil
Give to the weak, strength, my child
And the colors that come are good.
The Red of the cliffs at sunset,
Will come.
The Yellow of the shimmering sand,
Will come.
The Green of the plant life around,
Will come.
The Black of the thunderclouds heavy,
Will come.
All good colors will come, my child.
All good colors will come.
And do not try to match a color of the past.
>   This is a new day.
>   This is a new plant.
The colors that come forth are many,
None will be the same
And each that comes is good.
And each that comes is good.

Solar Dyeing Project

Here is a solar dye project that I have done with my class of early-childhood students in New Hampshire. The lesson can be expanded to fit any age group. If you are working with third-graders or older, for example, you might have each student choose a good dye from a variety of natural vegetation—certain flowers, berries, mosses, barks, roots, and so on. (A list of dye plants can be found at the end of this chapter.) For younger children, let them help you gather the materials—oak leaves, etc.—and then the class can watch as you prepare the dye bath and see the elements interacting over time on the window sill.

For this project we will solar dye three handfuls of washed and carded wool roving.

If you have a stovetop to use, you may also want to expand the project to include the dyeing of several cotton handkerchiefs.

Pre-mordanting the fibers

Wool

The wool can be solar pre-mordanted with cream of tartar (a few dashes of salt or vinegar may alternatively be used in exactly the same way, with varying results). Some strong traditional dye plants do not require pre-mordanting at all. Although tannins are less commonly used for wool, I have had some good results dyeing roving after treating it with a solar tea bath of oak leaves for several days.

Collect several quart-sized mason jars. (An expanded version of the project will, of course, require larger jars for pre-mordanting larger amounts of fibers).

Gathering oak leaves

Have the children help you gather a good handful of green oak leaves. Tear or crumble the leaves, place them in a jar, and fill the jar with warm water. Alternatively, you can have the children gather acorns and crush them. My students placed their acorns into depressions in granite boulders and happily mashed them with rocks. Place the crushed material, shells and all, into the jar.

Add the wool

Fill the jar with warm water. Put the lid on the jar loosely and set it in a sunny spot—on a windowsill, say—for a few days to a week or more. Do not screw the lid tight, but keep it loose enough so that if some fermentation occurs, the gasses can escape. With the protein fibers you can avoid having to use a stovetop altogether and just use solar heating to activate the dyeing process.

Pre-mordant with cream of tartar

Take an empty jar, and add a few tablespoons of cream of tartar. Partly fill with warm water, leaving room for the wool. Take three modest handfuls of washed and carded white wool (or your little hand-spun hanks of well-cleaned wool) and place them into the jar so they are completely submerged.

Separating the clumps of wool for the separate dye batches is best done while the wool is dry. The jar should not be stuffed so full that the water cannot circulate. Put the lid on the jar and set it in a sunny spot. The cream of tartar will not take as long as the tannin—which needs time to leach out of the vegetation—but it won't hurt the wool to soak for many days, in case you want to prepare both jars at the same time.

Cotton

If you are dyeing cotton handkerchiefs, be aware that cellulose fibers have a protective layer that must be broken down to absorb the tannins that attach to the dyes. For this reason, the cotton must be boiled in a tannin-rich sun tea, such as the liquid you derive from the soaked oak leaves or acorns.

Allow the cotton fabric to boil for around 45 minutes before you solar dye them.

Preparing the Dyestuff

Gather some plants and flowers

Have the children bring from home—or gather from the schoolyard under supervision—any of various child-friendly dye-plants. These could include **marigold flowers** or **red or yellow onionskins** for yellow, **hibiscus flowers** or **red cabbage leaves** for red or pink. For my class, I planted marigolds in the spring just for this purpose. Blues are harder to come by unless you happen to have one of the indigo-containing plant varieties growing in your area. Alternatively, you can order natural indigo from a number of companies.

Select two or three types of dyestuff to go in the jars. For example, you might choose marigolds for yellow, hibiscus for red. Tear or crumble each kind of vegetation and place a handful of it in a jar, labeling the jar. Fill with warm water, place the lids on loosely, and put in the sun for several days or a week or more.

From pre-mordant to dyebath

WOOL
Place one clump of the pre-mordanted wool into each dye-jar. Replace the lids loosely, and set the jars back in the sun. Leave them there for another few days or a week or more.

COTTON
If you are dyeing cotton handkerchiefs, remove them from the hot water with a stick and let them drip dry before placing them into the dyebath.

TIME IS YOUR AID
Allow Grandfather Time and the sun to do the work of solar-dyeing for you. The amount of time needed will vary depending of the amount of sunlight exposure, etc., and you can just experiment. Plant colors tend to brighten up a bit as the fibers dry.

VOILA!
On the day of the great reveal, remove the wool and handkerchiefs and allow them to dry on a towel. The wool might be streaky and dotted with bits of vegetation. Hand-card each colored clump for a while, and the color will smooth out, and the bits of debris will drop out. Finally, shape each into a mini-bat of roving that will now be ready for spinning or felting. If you dyed both cotton and wool, compare those from the same dyebath. The differences might be surprising!

Vinegar or baking soda is sometimes used as a post-mordant to enhance or alter the color results. For example, I obtained a deep green for wool when I followed up the dye bath of red onion skins with a dip in a baking soda solution.

Except for the vinegar, these natural solutions can be poured out in the yard to water plants or added to the compost. The vinegar mordant is good for keeping back weeds in a way that is harmless to the earth and our bodies. When using salt mordants, do not pour out in the garden, as salt is harmful to most plants.

When ready, remove the handkerchiefs and wool from the pre-mordant liquids once they have cooled down, gently squeeze out excess liquid, and lay the fiber on a towel for a few minutes to drip dry. Once desirable color results are obtained, it makes sense to expand into bigger vats for dyeing larger amounts of fiber at one time.

Other natural dye-plants and mordants

There are many books available on natural dyes, but often they call for alum or other even harsher metallic salts that some prefer not to use and that should not be brought into a grade-school classroom. You may want to expand upon this process by trying dye-plants you can obtain in your area in various experimental combinations with child-friendly mordants such as tannins, salt, vinegar, and cream of tartar. Be sure to clearly label everything! This is a wonderful class exercise, since each student can experiment with just one or two plants and the knowledge gained then pooled and organized and presented as a whole, very practical, body of knowledge. In this way we cultivate in our students and ourselves a true appreciation for traditional dye-plants and dyeing practices. Beautiful traditions, earth-friendly cultures, and community-oriented economies have formed around the harvesting of such gifts of color offered by nature. [Please note that dyeing—even with plants—is an activity that requires close adult supervision.]

As you continue upon your path of discovery of natural dyes, enjoy finding artistic ways to display the valuable knowledge gained from your experiments.

chapter three

Cultures and Their Colors

Cochineal

The microorganism that feeds off the Nopal cactus in the deserts of North America provides a broad spectrum of reddish dyes, from a rosy gold to deep purple. The tiny parasites are swept off the cactus-pads into baskets or clay pots, and then ground and prepared in various ways to make a variety of colors.

We delight in the beautiful colors with which Nature glorifies her plants and flowers, but most of those pigments cannot be transferred to cloth—at least not in any permanent way. You will notice that the scientific botanical names of many of the plants cited here contain the Latin word *tinctoria*, or *tinctorius*. This means that that plant, since ancient times, was recognized and used for its ability to permanently color cloth. However, many of the New World dye-plants may lack such designation because the botanists who named them might not have been familiar with all its native uses. Below is a list of some of the more common plants—out of the many hundreds known to produce some usable dye—that might be utilized by fiber artisans. These plants are loosely grouped by range of color, though the actual colors can vary widely depending on pre-and post-mordants, the type of fiber, and many other factors. Many of these plants might reasonably appear in several different color categories, but, for simplicity, each plant has been listed just once. In short, the list is not intended for use as an orderly paint-box—with each tube labeled with its precise hue, but as a resource to inspire your own experimentation.

While natural plant dyes cannot be precisely standardized in the way that synthetic dyes are, you may soon discover their innumerable charms. Just one example: It has been observed that, for some mysterious reason, the colors created by plant dyes all seem to naturally go together without clashing, contrary to what often happens with artificial dyes.

Reds, oranges, and reddish browns

Alder, *Alnus rubra* (bark)
Balm (flower)
Bamboo
Barberry, *Mahonia*—various species (any part of the plant)
Bedstraw, *Galium triflorum* (root)
Lady's Bedstraw, *Galium verum*
Beets (root)
Bloodroot, *Sanguinaria canadensis* (root)
Brazilwood
Burdock
Butternut tree, *Juglans cinerea* (bark, seed husks)
Carrot (root)
Cherries
Chicory
Chokeberries
Comfrey
Giant Coreopsis

Golden Marguerite, *Anthemis tinctoria* (fresh or dried flowers)
Crabapple (bark)
Dandelion (root)
Dock
Eucalyptus (leaves, bark)
Fennel
Geranium
Hibiscus flowers
Grand Fir (bark)
Hops
Japanese Yew (heartwood)
Juniper
Lichen
Lilac (twigs)
Madder (roots)
Wild Plum (root)
Pokeweed
Pomegranate (peel)
Poplar
Portulaca (dried flowers)
Raspberries
Sweet Woodruff, *Galium odoratum* (fresh roots
Safflower, *Carthamus tinctorius* (flowers)
Sassafras (leaves)
Sorrel
Strawberries
Sunflower
Sycamore (bark)
Turmeric
Weld, *Reseda luteola*

Hawaiians used a combination of native turmeric roots called *olean*, combined with the local noni plants and the fluid of the kupaoa vine to produce a yellow dye called "Malo of Aliʻi."

The Hawaiians even gave attention to the scents of their dyes. This dye-mixture was traditionally scented with ripened coconut flesh.

Yellows

Agrimony (fresh leaves, stems)
Alfalfa (seeds)
Bay leaves
Broom, *Cytisus scoparius* (fresh flowers)
Celery (leaves)
Crocus
Daffodil (withered flowers)
Dahlia flowers
Dandelion (fresh flowers)
Dyer's Greenwood, *Genista tinctoria* (shoots)
Fustic, *Chlorophora tinctoria* or *Maclura tinctorial* (wood)
Goldenrod (fresh flowers)
Grindelia
Heather
Hickory leaves
Lavender Cotton, *Santolina chamaecyparissus* (fresh flowers, leaves)
Marigold (flowers)
Mimosa (flowers)

Horseradish
Mullein (leaf and root)
Nettle, *Uritca dioica* (all plant, fresh)
Oregon Grape (roots)
Osage Orange (heartwood, wood chips, or sawdust)
Oxalis (also Wood Sorrels) (yellow flowers, stem)
Queen Anne's Lace
Paprika
Peach leaves
Plaintain, *Plantago major* (fresh, all plant)
Red Clover (whole blossom, leaves, and stem)
Saffron (stigmas)
Sage, *Salvia officinalis* (fresh tops)
Salsify
Syrian Rue
Tansy (tops)
White Mulberry (bark)
Willow (leaves)
Yarrow, *Achillea millefolium* (fresh flowers)
Yellow Coneflower (whole flower head)

The young leaves of woad, *Isatis tinctoria*, was made into a blue cloth dye and body paint by ancient Celts. The plant was brought to the New World from Europe by early settlers, but now that chemical dyes have supplanted plant dyes, it is considered an invasive species—so you may feel free to gather all you like from the wild!

Blues and purples
Blackberry (fruit)
Blueberries
Cherry (roots)
Cornflower (petals)
Dogwood (bark)
Elderberry
Geranium
Grapes
Hyacinth (flowers)
Huckleberries
Indigo, *Persicaria tinctoria* or *Indigofera tinctoria* (leaves)
Logwood
Red Cabbage
Red Cedar root
Red Maple (inner bark)
Mulberries
Nearly Black Iris
Purple Iris
Oregon Grape, *Mahonia aquifolium* (fresh fruit)
Smilex, *S. aspera*
Sweetgum (bark)
Woad, *Isatis tinctoria* (fresh young leaves)

Greens
Angelica
Artemisia
Artichokes
Bayberry, *Berberis vulgaris* (all plant: fresh or dried)
Betony, *Stachys officinalis* (all plant, fresh)
Black-eyed Susan, *Rudbeckia hirta*
Camellia (petals)
Chamomile (leaves)
Coneflower
Feverfew, *Tanacetum parthenium* (fresh leaves, stems)
Foxglove (flowers)
Grass
Hydrangea (flowers)
Larkspur
Majoram, *Origanum majorana* (fresh whole tops)
Mulga Acacia (seed pods)

Peony (flowers)
Peppermint
Pigweed (entire plant)
Purple Milkweed (flowers & leaves)
Red Pine (needles)
Rosemary, *Rosmarinus officinalis* (fresh flowers, leaves)
Snapdragon (flowers)
Spinach (leaves)
Tea Tree (flowers)
Uva Ursi, *Arctostaphylos uva-ursi* (fresh, all plant)
White Ash (bark)

Browns
Acorns (boiled)
Amur Maple, *Acer ginnala* (dried leaves)
Birch bark
Black tea
Coffee grounds
Colorado Fir (bark)
Hollyhock (petals)
Hops
Iris (roots)
Ivy (twigs)
Meadowsweet
Oak galls
Oregano (dried stalk)
Pine bark
Potentilla, *Potentilla verna* (fresh roots)
Walnut (husks)
Black Walnut (husks)
Weeping Willow (wood & bark)
White Maple (bark)

Black Walnut husks contain a lot of tannins and produce a deep brown dye. A dye bath made from them will prepare a fabric to take an over-dye, but the dark tannins will also affect the color outcome.

chapter four

Getting Started
with Intermediate Barehand Knitting

chapter four

This chapter begins with a review of some basic terminology from *Bare Hand Knitting* Book I, interwoven with some new terms for this second crafting book.

Geography of the Hand

Barehand crafting gives the artisan a direct relationship with the medium, the fibers that are knit and sculpted. To describe the techniques clear terminology is needed.

Right- and left-handedness

The dominant hand of the crafter is referred to as the Shuttle Hand and the non-dominant hand is referred to as the Loom Hand. This means that if you are right-handed, your "Shuttle" is your active right hand, and your "Loom" refers to your passive left hand. For the left-handed, Shuttle is left and Loom is right.

Whether the reader is right-handed or left-handed, these instructions will work for both. It is important that students learn to distinguish between the left and right hands, but this does not need to make instructions more complicated for left-handed people to follow.

Moving around the hand

Palm-side: inside or front side of the hand
Dorsal-side or Back-side: outer side of the hands
Pad-side: palm-side or inside of the finger
Knuckle-side: back or knuckle side of the fingers
Thumb-Notch: where Thumb and Pointer join
Arrow-Notch: where Pointer and Middler join
Center-Notch: where Middler and Ringa join
Pinky-Notch: where Ringa and Pinky join
Finger-Palm Crease: the arched crease between fingers & palm
Middle Gap: the gap between the Loom hand and the Shuttle and the midline between the left and right brain hemispheres.

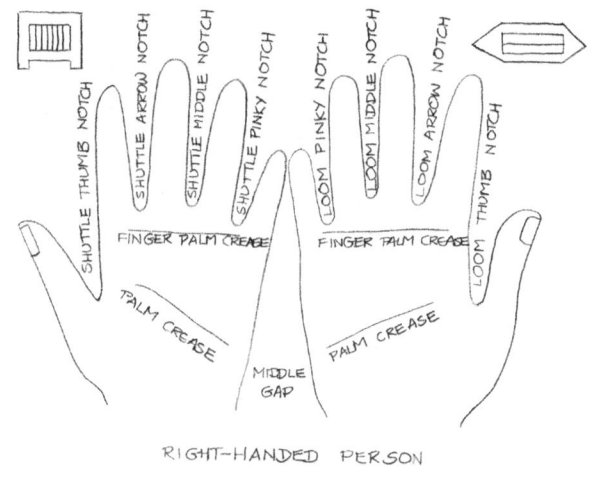

RIGHT-HANDED PERSON

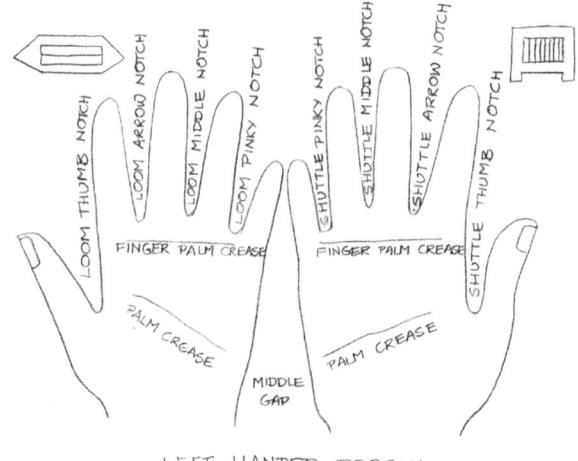

LEFT-HANDED PERSON

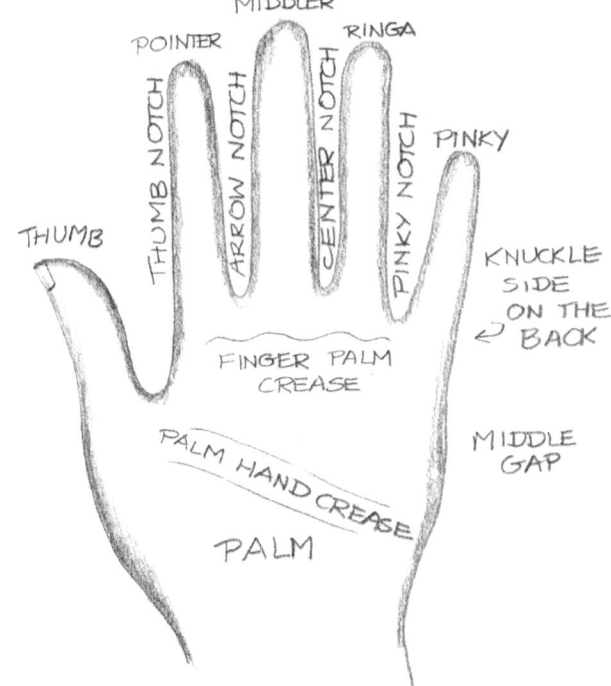

Getting Started: Barehand Knitting

Directionality

Thumbwise—moving in a line from the Pinky to Pointer

Pinkywise—moving in a line from the Pointer to Pinky

Tipwise—moving along a digit toward the tip

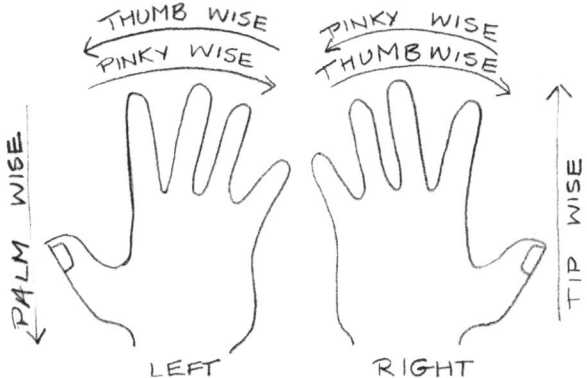

For some directions where the same standard must apply to everyone, such as those for spinning and those that involve two hands, the terms right and left and clockwise or counterclockwise become necessary to use.

Topwise and countertopwise

A right-handed child will naturally twirl the top so that it spins in a clockwise direction; a left-handed child will spin it counterclockwise. Therefore, instead of "clockwise" and "counterclockwise,"

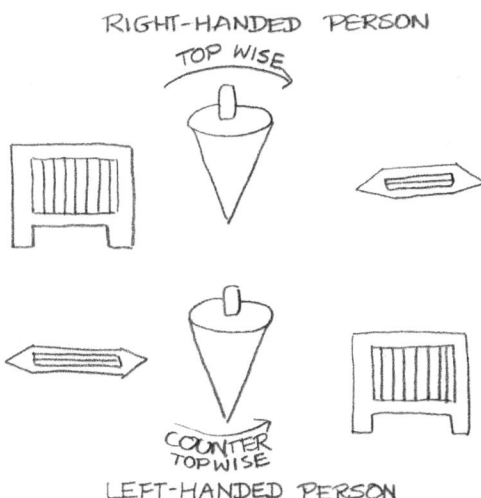

we use the terms "topwise" and "countertopwise." For the right-handed, "topwise" is the same as "clockwise;" for the left-handed, it is just the opposite. If you ever forget, just imagine twirling a top between your fingers, and it will be made clear.

Terms for bilateral techniques

For techniques that cross the midline, because both hands are more actively involved, our directions toward the Shuttle Hand or toward the Loom Hand sometimes express a general direction of horizontal movement, and the general term will be "Shuttlewise" or "Loomwise." In this way we can say, "Loomwise" even when working on the Loom Hand, for example because the term simply refers to a direction of movement on a line from Shuttle to Loom, or, "Shuttlewise," from Loom to Shuttle.

(These directional terms are independent of any fixed location. Stitches on your Shuttle Hand can move Shuttlewise because they are moving along an arrow going from Loom to Shuttle.)

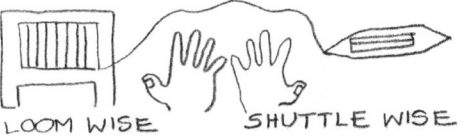

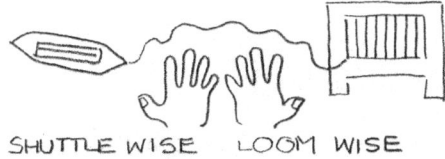

In a classroom setting, this terminology clears up confusion by eliminating the necessity of having to give a reversed set of instructions for left-handed students. This is the terminology used throughout this book. The terms Right and Left are used in some instances as bilateral techniques come in, but only where necessary.

Pinches

The main pinch that will be used for plucking and holding yarn is the bird-pinch, which comes most naturally. As your barehand knitting progresses, others will be called in for specialized actions. Students are likely to enjoy the introduction to some of the new pinches here that were not included in the first book on barehand knitting.

Bird-pinch: Thumb-tip touches tip of Pointer.
Fox-pinch: Thumb-tip touches tip of Middler

Coyote-pinch: Thumb-tip touches tip of Ringa
Peacock-pinch: Thumb-tip touches tip of Pinky

Measurements

Many common measurements—the inch, the foot, the yard—were originally based on body dimensions. Later these were standardized when there was a need for increased precision for interchangeability and fair trade. It is important for students to learn standardized measurements, but their use is not always relevant or convenient for projects. In this book both will be used where appropriate. When the indication does not require a standardized measurement, these individualized measurements are designated with the word *personal*: a personal inch, personal foot, personal yard.

Your *personal inch* can be measured off with the top segment of your Thumb.

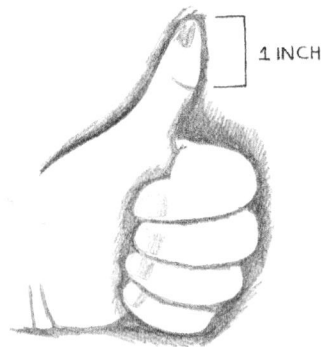

Your *personal foot* can be measured out by your foot or, perhaps more easily, by the distance from wrist to elbow.

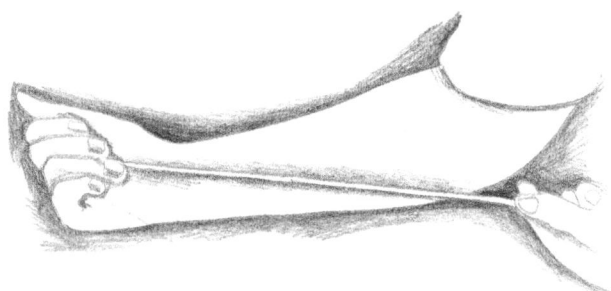

Your *personal yard* can be measured as the distance from your chin or mid chest, to the tip of the Thumb of your outstretched hand.

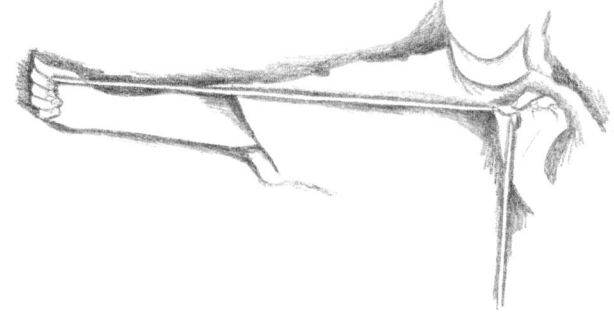

Yarn

Yarn sizes

Universally accepted yarn sizes have been designated as follows:

1. Super Fine (also called Sock, Fingering, and Baby)
2. Fine (also called Sport and Baby)
3. Light (also called DK, and Light-Worsted)
4. Medium (also called Worsted, Afghan and Aran)
5. Bulky (also called Chunky, Craft and Rug)
6. Super Bulky (also called Bulky and Roving)

Yarn terminology

The yarn terminology used throughout this book is mapped out below as a reminder from the first book, *Bare Hand Knitting*.

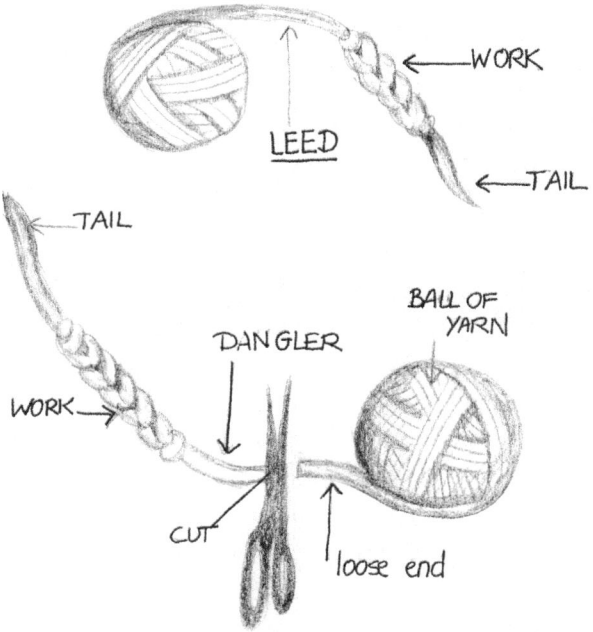

Geography of the Work

A knitted panel is sometimes referred to as a "knitted piece or panel", or "the work" or the "knitted fabric." In the case of embroidery, it becomes the "foundation fabric." All knitted work has a *start end* and a *finish end*. It has a selvage on each long side. Before the ends have been woven in, there is a tail coming out from the corner of the start end and a dangler coming out from the corner of the finish end.

Field stitches face down toward the Earth as you knit and *ripple stitches* face up like moonlight reflecting off of the ripples in the water. Field stitches generally become the topside or outside of a completed knitted piece and ripple stitches are generally on the underside or inside.

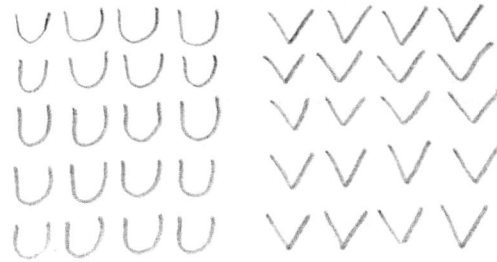

If you put your work down and resume later, be sure the ripple stitches are on the topside when you begin knitting again. Alternations are sometimes worked into a knitted garment intentionally.

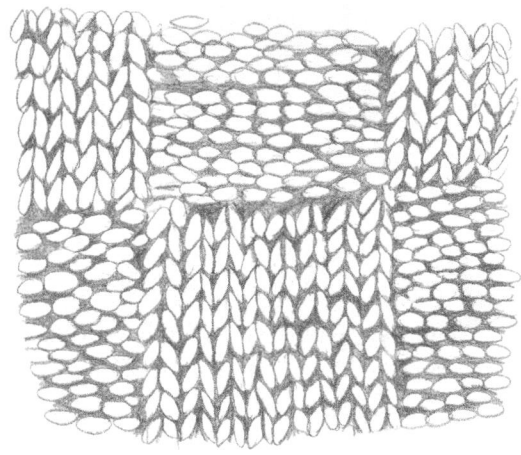

chapter four

Selvages: When you buy cloth from a fabric store, the piece has a cut edge where the salesperson snipped it to length for you (and another at the other end, where it was cut for the previous customer) and two strong clean edges, called selvages (from "self-edge"), along either side.

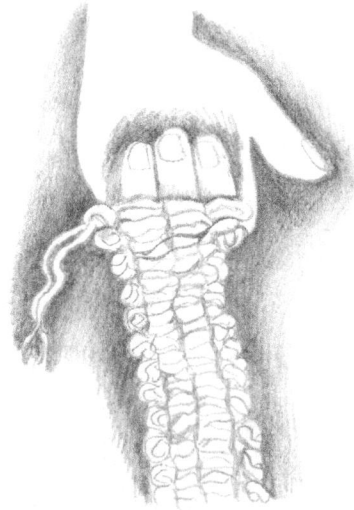

These strong, neat selvages are derived from the action on the loom when the weft-yarn from the shuttle wraps around the warp thread along the edge, rather than being cut and re-started.

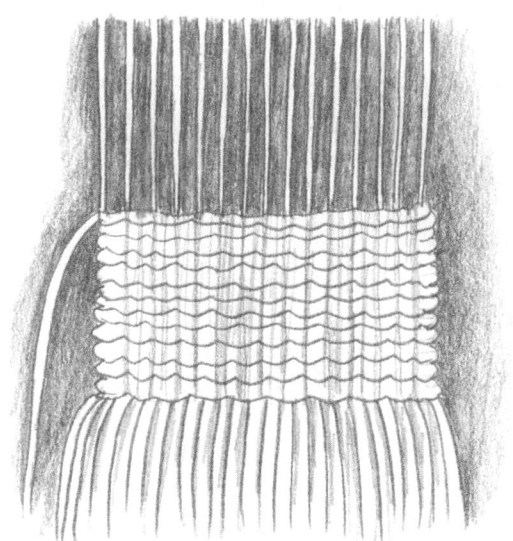

The *Spruce technique* introduced in this book makes it possible to connect several pieces, giving the barehand knitted fabric neat, trim start and finish edges between bridged panels.

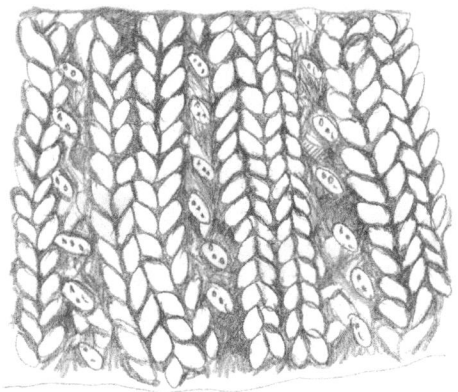

Choosing Our Materials

To be aware of the origins of the materials is important. Whether one is working with plant fibers or animal fibers, as we create yarn sculptors, we come into direct contact with our materials, reminding us of the intimate connection we have with their sources and the environment that sustains us. The fibers we spin and knit, the buttons we stitch, the beads we string, and the dyes we mix can all be collected in sustainable ways as they have been for millennia. It is an ongoing challenge to seek out products made closer to home and processed without the use of toxic materials or slave labor—those lacking huge smokestack industries in the chain of their manufacture.

In continuing along this path, however, I believe that together we will bring healing to the earth, to our society, and to our own bodies and minds. Whereas lively colors can be cheering, lately I find that I prefer the milder colors of plant-dyed and plain un-dyed yarns with their warm browns, soft greys and creamy whites. Bear in mind that it is not only the materials but especially it is the wholesome work of sculpting with yarn itself that is so deeply needed by folks in every walk of life. It is also important to consider that not everyone has a broad range of choice in their materials and this most especially applies to children. The statement of each and every artist is valid in its own right. In the end, I'd like to honor each artist's personal choices for colors.

Sources for fibers

Fiber Shed is an organization that can help connect knitters to their local suppliers of yarn and wool outlets. Other protein fibers and plant fibers are also obtainable through fiber sheds. A list of Fiber Shed locations is included in the back of this book. Look for upcoming wool festivals in your local area, where you can buy directly from local suppliers. Also check out your local yarn shop.

For larger amounts of yarn, you can often get discounts when buying directly from suppliers in bulk. Waldorf handwork teachers order in bulk at a discount from Brown Sheep Co. This company is based in the US and carries quality 100% wool yarn and a good selection of the bulky sizes called for in many projects for this book. The project prototypes for this publication were also made using their fine product.

Move even closer to the source of your materials by following the directions for spinning your own yarn in Chapter 2, From Sheep to Skein.

Heritage strains of cotton are making a comeback. These ancient varieties do not work for machine processing, but with their longer fibers they are superior for hand spinning. Another advantage is that the native cottons of old come in beautiful blues and golds and do not need to be dyed at all!

To spin your own yarn is also a wonderful and economical way for a barehand knitting enthusiast to keep up with their yarn requirements as described in the previous chapter.

Techniques

Combining technques

As you move through the lessons in the book and learn the techniques taught in previous chapters, you will discover that there are countless ways that the various stitches can be combined for projects. As is the case with any art form, there is no one way to create, and you are encouraged to develop your own ideas and methods. Such possibilities will be explored through some laid-out projects that use a combination of techniques. Still more suggestions for tried-and-true combinations and hints for how to attain them can be found toward the end of many chapters in this book.

Full, roll, and block your wool

Fulling

Bear in mind that barehand knitted fabrics made from wool yarn can be enhanced through the process of fulling. To full is to hand wash in warm water with soap that results in a very light felting. This process relaxes and strengthens the fibers.

Rolling

While it's still wet you may also want to sushi roll the fabric just a bit—but more rigorously along the start and finish ends, to shrink them down. You can accomplish this by rolling them out in a towel or a mat.

chapter four

Blocking

Find a clean flat surface and be sure your item is nicely blocked out before leaving it to air dry for 24 hours. To block a wet wool item means to carefully smooth it out and position it into the shape in which you want it to dry. These techniques were introduced in *Bare Hand Knitting Book I* and are relevant for all of the knitted items made from wool that we create.

Terms

Wherever possible we have used traditional knitting terms, but, in some cases, new terms had to be created for this medium. In the vocabulary review at the end of each chapter, you will find a listing with newly introduced terms that will be built upon in the chapters that follow.

Brief summary of steps

Operations:	specific movements relating to barehand knitting
Elements:	individual moves (likened to letters)
Stitches:	made up of one or two elements (likened to words)
Polystitches:	groups of elements or stitches in a certain order (likened to sentences)
Sequences:	longer grouping of stitches or poly stitches (likened to paragraphs)
Rows:	repeating series of stitches or poly stitches

Introductory instructions are very detailed. However, after a bit of practice, you can refer to the coded sequences placed in the text as shorthand reminders.

Chapter Review for "Getting Started"

Vocabulary	Hand-related terms	Barehand geography
hank	Thumb	Thumb-Notch
skein	Pointer	Arrow-Notch
leed	Middler	Center-Notch
tail	Ringa	Pinky-Notch
dangler	Pinky	Palm
loose end	bird-pinch	Finger-Palm Crease
bight	fox-pinch	under layer
weave	coyote-pinch	put-up
rolling	peacock-pinch	put-back stitches
fulling		

chapter five

Finger Crochet

chapter five

The Tail-tugger Slipknot

The first step in finger crochet is the tail-tugger slipknot. Normally, whether or not a slipknot is tightened by pulling on the tail is a coin-flip. Here the process is broken down into clearly definable steps so that, once learned, it will give a consistent and reliable result. This deliberate approach is the best way to introduce the slipknot to children once they are ready to make a slipknot for themselves, somewhere between ages seven and nine.

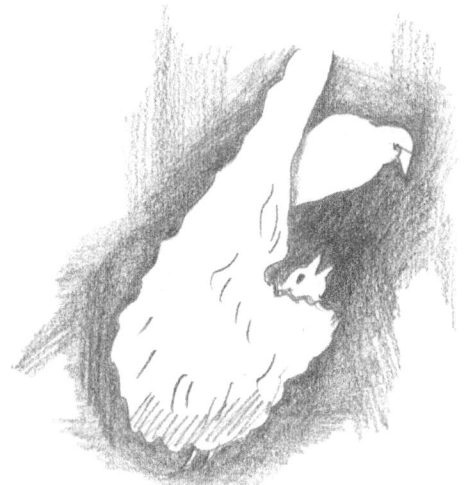

Rhyme for the cast-on slipknot

*A black feathered bird
With a bright yellow beak
Builds a hanging nest
Like a sack from a tree.
The baby bird is hungry.
He opens up wide,
Insisting—no, demanding
That a grub be put inside.
Searching along
Up under and through,
Mama Oropendula
Plucks up a worm for two.*

      – A.B.Akin

Instructions for the tail-tugger slipknot

Find a comfortable place to sit and place a yarn-ball in a basket, to your Shuttle side.

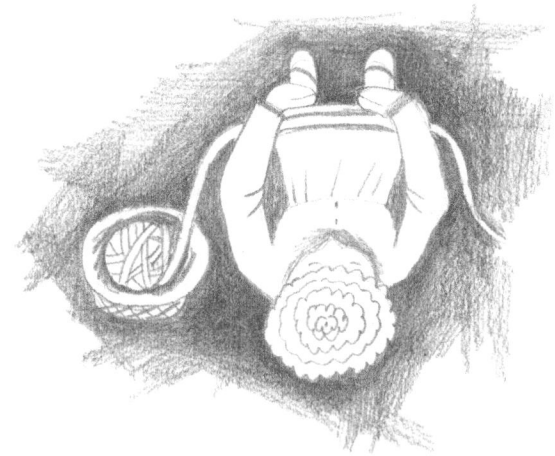

Lay the strand across your lap, so that the tail hangs slightly over your knee that is farthest from the ball of yarn. With your Loom Hand, lift the middle section of the yarn, about a foot above your lap.

Swivel your fingers slightly so that the tail of the yarn hangs farther from you and the leed, connecting to the ball, is closer to you.

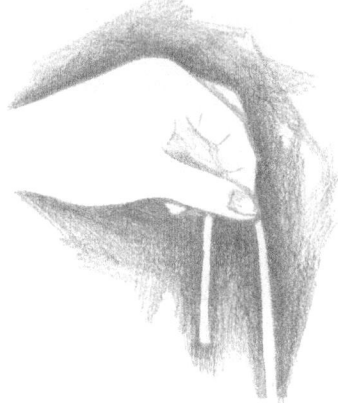

With your Shuttle Hand, grasp the parallel hanging strands, at about the midway point, letting your Shuttle Thumb rest between them to keep them from crossing. Now, let go with your Loom Hand.

Finger Crochet

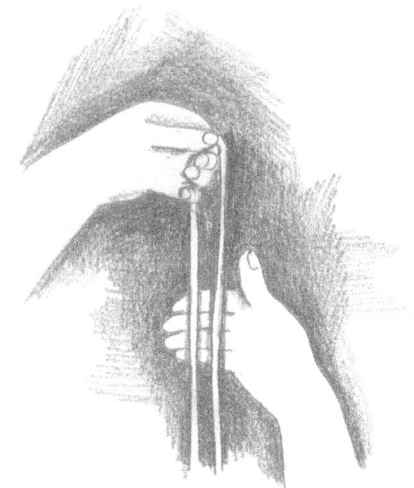

A droopy loop is now draped down over your hand.

Insert your Loom bird-pinch in through the loop, toward your Shuttle wrist and lower it down to rest at the bottom of the loop, spreading the fingers of the pinch apart to create a tall triangle.

Slowly lift your Loom Hand while, simultaneously, lowering your Shuttle Hand to create an upside-down triangle, against the Palm of your Loom Hand.

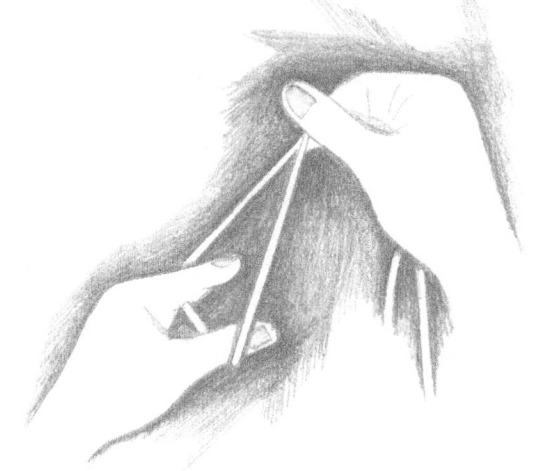

Once you have done this, the yarn will look something like the face of an ox, with the two ears around your Thumb and Pointer.

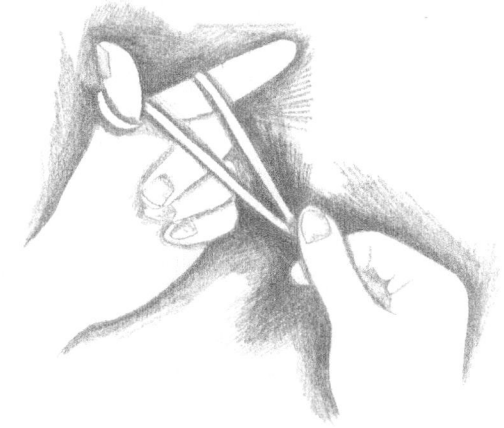

Let go with your Shuttle Hand.

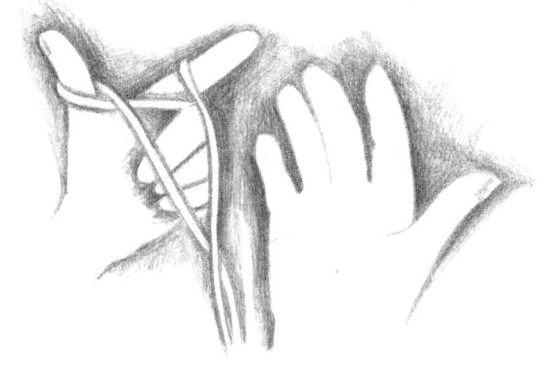

chapter five

Loosen the loop just enough to also fit your Shuttle Thumb.

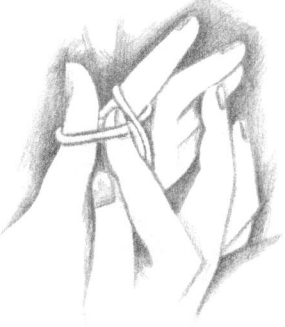

Poke your Shuttle bird-pinch up through the loop on your Loom Thumb.

Pluck the loop on your Loom Pointer with your Shuttle Bird-pinch.

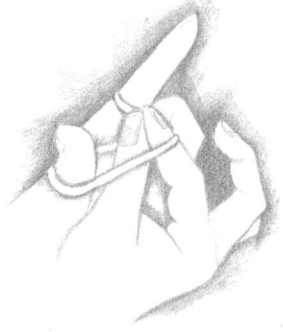

As you tug the yarn toward you, the loop on your Loom Thumb will naturally rise up off of it. Slip it off the end of the Thumb. Keep a good hold on the new loop with your Shuttle bird-pinch as you grasp the two dangling strands (the leed and tail) with your Loom-Fist.

Tug on the new loop with your Shuttle bird-pinch to tighten its base.

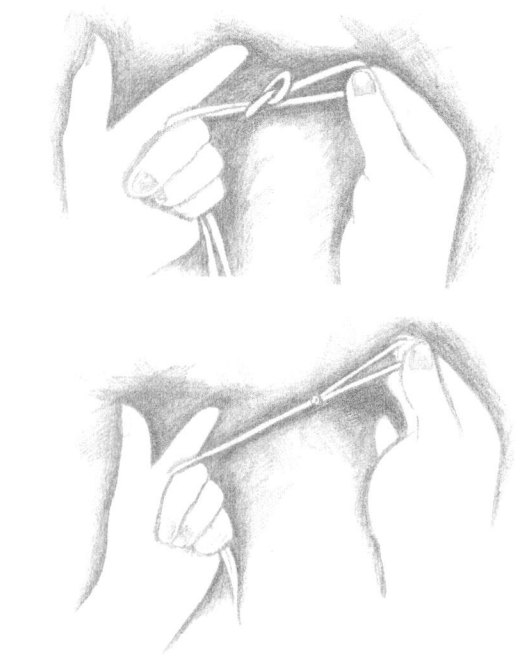

✶ You have just completed a tail-tugger slipknot.

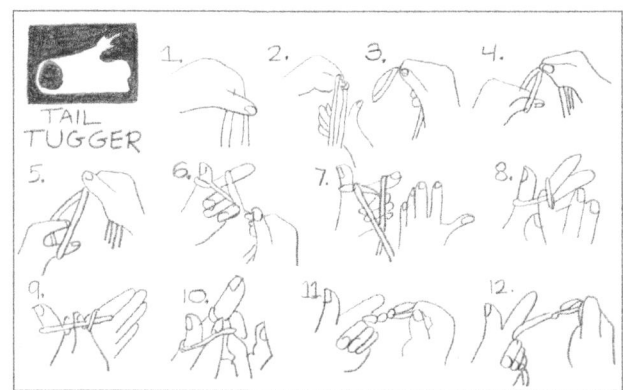

Adjusting your loop

Any slipknot can be tightened or loosened to a desired size. The beauty of this slipknot is that you can reliably tighten it by tugging on the tail, and loosen it by tugging on the loop itself, on the side connecting to the tail. If you tug on the other side, it only tightens the collar around the base of the knot.

Important: Once you have created a successful slipknot following this pattern, go ahead and repeat the sequence a dozen or more times, while the instructions are still fresh in your mind, until the movements become second-nature to you.

Finger Crochet

Crochet without a Hook

Barehand crochet is a versatile and yet simple technique that closely mimics large-needle crochet. With the hook of a single Pointer finger, an initial chain of yarn is created and re-entered into, and the piece builds with single-file rows of loops pulled through loops, creating either a rectangular-shaped panel, or, with a slight variation in the procedure, a circular panel.

Any natural, flexible, and touch-friendly yarn can be used for this technique. Finger-crochet projects are easy to start and easy to set aside. All the more reason to take your project along with you anywhere! Because the crochet piece grows as you work, but is never firmly attached to your finger, it is best to work while seated so you can rest it in your lap.

An overview of straight crochet

The initial practice project is one for straight crochet. This technique creates a long rectangular or square strip of fabric that is made by working back and forth along the width, each new row being linked, stitch-by-stitch, to the previous one. This means that the length of the first row of chain you make—called the *starter-chain*—will determine the *width* of the final scarf, and each row will have the same number of stitches as the previous row.

Once you have laid down the starter-chain, you will crochet into it a second row, called the *foundation row*. Finally, you will crochet rows of regular stitches until you have attained the desired length of your scarf.

As you reach the end of each row of *chain*, *foundation*, and *regular stitches*, the work will reverse direction along the piece like a farmer plowing a field. But this is accomplished by simply flipping the piece over each time, so that your *direction of working* will always be the same.

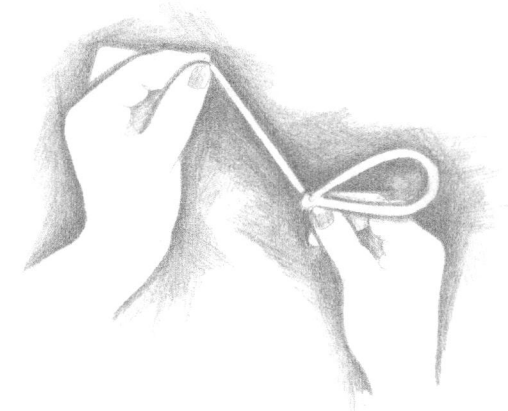

Preparing a tell-tail

Begin by preparing a pair of *tell-tails*—yarn-loops of a contrasting color to your work. (*Tell-tail* is a nautical term, referring to a strand of yarn tied to the rigging of a sailboat to indicate wind direction.) Make each tell-tail loop by doubling about a 12-inch strand, smoothing the ends together and tying a two-ply overhand knot near the ends.

You will be using your tell-tails to mark the beginnings and ends of rows, which will be a great help in keeping the number of stitches in each row consistent. Set down the tell-tail ties within grasping distance.

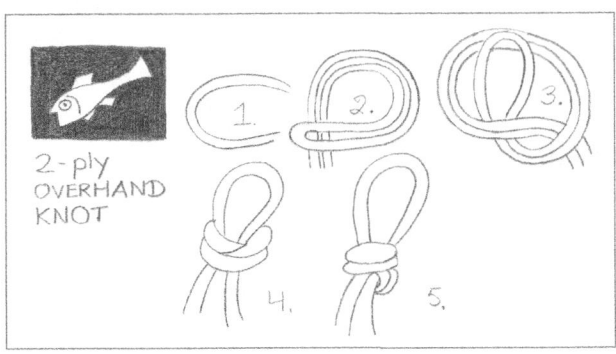

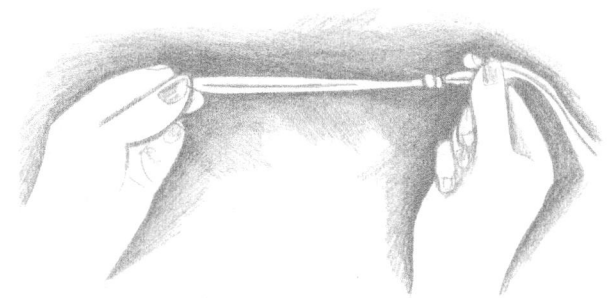

chapter five

Rhyme for finger crochet

Two foxes lope out of the forest one day,
And down to the pond where the children all play.
Their ears pricked up high, noses close to the ground,
They sit near the water and don't make a sound.
A child slides down the root of a tree;
Splashes into the pond, crying "Hey, look at me!"
He pulls out a frog and goes back to the top,
Another frog comes from behind with a hop!
This froggie ducks down through an old hollow log
And Foxy scoots up again close to the bog.
      – H. Akin and A.B. Akin

Creating an Autumn Scarf

While learning, it is best to use bulky weight yarn.

Create two tell-tail ties and set them aside. Find a comfortable place to sit and place the yarn-ball to your Loom side. Make a tail-tugger slipknot.

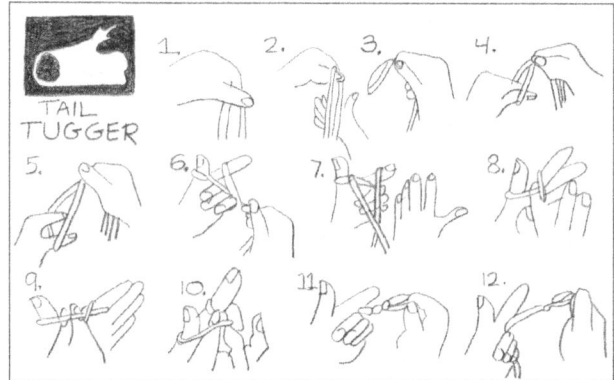

Recall the technique for finger knitting a regular chain introduced in *Bare Hand Knitting* Book I and then practice making a chain that is quite loose.

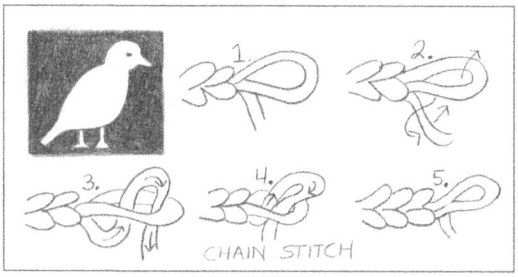

Starter chain

Creating a loose chain is the first step to beginning a finger-crochet project. To make a loose chain, begin by making a tail-tugger slipknot, and finger-knit just as you would a regular chain, except you will tug each new loop only down to the size that will allow your Pointer finger to just slip into it.

A loose chain

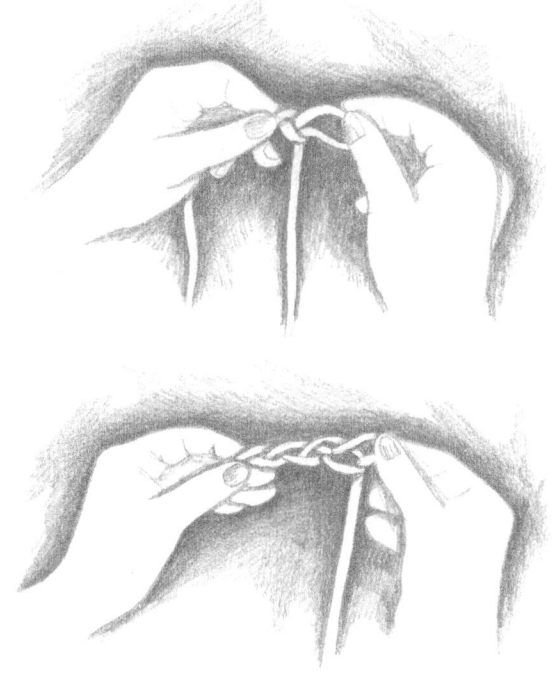

For this project, I suggest using a starter chain of 12 stitches. The length of this loose chain will then be the final width of your scarf. Chain-knit the 12 stitches as described above, and then close-off the starter-chain by adding a final *floater stitch*, (in this case, a 13th stitch) which is pulled fairly snug because it will not be linked into.

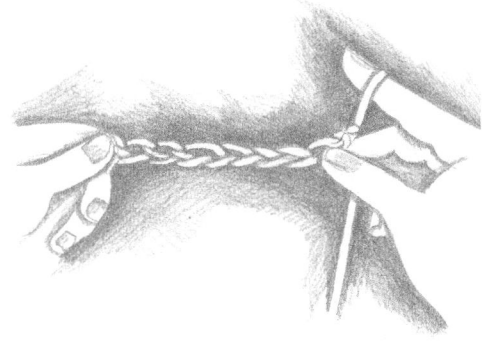

The floater stitch is used for "rounding the bend" to the next row.

* You have worked your first floater stitch.

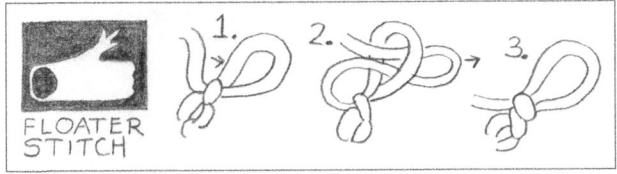

Your starter chain is now complete.

STARTER CHAIN SEQUENCE
- Tail-tugger code
- Starter chain code
- Floater stitch
- Flip the work

The form of each link

Notice that each link of the starter chain has three strands to it: two strands that cross each other and one "free-floater." Position the chain so that the crossed strands are on top.

Foundation row

Now is the time to crochet the *foundation row*. Place the yarn-loop onto Shuttle Pointer. Take hold of your knitted chain with the fox-pinches of both hands. Suspend the leed over the Knuckle-side of Loom Pointer and straighten that finger to create the necessary tension in the working yarn and to keep it out of the way.

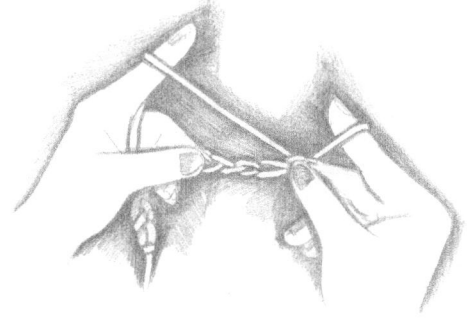

Note that the work is stretched between the fox-pinches of both hands and that both Pointers (representative of the fox's ears) are held upright and in readiness for working a stitch. This will be referred to as the *fox-chat* position.

With your Shuttle Pointer, poke around to find the final stitch of your starter chain—that is, the one just before the floater stitch. This will be the first stitch you will crochet into.

chapter five

Slip your Shuttle Pointer through the hole of that link, in the direction away from you.

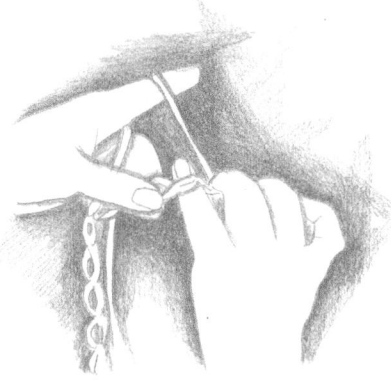

Hook the leed with Shuttle Pointer and pull it back toward you through the same hole, forming a new loop on Pointer.

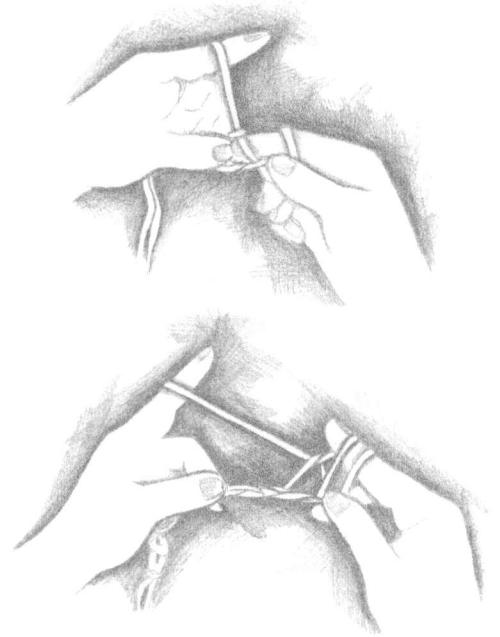

Note: There will now be two yarn-loops on Shuttle Pointer. Both fingers should now be straight and lifted again. (Like the pricked-up ears of alert foxes.)

Using your Loom Pointer, gently bring the leed back around the nail-side of Shuttle Pointer's tip, stretching it between the Pointers to keep the tension. You will bend Loom Pointer down and forward, slightly putting tension into that segment of leed to secure it from slipping.

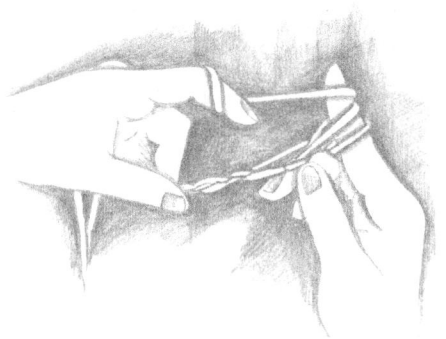

Loom bird-pinch the two yarn-loops on Shuttle Pointer, securing them for the next move.

Swivel your Shuttle Hand toward you slightly (counter-topwise), hooking the leed with the tip of Shuttle Pointer, pulling it down through both of the yarn-loops as they slip off the tip of Pointer. This will leave a new yarn-loop on Pointer.

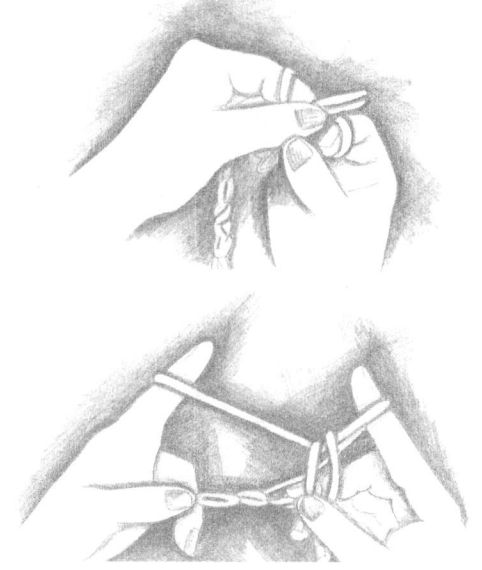

You should now have one yarn-loop on your Shuttle Pointer, and end up in fox-chat position, just as when you started.

✷ You have just completed your first foundation row crochet polystitch.

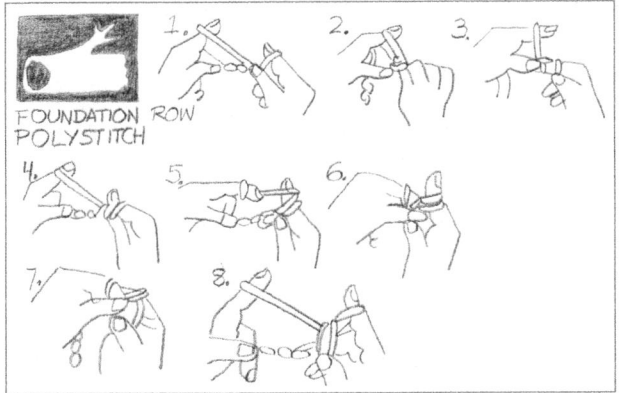

Find the next stitch over, and do a foundation row polystitch into it. Continue doing such polystitches until you have worked back to the beginning of the starter-chain.

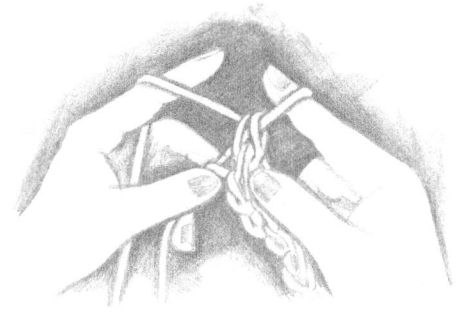

At this point, add a floater stitch for rounding the bend.

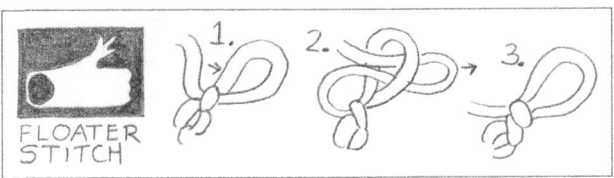

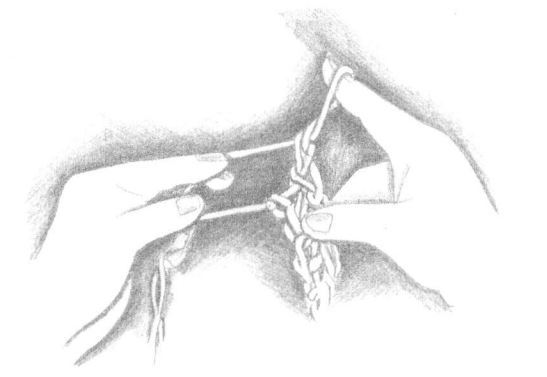

Now, flip your piece over in preparation for working a straight row of regular crochet polystitches.

✷ You have flipped your work.

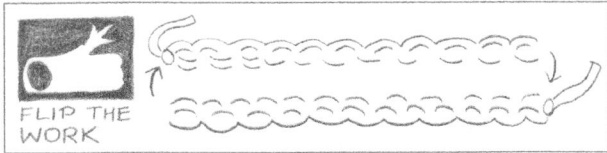

This completes the entire foundation row sequence.

FOUNDATION ROW SEQUENCE
- **Foundation row polystitch**
- **Floater stitch**
- **Flip the work**

Straight rows

Now you will be doing your first regular row, working into crochet stitches instead of into chain. Notice that the stitches of the foundation row you have just completed have a different appearance, having two upper ridges or "lips."

The shape of a stitch

Take a close look at a foundation row stitch. Identify two little bumps in the yarn forming a teardrop shape, called lips, making the top ridge of each stitch. Regular crochet stitches are worked under both lips of the ridge.

chapter five

Begin a new row

The first stitch of a new row is worked into the last stitch of the previous row, skipping the floater stitch.

For regular rows, the crochet stitches are worked under both lips. Poke through the hole under both lips and complete the steps of a crochet polystitch.

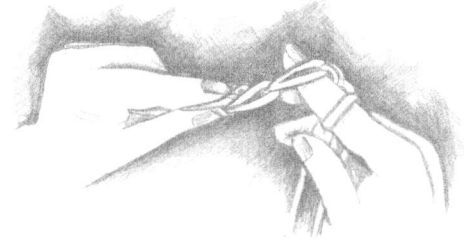

∗ The completed stitch is a regular crochet stitch for rows. Notice that only step two of this polystitch is distinct from the Foundation Row Polystitch in that Pointer passes under two lips.

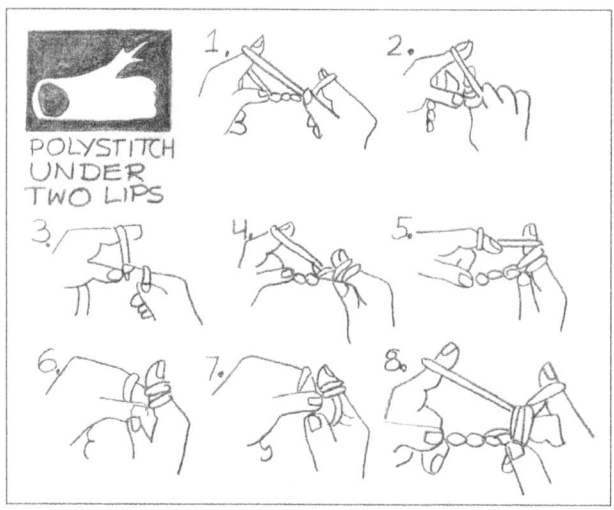

Keep working until you reach the end of the row; do a floater stitch, flip your work, and start on the next row.

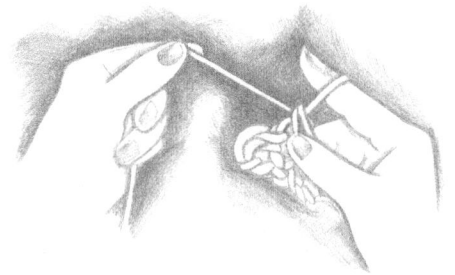

When you reach the end of each row it can be difficult to identify the last stitch of the previous row, as it tends to sink down into the edge of the work. Be sure to pull it up and stitch into it, otherwise you can lose stitches in a row and the width of the crocheted fabric begins to narrow. To avoid this, count your stitches at the end of each row, to make sure the number matches your foundation row. Do this by counting fishlip pairs along the ridge.

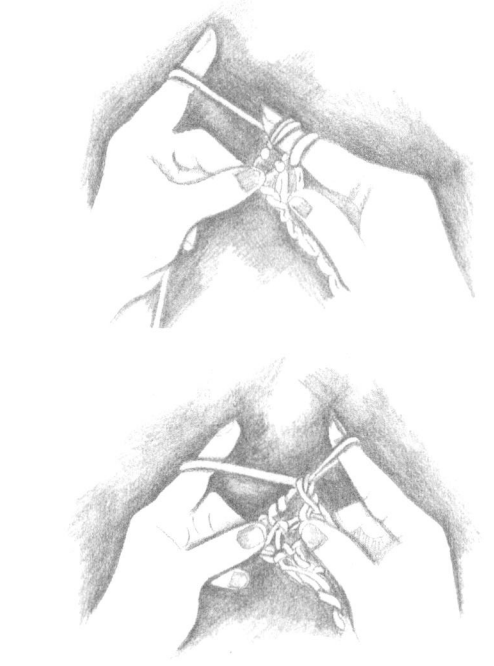

Add a floater stitch to the end of the row.

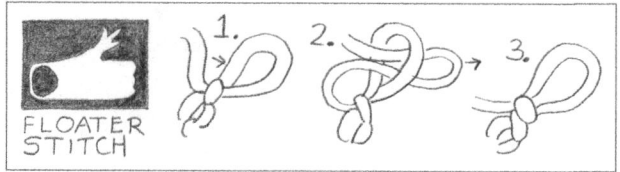

Flip the work in preparation for another row.

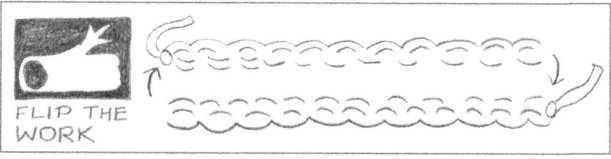

∗ This completes the repeating sequence for straight rows.

REPEATING SEQUENCE FOR STRAIGHT ROWS
- **Polystitch code for 2 fishlips**
- **Counting stitches from 1-9 plus floater**
- **Floater stitch**
- **Flip the work**

Row markers

An excellent method for keeping your rows even, is to attach a tell-tail to the first stitch of each row. As you complete the initial polystitch for a new row, fasten the tell-tail to the fishlips of the just-completed stitch, which is under and behind the active loop. After you have done this with both tell-tails, one at each end, you then re-use each tell-tail as you will find it just below the new stitch. Unfasten it and re-fasten it into the new stitch above. As you reach the end of each row, you will make a floater stitch, then flip your work and continue. By attaching a tell-tail into the first stitch, you will always have a tell-tail at either end of your work. And you will always know when you have reached the last stitch of the previous row.

This easy and fun system goes a long way to preventing unwanted decreases that so often plague those who do crochet.

Tensions

If the tensions of your work do not seem quite right, just allow some time for the fibers and tensions to relax into place. With more experience, you will find your tensions improving.

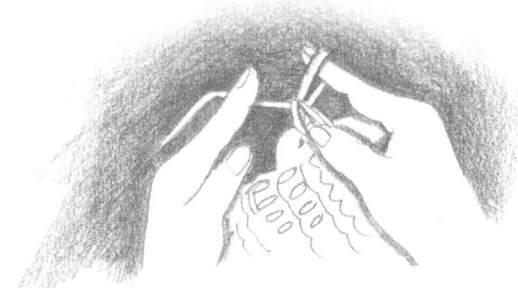

Finishing up

In crochet, unlike with knitting, there is no need for a casting-off sequence, as only one stitched is worked at a time. Once you have completed as many rows as you want, finish the final row and cut the leed, leaving a six-inch dangler, which you will put through the last loop.

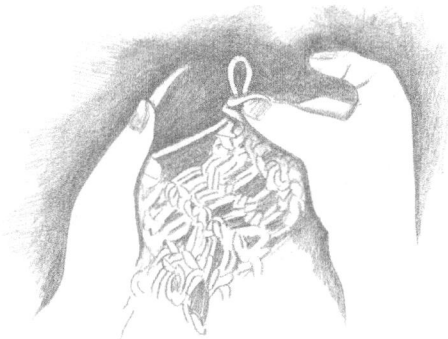

Tug gently on dangler to snug up the last stitch.

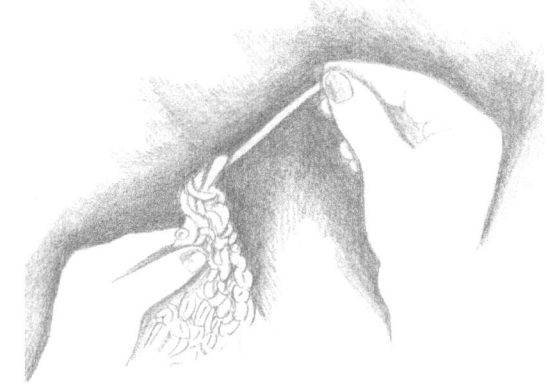

Continue to work rows, in keeping with the rows sequence, until your crocheted fabric is the desired length for a scarf.

chapter five

* You have cut the leed and tied off.

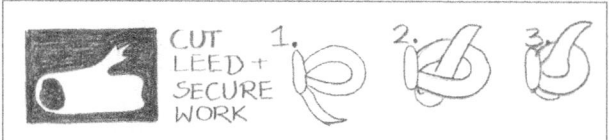

In order to hide your dangler and tail in the work, weave-in each and split-and-fasten the ends.

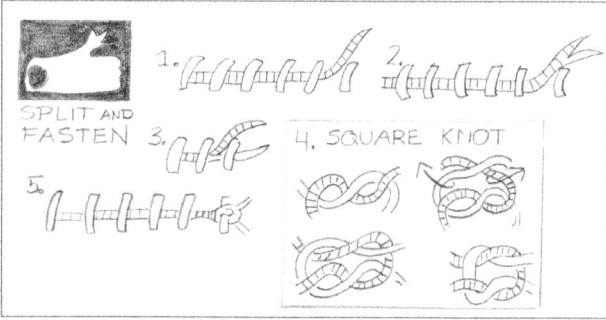

* This completes the entire sequence for straight crochet.

STRAIGHT CROCHET SEQUENCE
- **Tail-tugger**
- **Starter chain**
- **Foundation row**
- **Regular rows**
- **Cut and secure**
- **Split and fasten**
- **Adding fringe**

Adding fringe

Adding fringe to the ends of your autumn scarf can be a nice touch. For complete instructions refer to Chapter 7, in *Bare Hand Knitting* Book I.

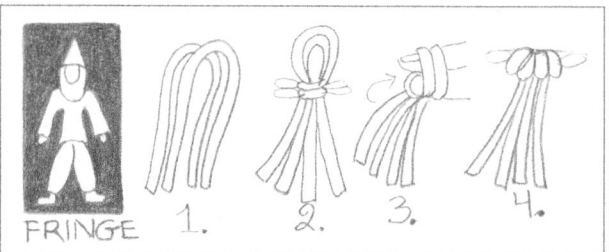

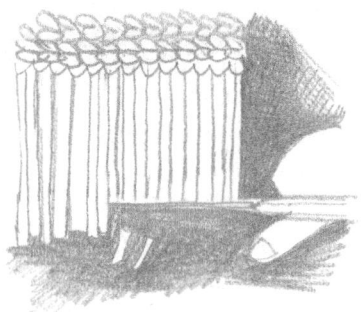

Congratulations, you have created a very nice, wearable scarf!

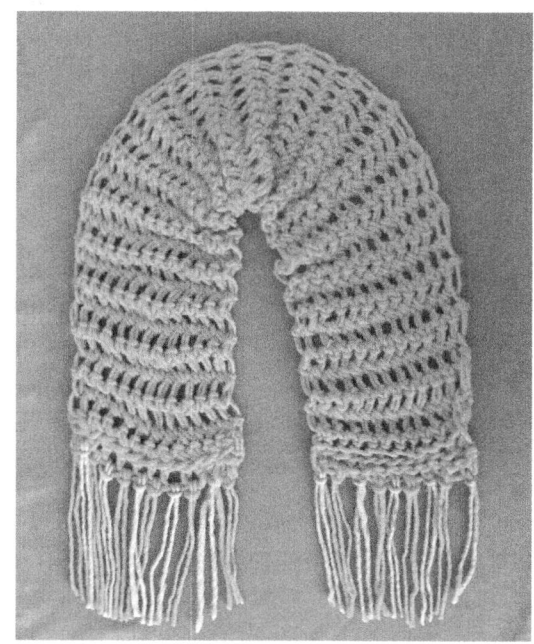

Practice makes natural

It is generally a good idea to complete a few projects using straight crochet before moving on to circular crochet. Only by practice will the process become natural, as your fingers become familiar with the subtle movements required and the tensions in the work even out.

Finger Crochet

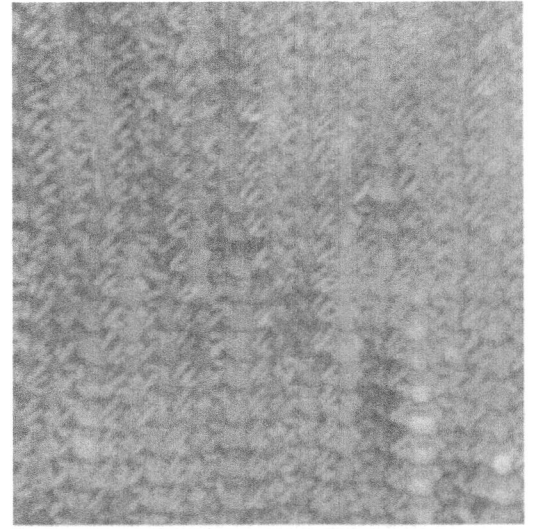

Doll's blanket made using barehand flat crochet.

Circular Crochet

This technique begins in the center and expands outward. Your starter-loop—the tailtugger slipknot—provides the initial framework. Around that, you will crochet an orbiting *foundation row*, followed by as many *regular rows* as you'll need for the size of your piece.

As each successive orbit gets larger, the rows get longer, and so special additional stitches, called *increases*, must be added, as will be described. You will also be attaching a *tell-tail* as a signal-flag to indicate when each orbit has been completed. At the end of the project, the tell-tail is removed.

While the rows in straight crochet go back and forth, the rows of circular crochet always build in the same, countertopwise, orbital direction. For example, in the project below, the work starts in the center of the top of the hat, crocheting a flat disk, and then making an adjustment that allows the work to form a bowl shape.

Poem for circular crochet

Two by two
Go the pairs
Whether they have
Scales or hairs.
Animal [enter animal type for row] ma,
Animal [enter animal type for row] pop,
Into the arch
With the pointed rooftop.
　　　　　　　　– A.B. Akin

chapter five

Crocheting a Hat

For the practice project you will make a hat.

Materials: One ball bulky weight yarn. About 14 inches of yarn in a contrasting color for the tell-tail.

Begin with a starter-loop

Create the starter-loop by making a tail-tugger slipknot with the knot at least six inches in from the tail of your working yarn.

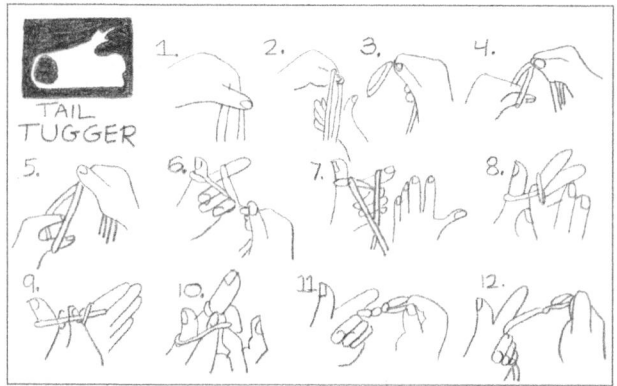

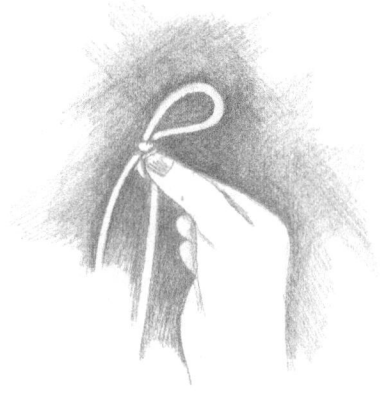

Adjust the loop so that it is the about the size of a lemon.

Test the knot to make certain it is a tail-tugger—this is critical for the last step of the project when it would be too late to think about starting over.

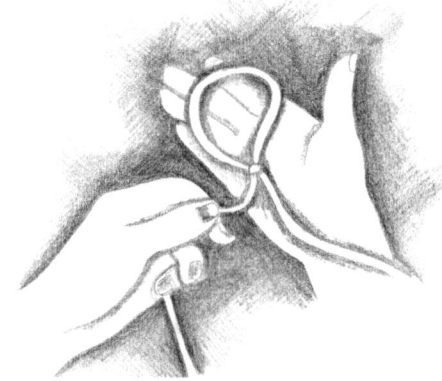

Using your Shuttle fox-pinch, grip the tail below the knot, while your Loom fox-pinch grasps the top of the loop, about a third of the way around, so that when the top strand is drawn taut between the pinches, the bottom of the loop sags open below.

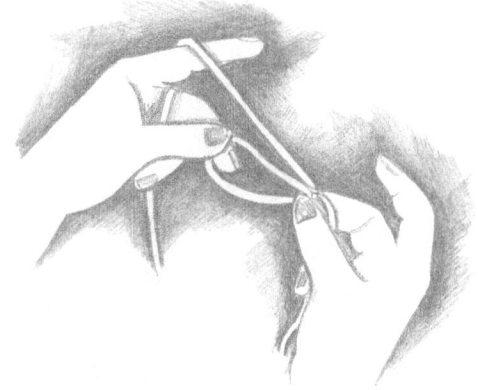

Now, straighten your Pointer fingers in readiness just as you would in fox-chat position—only here there isn't a loop on Pointer yet, and you are gripping a loop instead of a chain.

This first stitch is very much like a regular crochet polystitch, only you are starting without a loop on Pointer. Treating the starter-loop like the smaller hole of a starter-chain in straight crochet, insert your Shuttle Pointer into the starter-loop, going outward, away from you, passing above the leed.

Bending Pointer down, hook the leed and draw it toward you through the loop.

Finger Crochet

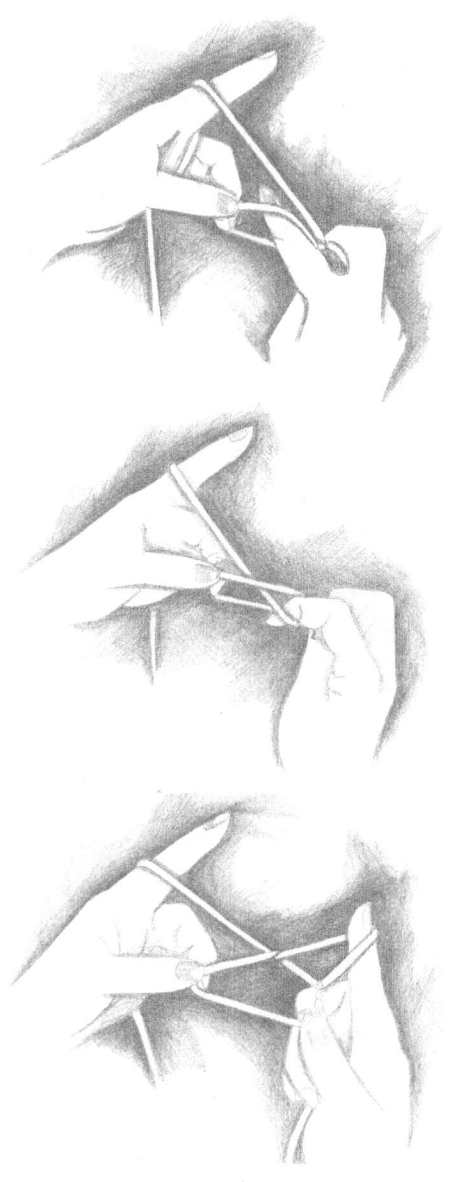

Bring Loom Pointer down in front of the leed, and Loom bird-pinch the single loop on Shuttle Pointer. Swivel your Shuttle Hand toward you slightly (countertopwise), hooking the leed with the tip of Shuttle Pointer, pulling it down through the loop as it slips off the tip of Pointer. This will leave a new yarn-loop on Pointer, and you will end up in fox-chat position, as when you started.

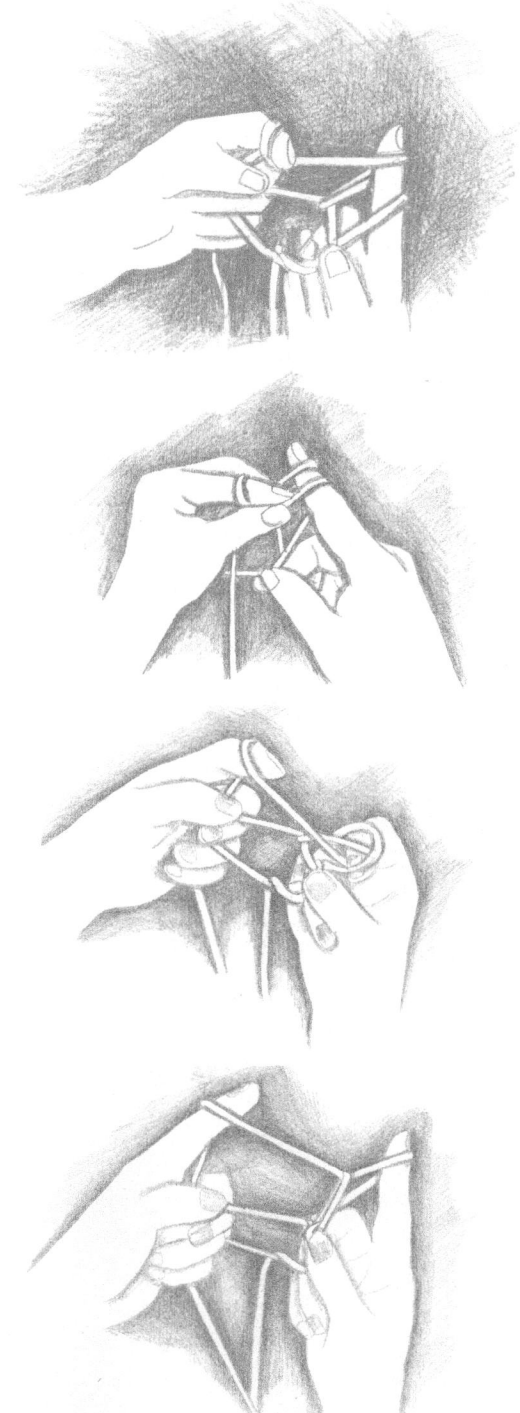

Now, using your Loom Hand, maneuver the leed that is coming off Loom Pointer around the nail-side of Shuttle Pointer.

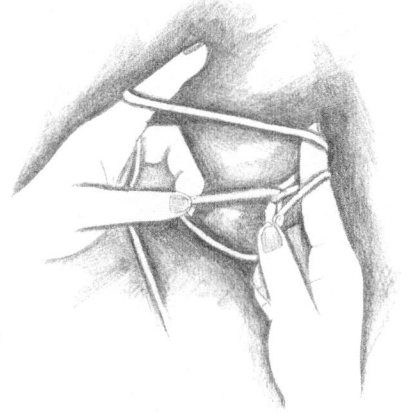

chapter five

✳ You have just worked the *anchor stitch*—the first circular crochet polystitch.

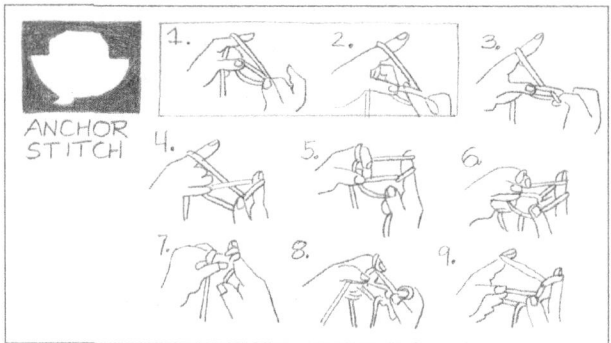

Assume fox-chat position in readiness for another stitch.

With the active loop on Pointer, you will now poke the tip of Shuttle Pointer under the ridge of the starter-loop and complete a regular crochet polystitch, as follows:

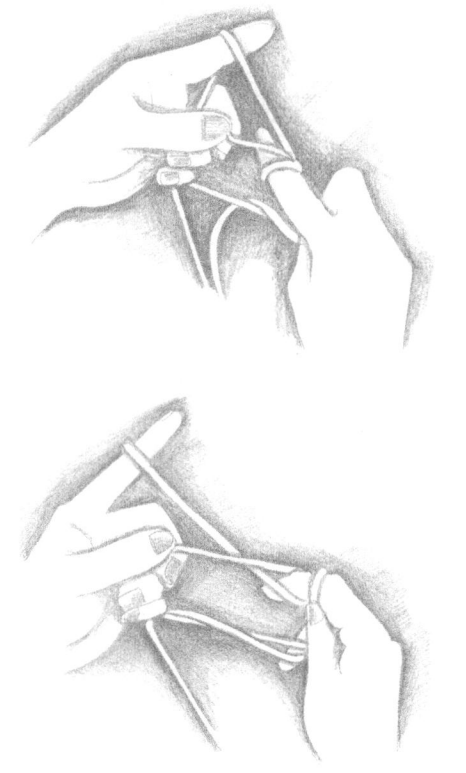

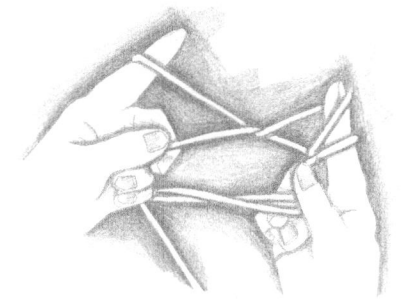

With Loom Pointer, bring the leed back around the back side of Shuttle Pointer.

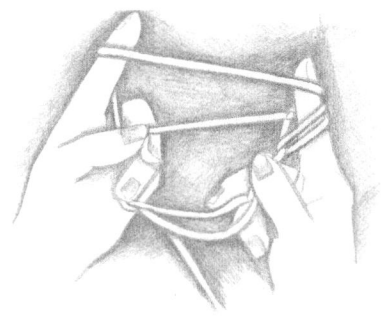

Bend Loom Pointer to hold the leed in place, and with Loom bird-pinch, secure yarn-loops on Shuttle Pointer.

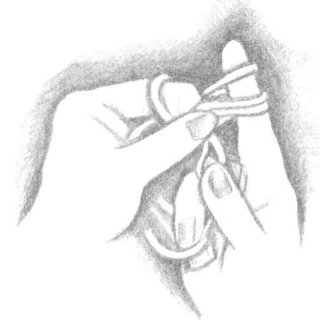

Hook down the leed with Shuttle Pointer and pull it down through both yarn-loops, creating a new yarn-ring on Pointer.

Finger Crochet

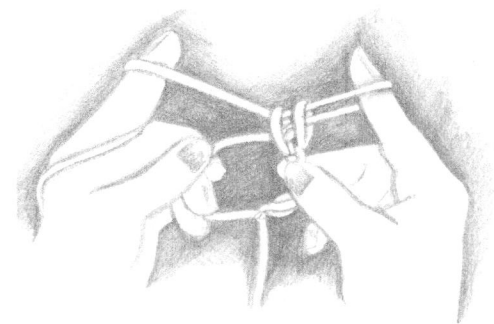

∗ You have now worked a regular crochet polystitch into a starter-loop.

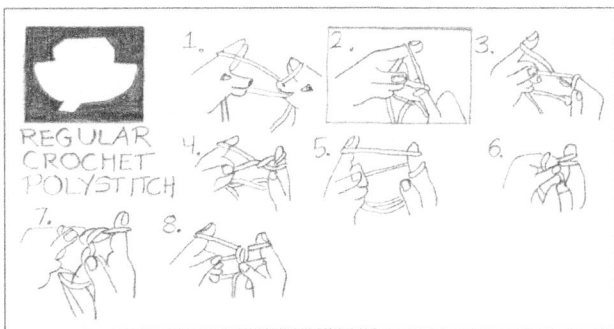

This was the second stitch of six that will make up your *circular foundation row*.

Do four more such stitches into the starter-loop. You now have six stitches, including the anchor stitch, completing your first circular foundation row.

Six is a very significant number in crocheting circles, and for circles in general.

Note: When you have gotten this far, you will likely have a bit of the starter-loop left bare, with no stitches on it. That is okay. Tug lightly on the tail of your original starter-loop to draw-in just enough slack for the stitches to meet, but no further. Resist the temptation to cinch everything up; that would make it too cramped to work the next row. Save the final tightening for when your crocheted work is completed.

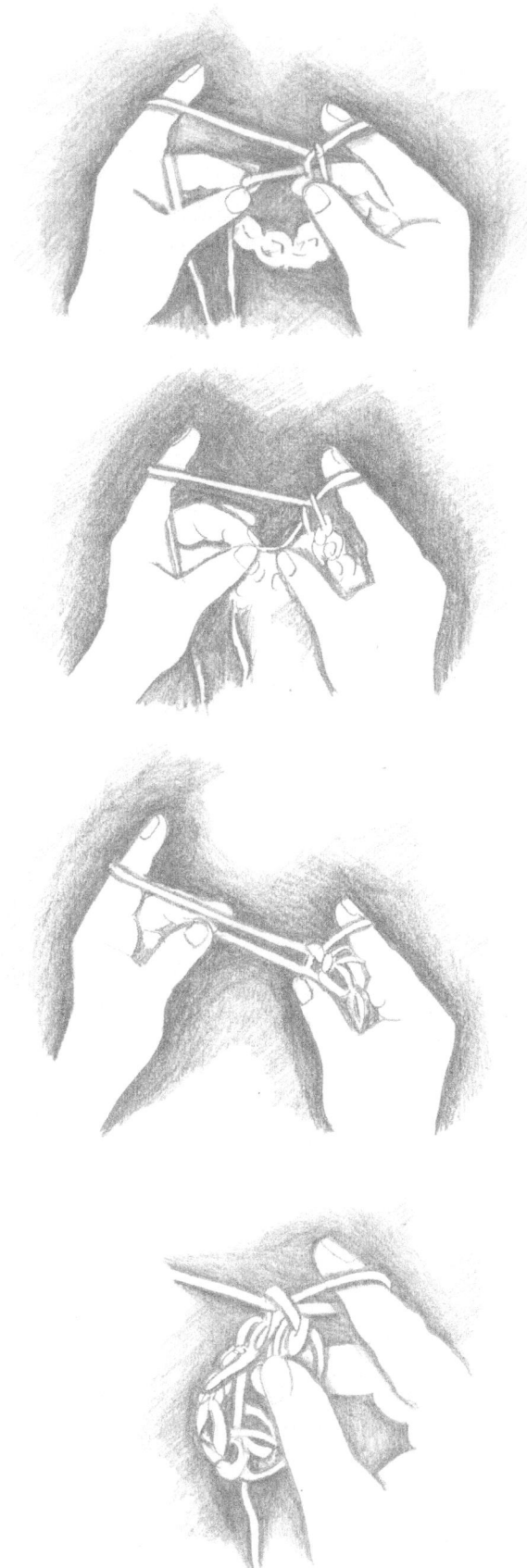

71

chapter five

Attaching the tell-tail

Identify the anchor stitch—the first stitch in the ring of six, which looks different from the others (two simple open lips). Pick up the tell-tail loop which you had set aside, and insert it knot-first through the lips of the anchor stitch, then draw it by its knot up through itself into a lark's-head knot that it is fastened to the upper lip of the anchor stitch. The little overhand knot near the tip of your tell-tail should wind up on the outside, away from the work.

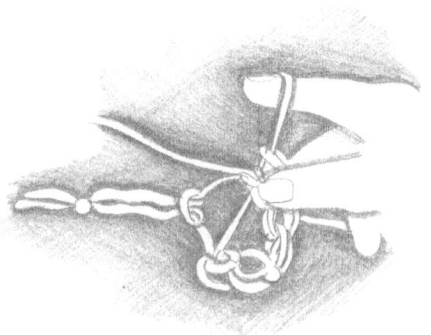

Slide the lark's-head knot Shuttlewise, so that it rests in that corner of the anchor stitch. Finally, tuck the tell-tail out of the way between your Shuttle Palm and the work.

Starting a new orbiting row

You will now be working two consecutive crochet polystitches into each stitch of the previous row in order to keep the work flat. In other words, you will do one regular stitch and one *increase stitch* into each of the six stitches of the foundation row.

Since the anchor stitch—the first stitch—is unique in that it has only one upper lip, work a stitch under that single ridge and complete a crochet polystitch follows.

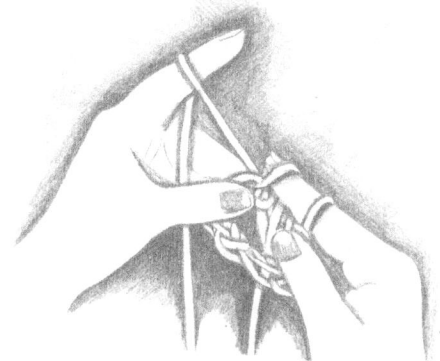

Hook the leed and pull back through the two yarn-loops on Shuttle Pointer.

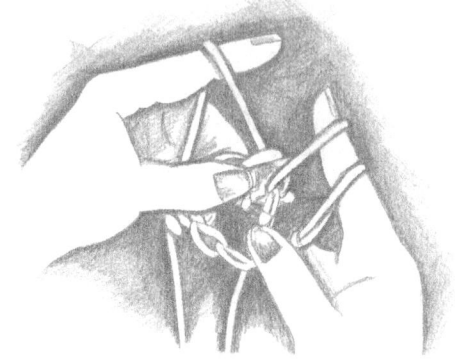

With Loom Pointer, bring the leed around the back side of Shuttle Pointer.

Bend and swivel Loom Pointer to secure the leed from slipping.

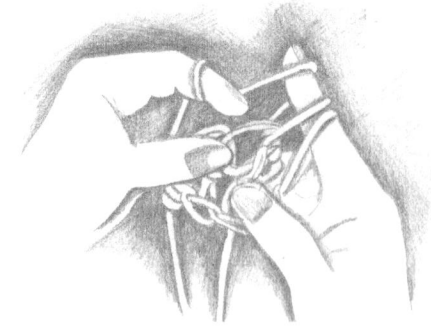

With Loom bird-pinch, secure yarn-loops on Shuttle Pointer.

Finger Crochet

Hook the leed with Shuttle Pointer and pull it down through both yarn-loops, creating a new yarn-loop on Pointer.

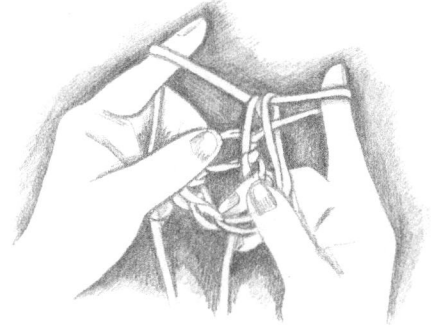

✳ You have worked the initial foundation row polystitch into the anchor stitch.

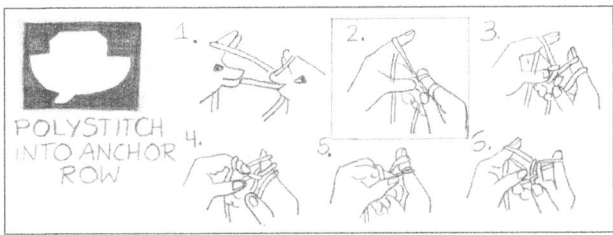

Pull the tell-tail up through the just-completed stitch to mark the beginning of your new row.

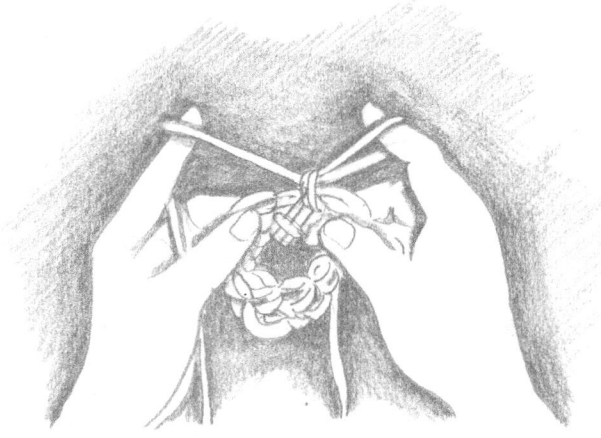

Increase

Work a second crochet polystitch into the single lip of the anchor stitch.

✳ You have worked your first increase.

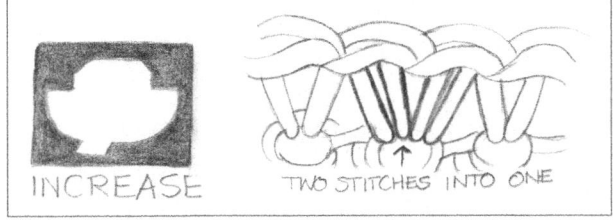

Continue to work your way around the foundation row, countertopwise, doing increases (two-in-one stitches) into every foundation stitch, for a total of twelve stitches.

These polystitches into the foundation row are done exactly as those described previously, except you will observe that when you were stitching into the starter-loop, you took the leed beneath a single strand; but now that you are stitching into full stitches, the leed passes under two lips. In this way you will now be working regular crochet polystitches under two lips, as is done in straight crochet.

chapter five

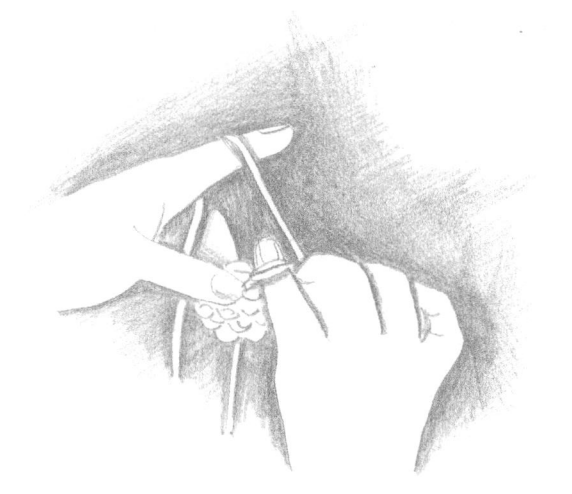

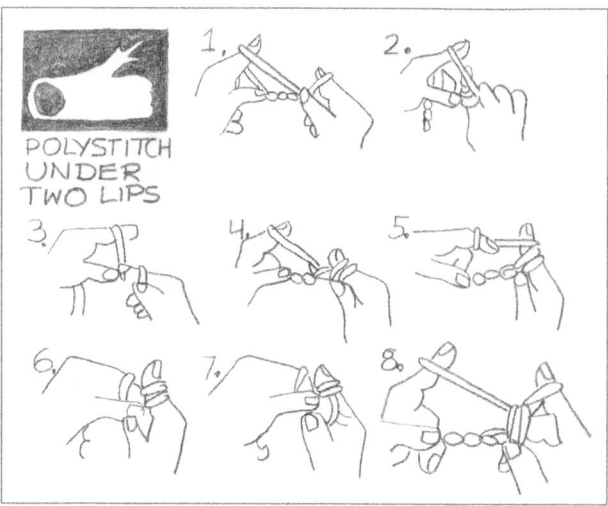

When you have crocheted around in a circle, you will know each row is complete when you come back to the tell-tail.

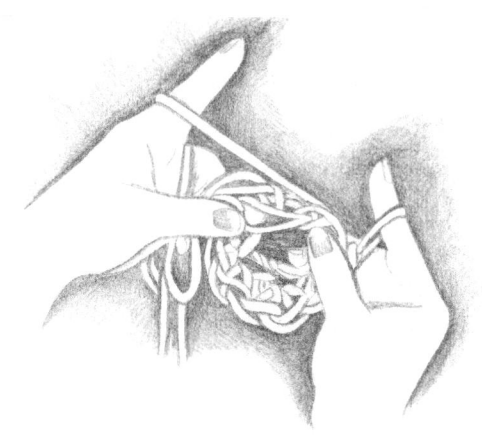

Patterned increases

When creating a piece that is both circular and flat, it is necessary to add stitches to each succeeding circle as the work grows outward. In other words, when doing straight rows, each stitch along the edge has one and only one stitch linked into it, but when working in a ring it is necessary to add stitches as the circles get larger. This two-into-one stitch is traditionally called an *increase*. As it turns out, six is the magic number for keeping a circle flat. You only need six increases added for each succeeding circular row, no matter how large your piece becomes.

Third orbit

Begin your third row by working a single crochet polystitch into the very same stitch that your tell-tail is coming out of—the first stitch of the previous row. Next, draw the tell-tail up through the just-completed stitch to mark the beginning of your new row.

(In the first regular row, you worked two stitches into every foundation row stitch. Now that you are on your second regular row, you must work one increase stitch into *every other stitch*, as will be explained shortly.) Work two crochet polystitches into the next stitch, creating an increase. Continue in a topwise direction working increases into every other stitch of the previous row. (All of your flat circular rows will have six equally distributed increase stitches in them.)

Recognizing where you are

When adding increases—two-into-one—it can be tricky at first to recognize which stitch to crochet into next. When you want to work a stitch into the next stitch over, straighten Shuttle Pointer so that the working loop is just above the stitch you worked into. Look for two little lines stretching Loomwise and a teardrop-shaped hole and work into it. When you want to work a second stitch into the same stitch, look for the pointy top of a pentagonal-shaped hole—like the roof-peak of a house. (I always think of the peak of the cabin on Noah's Ark, because of all the animals going two-by-two, which you will soon encounter.) Then, when you want to work a stitch into the next stitch over, lean Pointer workwise and look for two little lines stretching Loomwise and a teardrop-shaped hole and work into it. This pentagonal hole is just under the active loop. The difference is subtle at first but with a little time and practice you will recognize the difference with ease.

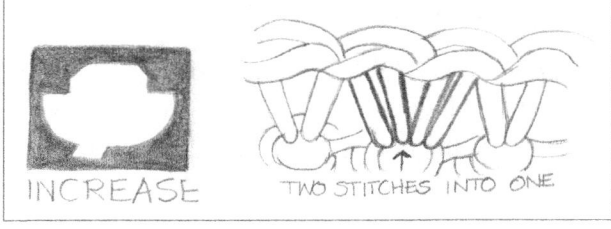

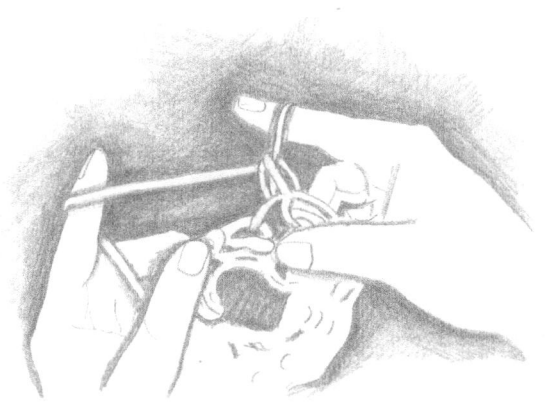

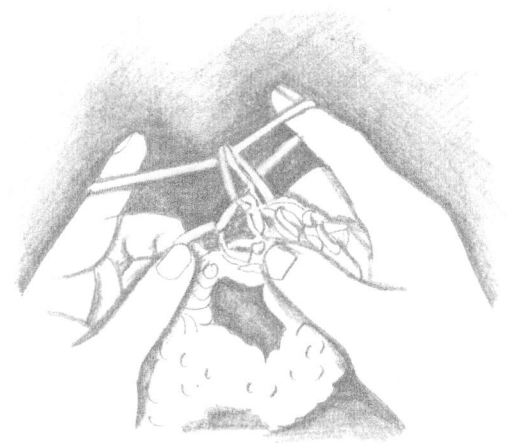

Continue rows

Continue to work rows. While on your third row, you work an increase into every second stitch of the previous row. For your fourth row, you will be working an increase into every third stitch, and so on.

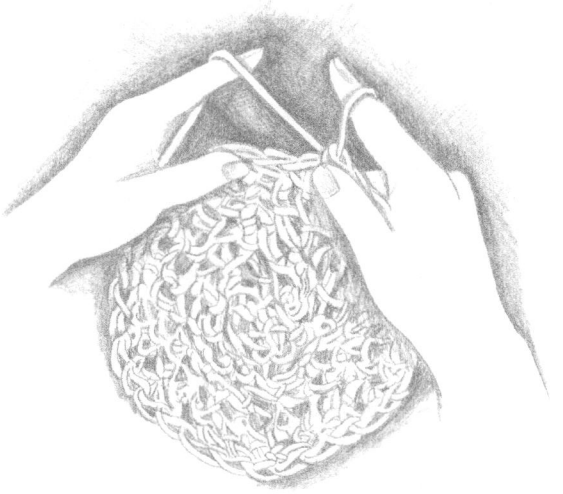

The Animal-Alphabet System for keeping track of increases

Below is the pattern of regular stitches and increase stitches as your flat circle grows outward. Your foundation row has six normal crochet stitches, your second row (orbit) will have six normal stitches paired with six increase stitches. Your third orbit will have the same number of stitches as the second plus an added six increase stitches, and so on. With 1 meaning a normal crochet stitch, and 2 meaning an increase stitch (two-into-one stitch), your pattern of stitches goes like this:

Foundation Row: 1, 1, 1, 1, 1, 1

Row A (Alligator): 2, 2, 2, 2, 2, 2

Row B (Bear): 1,2, 1,2, 1,2, 1,2, 1,2, 1,2

Row C (Camel): 1,1,2, 1,1,2, 1,1,2, 1,1,2, 1,1,2, 1,1,2

Row D (Duck): 1,1,1,2, 1,1,1,2, 1,1,1,2, 1,1,1,2, 1,1,1,2, 1,1,1,2

Row E (Elephant): 1,1,1,1,2, 1,1,1,1,2, 1,1,1,1,2, 1,1,1,1,2, 1,1,1,1,2, 1,1,1,1,2

chapter five

Row F (Fox): 1,1,1,1,1,2, 1,1,1,1,1,2, 1,1,1,1,1,2, 1,1,1,1,1,2, 1,1,1,1,1,2, 1,1,1,1,1,2

Row G (Giraffe): 1,1,1,1,1,1,2, 1,1,1,1,1,1,2, 1,1,1,1,1,1,2, 1,1,1,1,1,1,2, 1,1,1,1,1,1,2, 1,1,1,1,1,1,2

Row H (Hippo): etc.

When actually applying these principles, and the pattern above, it could be easy to get lost, and you'd find, despite your best efforts, your hoped-to-be-flat piece beginning to bend up into a bowl shape (too few increases) or acquiring ripples that radiate from the center (too many increases). Managing increases is like being the ringmaster of a three-ring circus—except that we have a lot more than three rings!

Fortunately, there is a practical system, one that has been taught successfully, that makes it easy to know what to do, when. And, speaking of circuses, this system employs a lot of exotic animals!

By listing the animals in alphabetical order, we call the first row following the foundation row, the "Alligator Row," the next row outward, the "Bear Row," followed by the "Camel Row," the "Duck Row," the "Elephant Row," and so on.

For whatever row you are working on, recite the letters of the alphabet, doing a single stitch for each letter, until you get to the letter of the animal whose row it is. Then say that animal's name twice and do a two-into-one stitch at that point. Then starting at A again, repeat the sequence. Here is what it sounds like for the first six rows:

Alligator Row: "Alligator-Alligator; Alligator-Alligator; Alligator-Alligator; Alligator-Alligator; Alligator-Alligator; Alligator-Alligator" (Do 2 stitches into each foundation stitch.)

Bear Row: "A, Bear-Bear; A, Bear-Bear; A, Bear-Bear; A, Bear-Bear; A, Bear-Bear; A, Bear-Bear" (Single stitch, two-into-one; single stitch, two-into-one; etc.)

Camel Row: "A, B, Camel-Camel; A, B, Camel-Camel; A, B, Camel-Camel; A, B, Camel-Camel; A, B, Camel-Camel; A, B, Camel-Camel"

Duck Row: "A, B, C, Duck-Duck; A, B, C, Duck-Duck; A, B, C, Duck-Duck; A, B, C, Duck-Duck; A, B, C, Duck-Duck; A, B, C, Duck-Duck"

Elephant Row: "A, B, C, D, Elephant-Elephant; A, B, C, D, Elephant-Elephant; A, B, C, D, Elephant-Elephant; A, B, C, D, Elephant-Elephant; A, B, C, D, Elephant-Elephant; A, B, C, D, Elephant-Elephant"

Fox Row: "A, B, C, D, E, Fox-Fox; A, B, C, D, E, Fox-Fox; A, B, C, D, E, Fox-Fox; A, B, C, D, E, Fox-Fox; A, B, C, D, E, Fox-Fox; A, B, C, D, E, Fox-Fox"

These rows are followed, if needed, by Giraffe, Hippo, Iguana, Jackal, Kangaroo, Lion, Monkey, Newt, Ostrich, Porcupine, Quail, Raccoon, Snake, Tiger—which should be plenty of rows for just about any project. (And a good thing, too—since U is a toughie!)

Helpful modification

This system works very well, but you might find you will sometimes lose track of whether you are doing the first or second Elephant or whatever. To fix this problem, try introducing the animals as "Papa" and "Mama." Instead of saying "Alligator, Alligator, Bear-Bear, Camel-Camel," use the following method:

Alligator-Daddy, Alligator-Mommy, etc.
A, Bear-Papa, Bear-Mama, etc.
A, B, Camel-Daddy, Camel-Mommy, etc.
A, B, C, Duck-Daddy, Duck-Mommy, etc.
A, B, C, D, Elephant-Dad, Elephant-Mom, etc.
A, B, C, D, E, Fox-Daddy, Fox-Mama, etc.
…and so on.

You can customize the titles of your animal pairs in any way you like. With the above technique, whenever you get to the Mama Animal, you know that is your increase stitch—the one that goes into the same stitch as the previous one.

An added advantage of the Animal-Alphabet system is that we can measure the sizes of our pieces in letters that can then be associated with animals: A small child might be fitted with a cap that goes out to D, for Duck before it tapers, while an adult might wear a size F for Fox or G for Giraffe. The thickness of the yarns used will also affect the sizes, of course.

Why six?

Look at the Animal-Alphabet diagram above. It is divided into six segments, and looking at just one segment, notice that the innermost ring has one animal-tile in that segment, the next row outward has two, next three, then four, and if it were larger, it would continue for five, six, seven and so on as far out as you like. That means, when you add a new ring to the outside of your circle, you will be adding six more stitches than the previous ring— one for each segment. This will continue to be true no matter how large your piece gets. Even if the piece were a hundred miles across, the next outer ring would only need six more stitches than the previous one!

Technically, to make a perfect circle would require "fractional stitches" to be added, or an extra full stitch every few rows. (The number 6 is mathematically related to 2π, which is 6.2831….) The shape we are actually creating is not a perfect circle, but a hexagon, which, for most purposes, can approximate a circle, since crocheted fabric is flexible. For a hexagon, there is no leftover fraction, and no additional increases need be added.

Going from flat circle to bowl

When you want your piece to stop expanding in a flat plane, but instead to start forming a bowl or tunnel—for example, when making the lower part of a cap—just stop doing two-into-one stitches. At the point where you are adding zero increase stitches, your work will form a tube with parallel sides.

For this project, after the fourth row expanding outward, you can now stop adding increases, and the rest of the rows will form a cylinder. Crochet is flexible enough that the top of the hat will smoothly curve downward into the sides. (As you work on future projects, you can experiment with the adding and subtracting of increase stitches

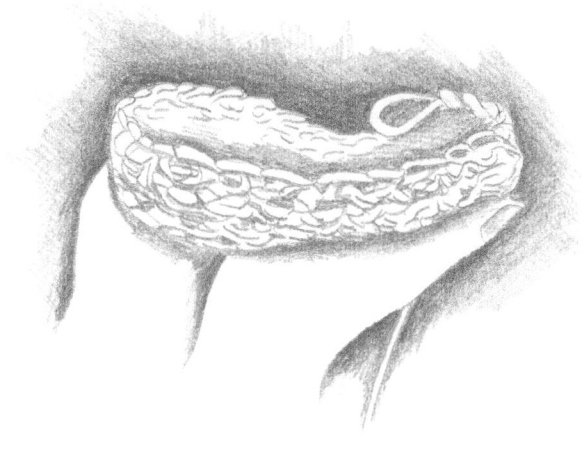

chapter five

more gradually, or in different patterns, as one technique in the creative sculpting of shapes in this flexible medium.)

Crocheting a finished-edge

When your hat has reached the desired size, you can complete the rim with a *finished-edge*. In order to complete the last row along the edge of the hat you will do a final orbit in exactly the same way as before, except that you'll work each new stitch under just one lip of the stitches of the previous row, rather than under two.

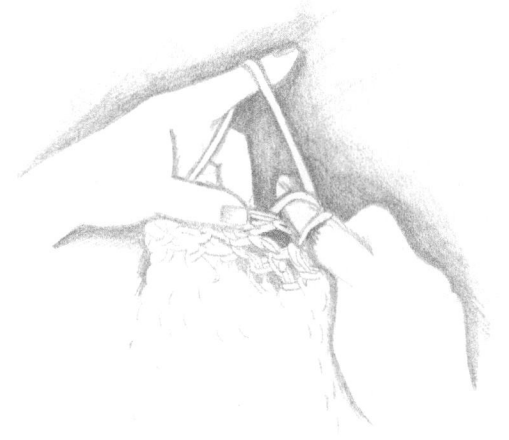

✶ This is how you do a *finished-edge crochet stitch*.

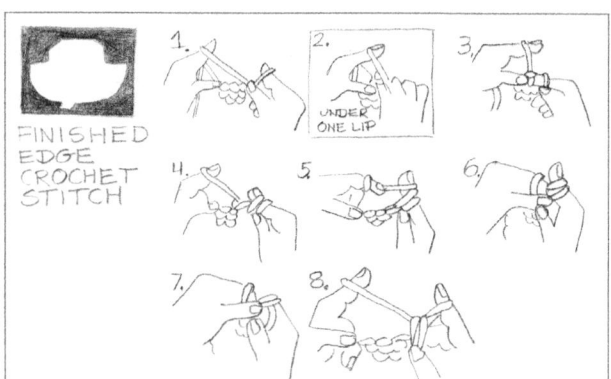

Tying-off

When your project is complete, cut the leed at eight inches and secure the work. Weave-in the dangler and do a split-and-fasten.

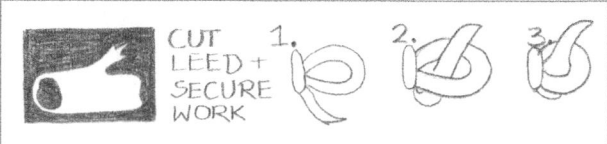

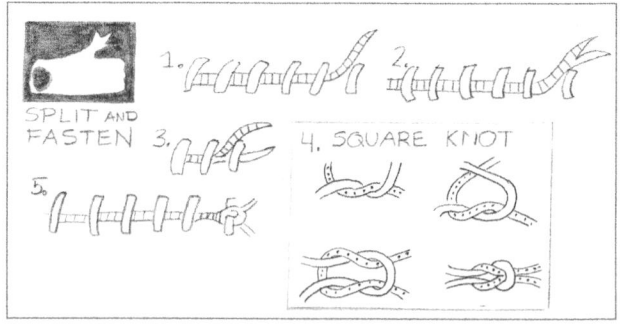

Remove the tell-tail

Loosen the lark's-head knot that secures the tell-tail to the anchor stitch, and draw it out of the work.

Closing the hole

This project began with a tail-tugger slipknot, and now comes the time to tug that tail! The top of your hat has an opening with the tail-tugger tail coming off of it. Gently pull the tail to snug up the hole, getting it as tight as you can without risk of breaking the yarn, then tying it off on the nearest stitch. One way to tie-off is to draw a bight of the tail through a nearby stitch, then poke the end of the tail through the bight and draw tight. Snip the tail two inches past the knot, and poke that bit back through.

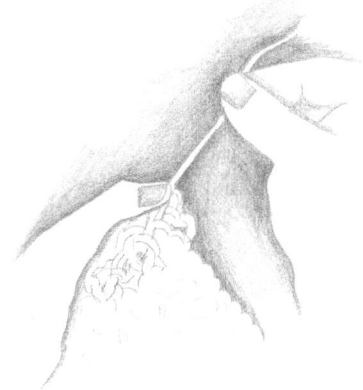

✳ You have drawn in the hole.

Ring charm

Now that you have done your first projects in finger crochet, you might like to try using your *ring charm* next time (as described in Book I, Chapter 7, page 125), and see if it makes it easier for you. Place the ring charm on Loom Pointer and draw the leed through it. The ring charm helps to secure the leed, keeping it out of the way while you work.

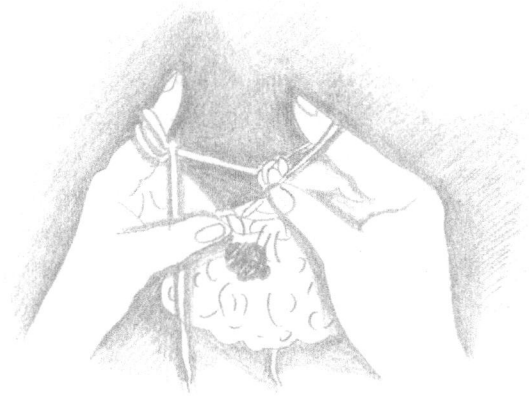

Variations

Color changes in finger crochet can produce pleasing effects, such as with the trivet in the picture on page 81.

By turning on and off the increase stitches, you can do creative tubular shapes with bulges and flares, similar to what a potter might make on the wheel.

You can insert a nifty vertical slit in a piece by alternating direction for several rows.

If you are familiar with traditional crochet, or should you obtain a book on the subject, you might like to try adapting some of the variations on the common crochet stitch to finger crochet.

chapter five

Vocabulary Review for "Finger Crochet"

finger crochet
fox-chat
crochet polystitch
straight rows
starter-chain

foundation row
floater stitch
circular crochet
tell-tail

slipknot
tail-tugger
circular rows
starter-loop

anchor stitch
orbiting row
increase stitches
finished-edge

Crochet Polystitches

The first two steps are the same for all polystitches. It is the third step that varies, depending on the type of polystitch. These alternatives are divided into two main groups: *straight crochet* and *circular crochet*. Straight crochet stitches can be further broken down into *foundation row* and *regular row* stitches. Circular-row stitches can be broken down into the *anchor stitch*, *foundation row*, and *regular row stitches*.

Finally, we have the *finished-edge crochet polystitch* for either straight or circular crochet.

First two steps for all polystitches

1. Place loop 1 on Pointer (unless this is a circular crochet anchoring stitch).

2. Take hold of your work (*the starter chain or loop, or the straight rows or circular rows*) with the fox-pinches of both hands, straightening both Pointer fingers to assume fox-chat position.

For straight crochet

3. For *Straight Crochet Foundation Stitches*: Slip loop-bedecked Shuttle Pointer through the single ridge along the starter chain.

3. For *Straight Crochet Regular Rows*: Slip loop-bedecked Shuttle Pointer just under the two lips of a regular stitch of the previous row.

For circular crochet

3. For *Anchor Stitch*: Slip loop-bedecked Shuttle Pointer through the *single ridge* of the starter-loop.

3. For *Orbiting Foundation Row*: Slip loop-bedecked Shuttle Pointer *through the starter-loop*.

3. For *Orbiting Regular Rows*: Slip loop-bedecked Shuttle Pointer through the *two lips of a regular stitch of the previous orbiting row*.

3. For *Finished-Edge Stitch* for Straight or Circular Crochet: Slip loop-bedecked Shuttle Pointer through the *top lip only* (or, alternatively, the bottom lip only) of a stitch of the previous row.

Continuing polystitch sequence: Step-4

4. Hook leed and pull back through the two yarn-loops (loops 1 and 2) on Shuttle Pointer (or a single yarn loop in the case of an anchor stitch).

5. With Loom Pointer, bring leed around back side of Shuttle Pointer.

6. With Loom Pointer, rotate and bend to secure leed from slippage, while, with Loom bird-pinch, secure yarn-rings on Shuttle Pointer (or a single ring, in the case of an anchor stitch).

7. Hook leed with Shuttle Pointer to pull leed down through both yarn-rings, creating a new yarn-loop on Pointer to complete the stitch.

Straight crochet rows sequence

- Work a single crochet polystitch under both lips of each stitch of previous row, Loomwise.
- Count stitches in rows-sequence to be sure none were missed.
- Add one floater stitch prior to beginning next row.
- Flip the work.

Circular tunneling crochet rows sequence

- Crochet orbiting rows countertopwise.

Circular-flat crochet rows sequence

- The initial row consists of six stitches
- Crochet orbiting rows counterclockwise working 6 evenly-distributed increase stitches into stitches of the previous row.
- The row ends where the tell-tail is met.
- Bring tell-tail up through the last stitch of the completed row to mark the start of the next row.

Projects

Making a doll blanket

Materials

1 skein of medium wool yarn.

Steps

1. Finger-knit a starter-chain, 25 stitches in length.
2. Add one floater stitch.
3. Crochet straight rows of regular crochet polystitches, or just until your regular sized ball of yarn runs out—roughly 50 rows. Note: Remember to add one floater stitch at the completion of each row, just before flipping your work.
4. Tie-off.
5. For adding fringe, loop on a length of yarn to each stitch in your start-row and end-row.

Making a trivet

Materials

½ skein (around 65 personal yards) bulky wool yarn
An 8-inch length of yarn of a contrasting color for tell-tail

Steps

1. Make a tail-tugger slipknot.
2. Work the foundation row of 6 stitches.
3. Add a tell-tail.
4. Crochet five flat circular rows, the final row being barehand crochet size E (Elephant).

chapter five

Optional color change

To do a color change for the rim, felt-splice or tie on yarn of a different color but same thickness, using the *felt splice* if your yarn is 100% wool or the *magic knot* for any type of yarn.

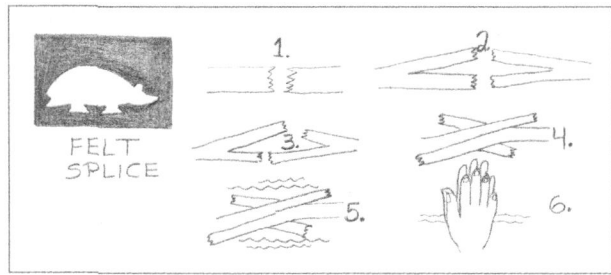

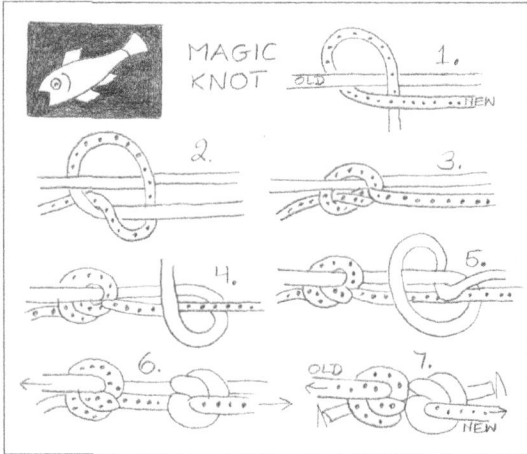

Crochet one additional flat orbiting row on row F.

After one orbit, place the last stitch into the first stitch of the rim color.

5. Snip the yarn and tie-off. Weave-in the end into the work of the same color.

6. Remove the tell-tail from the center of the piece.

7. Carefully draw-in the tail of the initial tail-tugger slipknot until it is closed up, and tie-off on the nearest stitch.

Making a light shoulder bag with drawstring

This project can produce a large shoulder bag with a strap or a small draw-string pouch, depending on how many stitches you put into it.

Materials

One skein of medium wool for the large bag, or about ¼ as much for the pouch. The thicker the yarn you use, the larger your bag will be.

Steps

1. Make a tail-tugger slipknot.

2. Work the foundation row of 6 stitches.

3. Add the tell-tail.

4. For the large shoulder bag, crochet four flat circular rows, the final row being finger crochet size D. For the small pouch, crochet just two rows, ending with row B.

5. For the large shoulder bag, crochet 18 Tunnel-rows (zero increases per row) of regular crochet polystitches. Note: There is no longer a need to pull the tell-tail through the beginning of each new row.

   For the small pouch, crochet just four Tunnel-rows or until the bag has the desired depth.

6. Draw a line with your mind's eye to check that the last row ends in alignment with the tell-tail. Do not cut your leed.

Creating the drawstring

Note: When you have completed your last stitch, without cutting the leed, use the last loop as the first loop for knitting a chain.

7. Chain-knit a length that is twice the circumference of the top ridge of your bag.

8. Cut the leed, tie-off the dangler, and tie an overhand knot in the chain near the end.

9. Where the chain sprouts from the pouch, pull a bight of it into a loop and tie a two-ply overhand knot, creating a loop, as snug against the bag as you can. Take the end of the chain

and, starting next to the chain-loop, weave it in and out through stitches all around near the top of the bag. When you come around to the chain-loop again, poke it through. Your pouch is done!

Strap for shoulder bag

10. Choose the yarn you want for your strap—best to use a different shade or color from the bag. Make a starter-chain 6 stitches long.

11. Crochet 40 straight rows of regular crochet stitches.

12. Cut the leed and tie-off, weaving-in the dangler.

13. Using the caterpillar stitch—also called a running stitch—stitch one end of the strap to 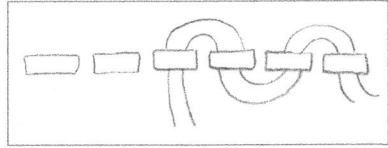 the inner side of your crochet bag at the fourth row down from the top ridge of the bag—the row just below the drawstring—at a point that is 90 degrees away from the drawstring loop; so that the loop ends up at the front of the bag.

14. Stitch-on the other end of your strap to the same row on the opposite side of your bag, in the same way. Your shoulder bag is done!

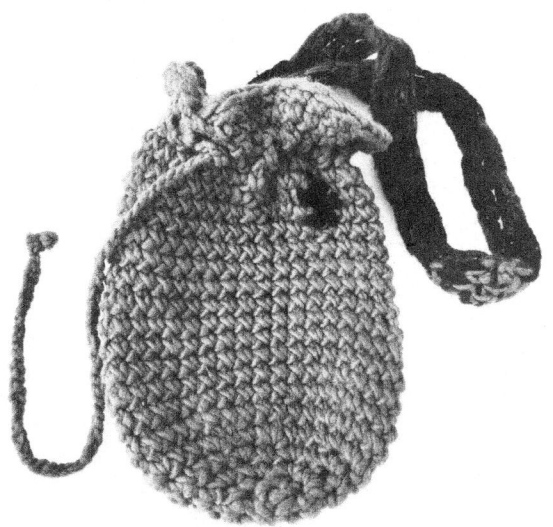

chapter six

Rooted Stitches

chapter six

Casting On and Casting Off for Barehand Knitting

When you knit with needles, you start with a *cast-on row*: a series of connected loops strung out along the length of the needle that provides the starting-edge for your piece. You then work a series of rows, each parallel to the cast-on row, and parallel to the needle, and each linked into the previous row.

With barehand knitting, the cast-on row is strung out along a line that is parallel to your Finger-Palm Crease. In other words, if you were to lay a knitting needle along the Finger-Palm Crease, the work that in normal knitting would grow out of the side of that needle is duplicated by the work that grows out of the back of your hand in barehand knitting.

The cast-on row (the first row) is the row of loops cast-on to each finger in turn. *Cast-on* and *cast-off rows* essentially comprise a chain of horizontally connected interlinking loops that create tidier start and finish ends for your knitted piece. Basic leapstitch rows used here are just the same as those introduced in *Bare Hand Knitting* Book I.

Whenever an initial stitch is secured around a bare finger, it is a *cast-on stitch*. When a stitch is secured-off, leaving the finger bare, it is a *cast-off stitch*.

Casting on in this way roots the initial row to your fingers in such a way as to allow for countless variations, including the two-handed multilevel and three-dimensional techniques that come later in this book.

The cast-on technique is rather tricky at first try. The movements call for some degree of dexterity, coordination, and flexibility in the fingers. Your manipulations will become more fluid with a bit of practice. Mastery of the cast-on is satisfying, and its practice soon becomes nothing short of fun!

The Woodchuck Family

(Rhyme for Cast-on)

Mama Woodchuck pops through a hole in the ground;
She feels a cold wind blowing all around.
She lifts her scarf up over her head,
And says, "Come Brother, get out of bed!"

Brother pokes up through the very same hole;
A cold wind circles from the far North Pole.
He wraps his scarf beneath his chin,
And says, "The cold's still getting in!"
He lifts another loop over his head,
And says, "Come, Sister, get out of bed!"

Sister pops up through the very same hole,
A cold wind curls from the far North Pole.
She wraps her scarf beneath her chin,
And says, "The cold's still getting in!"
She lifts another loop over her head,
And says, "Come, Baby, get out of bed!"

Baby pops up through the very same hole,
A cold wind curls from the far North Pole.
Sister wraps Baby's scarf beneath his chin,
Baby says, "Wapagain cuz da co'des gettin in!"
Sister lifts another loop over his head,
Baby says, "Now, wet's eat jam and bwead!"

– A.B. Akin and H. Akin

Creating a double-wrap winter scarf

Materials: You will need one ball of yarn. Choose a medium- to bulky-weight wool yarn while you are learning.

Casting On

Place the yarn-ball to your Loom side. Create a tail-tugger slipknot as introduced on page 56 of the previous chapter.

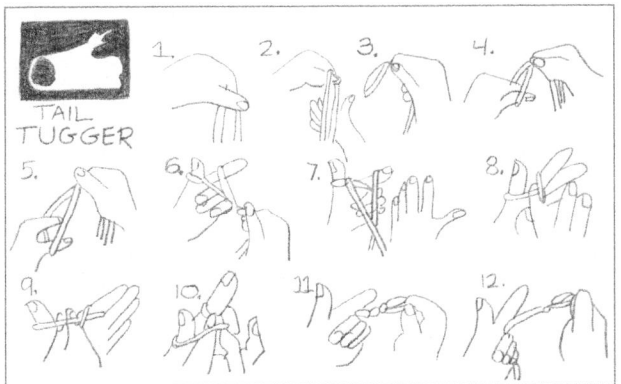

Hold up your Shuttle Hand in Palm Heart position; fingers upward and the Palm facing your heart.

Place the slipknot on Loom Pointer, and snug up the loop a bit—not too tight—allowing the tail and leed to fall down the back of the hand.

✸ You have anchored the cast-on row.

Slip Middler into the yarn-ring that is on Pointer.

✸ Middler has *snugged-up* into the ring on Pointer.

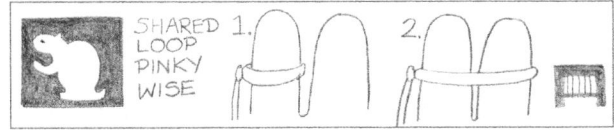

chapter six

Bring the leed toward you, through the Arrow Notch.

Lift the yarn-ring that is shared by both fingers over the leed that is lying against Middler, up and over the top of Middler only. You may have to bend Middler down slightly to accomplish this.

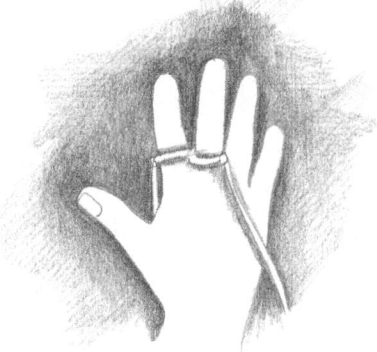

This step is called a *leap-twist*, because it leaves the loop twisted into a figure-eight. Leap-twists only occur when leaping with a loop that goes around two fingers.

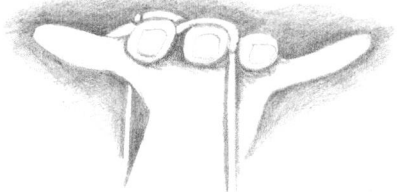

∗ You have done a Pinkywise leap-twist.

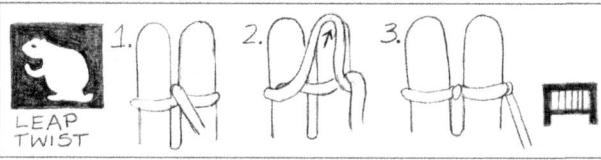

In one fluid movement bring the leed in through the Arrow Notch, around the front of Middler and then out again through the Center Notch, letting it hang down the back of the hand.

Take-up the lower yarn-ring on Middler and do a leapstitch by giving it a little tug and lifting it over the top yarn segment and over the top of Middler.

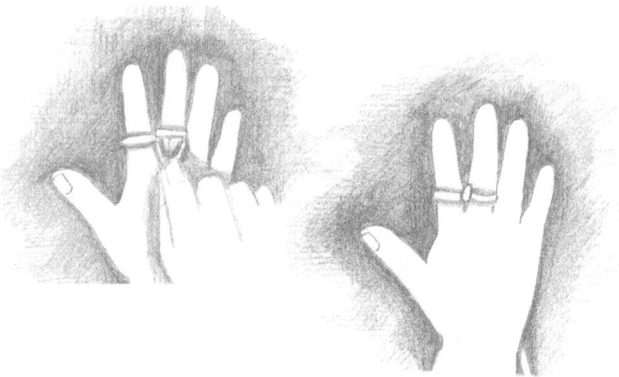

∗ You have done a Pinkywise U-turn leapstitch.

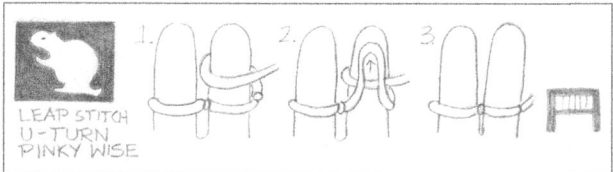

✻ You have completed a Pinkywise cast-on polystitch, or *cast-on stitch*, for short.

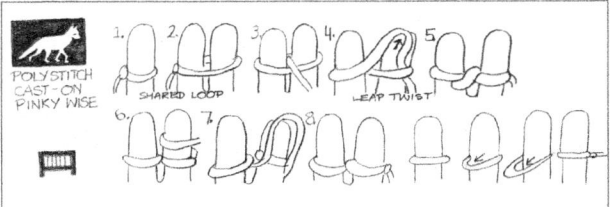

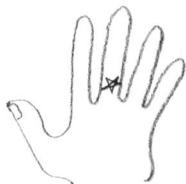

At this point, deslack the yarn-ring on Middler by giving a firm tug to that ring at a point that lies inside your Arrow Notch. This will snug up the cast-on polystitch just created.

Remove the slack from the yarn-ring by bringing it into the leed with a gentle tug.

✻ You have deslacked a cast-on stitch.

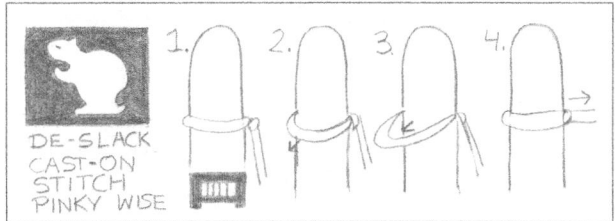

Now, cast-on to Ringa as you did onto Pointer: Snug up Ringa into the same yarn-ring that is around Middler, exactly as you had done with Middler against Pointer.

Bring the leed in through your Center Notch, lay it Pinkywise and do a leap-twist. Do a U-turn leapstitch.

Remember to deslack the cast-on stitch you have just made.

Cast-on to Pinky in exactly the same way: Snug up Pinky into the same yarn-ring that is around Ringa. Bring the leed in through your Pinky-Notch and do a leap-twist, followed by a Pinkywise U-turn leapstitch.

This completes the out row of cast-on stitches.

chapter six

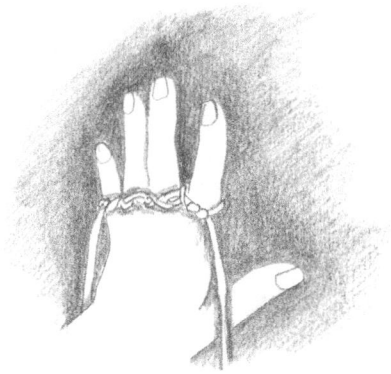

Lay the leed Thumbwise and do regular Thumbwise leapstitches (lift the yarn-ring over the leed and the top of each finger) on Pinky, Ringa, Middler, and then Pointer to knit the return row.

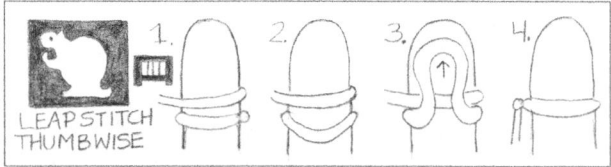

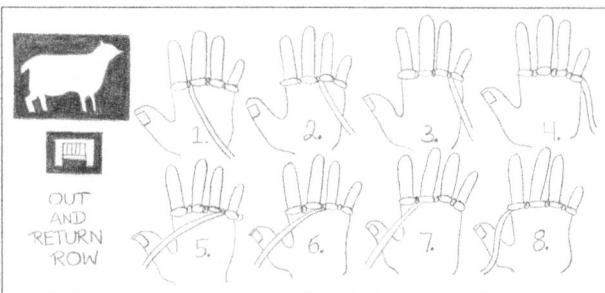

Deslack the cast-on return row, Thumbwise, beginning with Pinky and ending on Pointer.

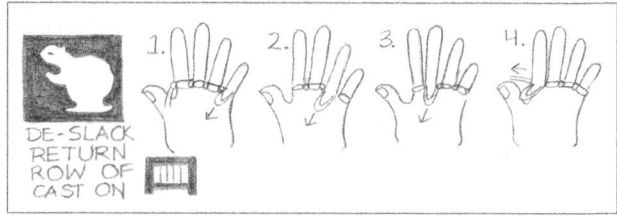

At any time now, you may tug on the tail to tighten the original slipknot, snugging-up that corner.

✻ You have now completed the entire *cast-on sequence* to the four fingers of your Loom Hand.

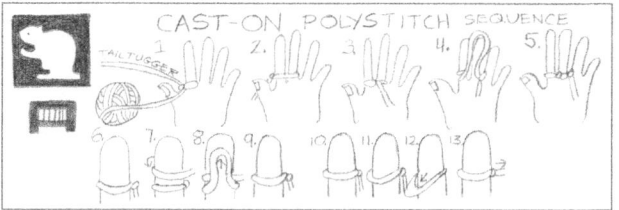

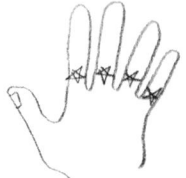

Note: The next out row will count as your first regular row and count as row number-one for counting purposes. This means that all out rows will fall on odd numbers and all return rows will fall on even numbers.

Rows

Now we shall leave the specialized cast-on stitches—*leap-twists* and *leap-rings*—behind, and, beginning Pinkywise, start doing regular rows of *leapstitches*.

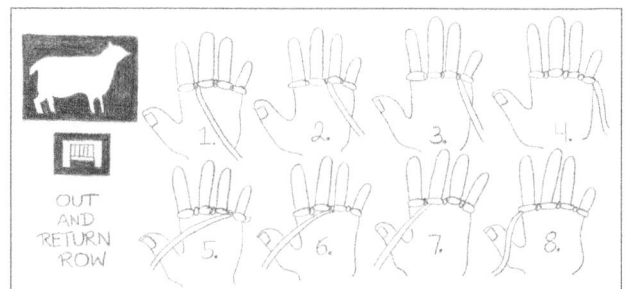

From time-to-time, you may find the yarn-rings trying to work their way up and off the tips of your fingers. Interleave the fingers of both hands and tamp down with your Shuttle fingers to push the rings back in place.

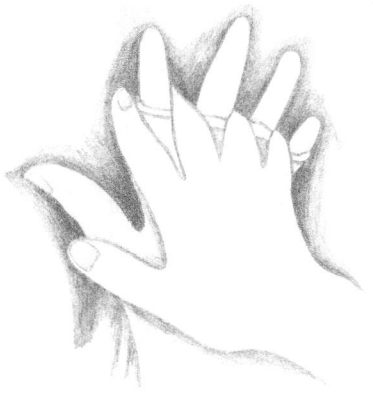

Continue until you have knit 50 rows (25 out-and-return rows) of leapstitches.

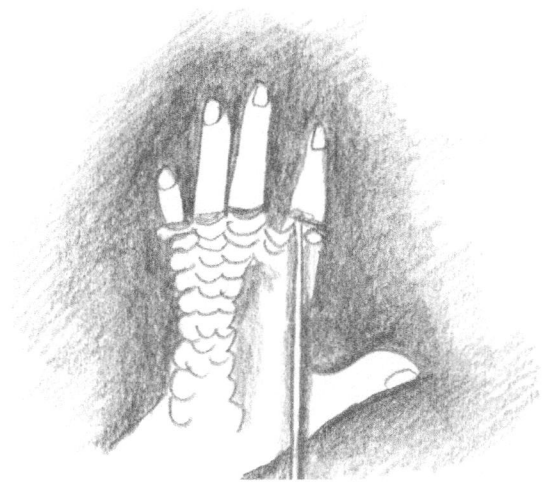

Casting Off: Flying Squirrel

Riddle-rhyme for casting off
(Guess the secret name of the new polystitch.)

Lift a loop to the next finger:
I can fly, but I'm no singer.

The second move is a leap-ring:
I have no feathers on my wing.

A workwise leapstitch follows-on:
I do not work from dark to dawn.

Leapstitch back the other way:
The best of meals is nuts, I say!

– H. Akin

(Answer: Flying-Squirrel Stitch)

The flying-squirrel cast-off is fun! The process creates a tidy chain of horizontally-linked loops that are sealed-off and fall from your fingers as you cast them. Only when the last loop of the row is securely tied-off is the entire row then truly safeguarded against unraveling. We begin the sequence with a lone flying-squirrel stitch, and then continue just as presented in the poem above.

Cast-off: Although you can begin the cast-off sequence from either end, for teaching purposes, we will begin with Pointer and work toward Pinky.

chapter six

Launch the cast-off

When you decide you have enough rows, run your last row Thumbwise, with the final stitch on Pointer.

Deslack the stitches of this return row, Thumbwise. (If in the future you should decide to cast-off in the opposite direction, just deslack the work flowwise in whatever direction you knitted the last row.)

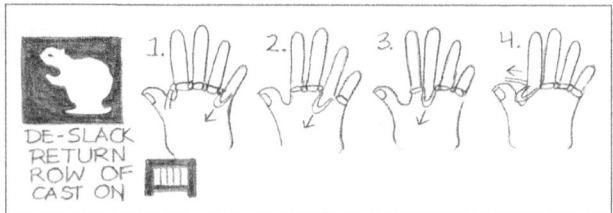

Do a Pinkywise leapstitch on Pointer, and let the leed hang down the back of the hand.

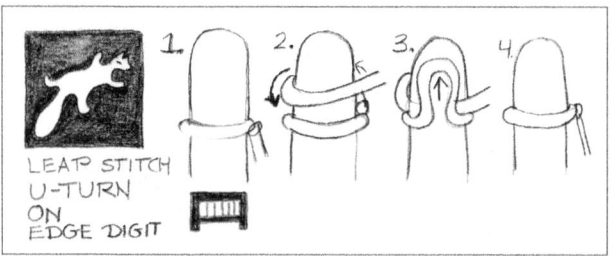

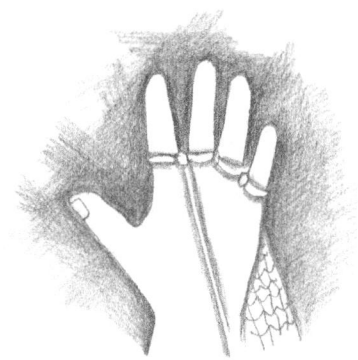

✳ You have just launched the cast-off row and now you can begin casting off.

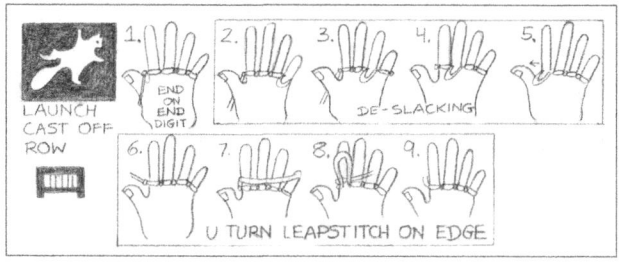

Now, do a flying-squirrel stitch: Lift the yarn-ring off Pointer, and carefully set it down on Middler, being attentive that it does not flip or twist it in any way. (The squirrel, which is flying from one tree to the next, needs to land feet first.) This will leave Pointer bare.

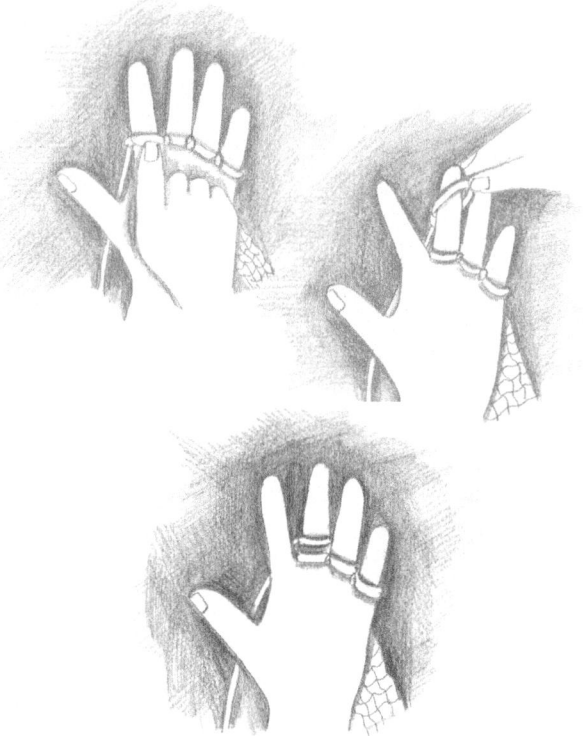

✳ You have now completed your first *flying-squirrel stitch*—or *flying stitch* for short. Note: In this example, Pointer is the resting finger and Middler is the active finger.

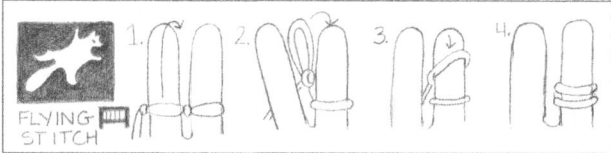

Lift the bottom yarn-ring on Middler up over the top yarn-ring on Middler.

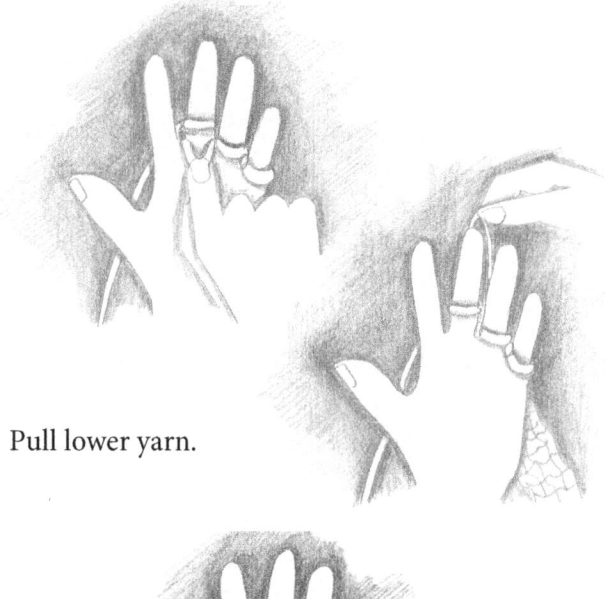

Pull lower yarn.

✷ You have just completed your first *leap-ring*.

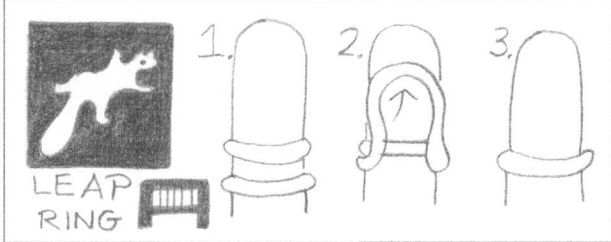

Do a Pinkywise leapstitch on Middler followed by a Thumbwise leapstitch on Middler.

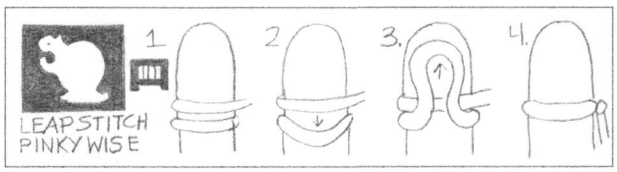

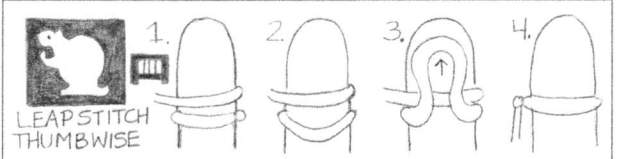

✷ You have completed a cast-off polystitch.

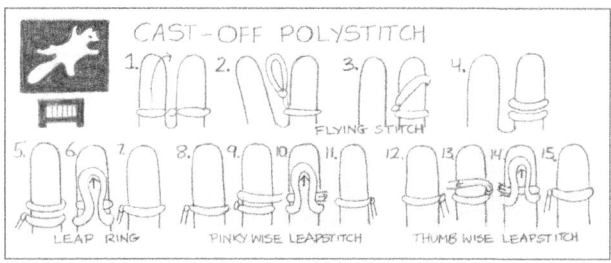

Keywords Reminder

When casting off, it can really help to recite the stitches of the sequence out loud as you go:

Flying stitch – Leap-ring – Pinkywise leapstitch – Thumbwise leapstitch

Do another cast-off polystitch from Middler to Ringa as follows: Do a flying stitch from Middler to Ringa, followed by a leap-ring on Ringa, followed by a Pinkywise leapstitch, followed by a Thumbwise leapstitch on Ringa.

Secure off row

You will now end the cast-off row as follows: Do a flying stitch from Ringa to Pinky.

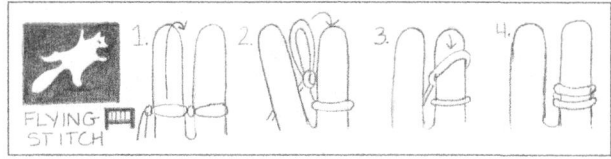

Do a leap-ring on Pinky.

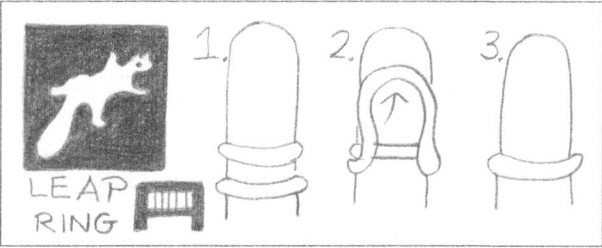

chapter six

Do a last Pinkywise leapstitch, and then *tie-off*, as will be described. Notice there is no Thumbwise leapstitch on the last cast-off stitch of a row; the tie-off takes its place.

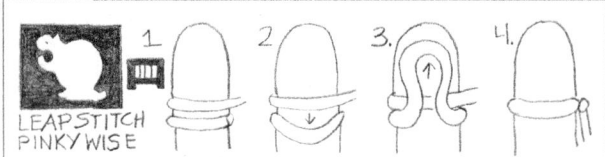

Tie-off

Now, your work is only attached to you at Pinky. At this point, snip the leed from your work, leaving about a foot dangling. Poke the end of the dangler up through the yarn-ring on Pinky, then slip the yarn-ring off while tugging on the dangler to snug-it-up.

* You have done an end cast-off polystitch.

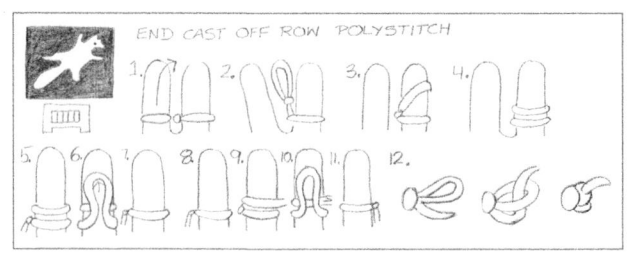

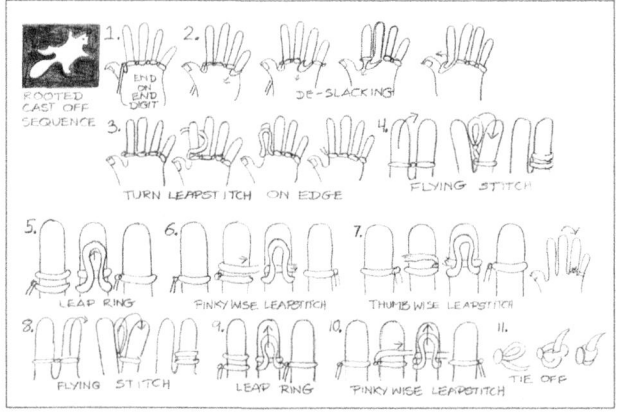

Weave-in and split-and-fasten the tail and dangler.

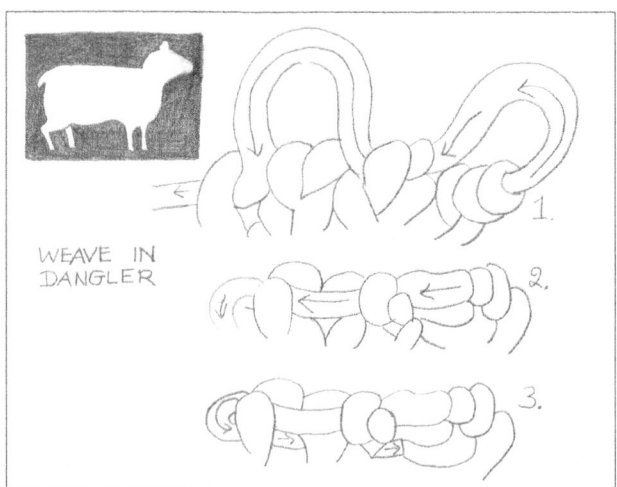

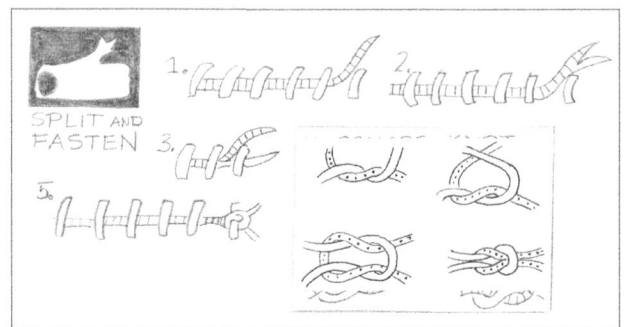

Rooted Stitches

You have completed your scarf! Remember to wear it when the winter winds come.

Here are the different effects that result from these two types of reverses: With *pylon turns* your piece is slightly narrower than with the *doubleback*, has a looser selvage, and fewer stitches along the edge—which will matter when you are joining two panels along their selvages. Also, when you examine a pylon selvage, instead of the fishlips and fishtails that you have with the doubleback edge, you will see only fishlips.

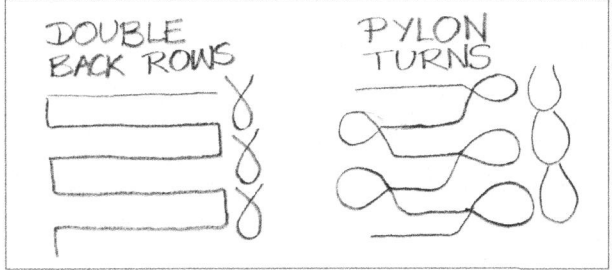

Tail-join tuck?

When starting a piece, you always have the option of doing a *tail-join*: After casting on, when your first return row again encounters the tail, simply smooth the tail and leed together, and proceed as if they are one strand. The tail-join was introduced in *Bare Hand Knitting* Book I.

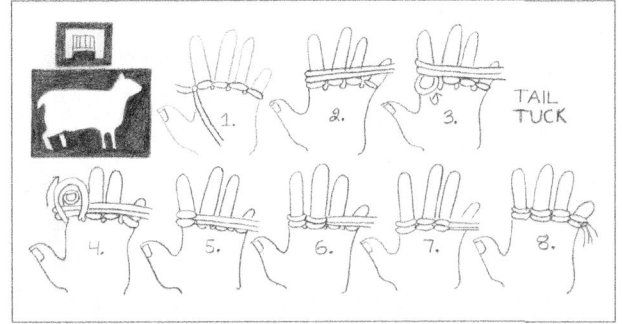

Variations

Two kinds of row-return

The regular rows in barehand knitting go back and forth, alternating direction at the ends. There are two ways to do this turnabout: *doubleback* and *pylon turns*.

Doubleback

You will notice as you knit rows that when you get to an edge-finger—Pointer or Pinky in this case—you do one stitch on the edge-finger, reverse direction, and do another stitch on that same finger as you head back the other way. This is a *doubleback*.

Pylon turns

The other way to reverse direction is to wrap the leed once around the edge-finger, do a leapstitch, and then continue in the reversed direction. This is a *pylon turn*.

Once these barehand techniques become second nature, they can be performed while sitting or standing, listening to music, or even taking a stroll. As you progress, you will find you can accomplish projects that are quite large and elaborate. Music can be a wonderful accompaniment to knitting and has the potential to enhance your enjoyment of this art form. Perhaps that is because this handicraft seems to have a rhythm, and even a melody.

chapter six

Chapter Review for "Rooting Stitches"

Vocabulary

anchor
shared loop
leap-twist
tail-tuck
flying stitch
pylon turns
doubleback rows

Elements

Anchor the Cast-On Row:
Place a tugger slipknot on your starting finger.

Shared Loop:
Bring neighboring digit, flowwise into the same loop on active digit.

Leap-twist:
Bring leed in through the active notch laying it workwise over a shared loop; lift the shared loop over the yarn segment and place it over the top of the active finger.

Topwise U-Turn Leapstitch:
When the leed hangs off the back of the hand and is brought in to pass topwise in front of the yarn-ring bedecked active finger and out again through the next notch, followed by a leapstitch.

Pinkywise Cast-On Polystitch:
Share a loop with neighboring finger, flowwise. Do a leap-twist. Do a topwise U-turn leapstitch.

Cast-On Row Sequence:
- Create a tail-tugger slipknot.
- Anchor the cast-on row to starting finger.
- Do a topwise U-turn polystitch on the starting finger.
- Do a cast-on polystitch onto neighboring finger, until the edge digit is reached.
- Do a return row of regular leapstitches.
- Deslack the return row.
- Launch the cast-off.
- End row at edge digit.
- Deslack final return row.
- Do a topwise U-turn leapstitch on edge-digit.

Leap-ring:
Leap bottom yarn-ring over top yarn-ring on the newly active finger.

Flying-Squirrel Stitch:
Lift yarn-ring from active finger and place it onto the neighboring finger flowwise.

Cast-Off Polystitch:
- Do a flowwise flying stitch from the resting finger to the active finger.
- Do a leap-ring on the newly-active finger.
- Do a flowwise leapstitch on the active finger.
- Do a counter-flowwise leapstitch on the active finger.

Entire Cast-Off Sequence:
- Launch cast-off on start-finger.
- Cast-off polystitches on each finger of cast-off row, flowwise, except for the edge-finger.
- Do secure cast-off stitch on edge-finger.

Row Reversals:

Doubleback:
Row ends with a leapstitch on edge-finger, followed by another leapstitch in the reverse direction.

Pylon Turn:
Takes the leed in front of the edge-finger and wraps around once, followed by a single leapstitch.

Stitches

Topwise U-turn Leapstitch:
Allow leed to hang off from the back of the hand; bring leed in to pass topwise in front of the yarn-ring bedecked active finger and out again through the next notch. Do a leapstitch.

Rooted Cast-On Polystitch Flowwise:
Share a loop with neighboring finger, flowwise. Do a leap-twist. Do a topwise U-turn leapstitch.

Rooted Cast-Off Polystitch Flowwise:
Do a flowwise flying stitch from the resting finger to the active finger. Do a leap-ring on the newly-active finger. Do a flowwise leapstitch on the active finger. Do a counter-flowwise leapstitch on the active finger.

Doubleback Stitch:
Row ends with a leapstitch on edge digit, followed by another leapstitch in the reverse direction.

Flying-Squirrel Stitch:
Lift yarn-ring from active finger and place it onto the neighboring finger flowwise; do a leap-ring (Leap bottom yarn-ring over top yarn-ring on newly-active finger).

Pylon Turn:
Take the leed in front of the edge-finger and wrap around once, followed by a single leapstitch.

Sequences

Rooted Cast-on Sequence:
- Create a tail-tugger slipknot.
- Anchor the cast-on row to starting finger.
- Do a topwise U-turn polystitch on the starting finger.
- Do a cast-on polystitch onto neighboring finger, until the edge digit is reached.
- Do a return row of regular leapstitches.
- Deslack the return row.

Launch the Rooted Cast-off Sequence:
Launch the cast-off by ending the final row at an edge digit; deslack final return row. Do a topwise U-turn leapstitch on edge-digit.

Entire Rooted Cast-Off Sequence:
- Launch cast-off on start-finger.
- Cast-off polystitches on each finger of cast-off row, flowwise, except for the edge digit.
- Do secure cast-off stitch on edge-finger.

chapter seven

Tunnel Knitting

chapter seven

The introduction to three-dimensional techniques begins with a narrow tunnel. You are invited to pass through the threshold and discover what's on the other side.

Over-rows and under-rows

You have previously worked outbound rows and return rows. In addition to those, tunnel knitting, also uses *over-rows* and *under-rows*. The under-rows are the same as the over-rows, except that they require special handling due to the overburden of the over-row stitches, as you'll see.

Story for the sneaky-fox stitch

A fox that had been chased out of town by the local farmers returned a few years later. He had been stealing their eggs to bring home to his family. This time, he did not want the farmers to know he was back in town, so he used the following method: He would quietly unlatch and lift the lids of the coops, but only take one egg from each. The farmers—who might get from each coop five eggs one day, and another day, seven—never knew when one egg was missing.

Sneaky-fox rhyme

The sneaky fox does not alert
The farmer that he's back in town
He lifts the lid and takes an egg,
Then sets the lid back down.

– H. Akin and A.B. Akin

Creating a Scrunchy with the Two-digit Tunnel

Materials
A ball of somewhat bulky yarn of the desired color.

Set-up
Place the yarn-ball in a basket to your Loom side. For your practice swatch, you will knit a tunnel that is two fingers wide—that is, a two-digit tunnel. (Later on, you will learn to create a four-digit tunnel and wider.)

The following steps are the same you used to cast-on in the previous chapter for Rooted Stitches, only you will be including the Thumb, and working across the Thumb Notch.

Cast-on

Begin by making a tail-tugger slipknot, and place it onto your Loom Thumb.

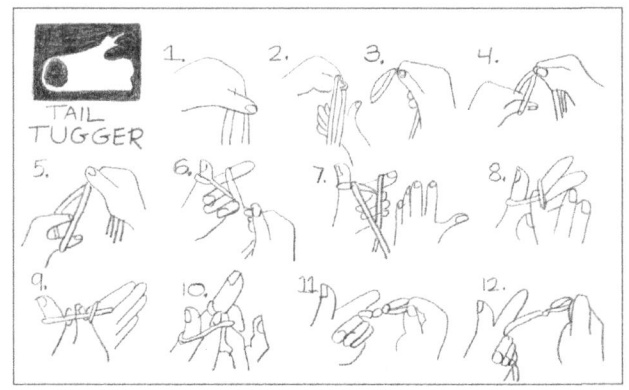

Tunnel Knitting

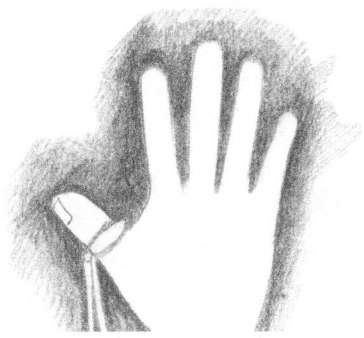

✻ You have anchored the cast-on row on Thumb.

Share a loop

Share a loop, Pinkywise, with Pointer.

✻ You have shared a loop across Thumb Notch.

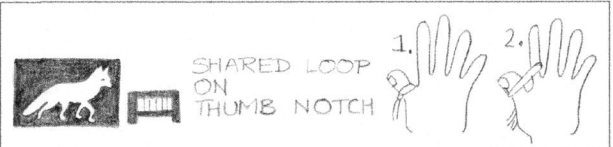

Leap-twist

Do a Pinkywise leap-twist with Pointer, as follows: Bring the leed forward through Thumb Notch and lay it Pinkywise.

Leapstitch the shared loop over Pointer only.

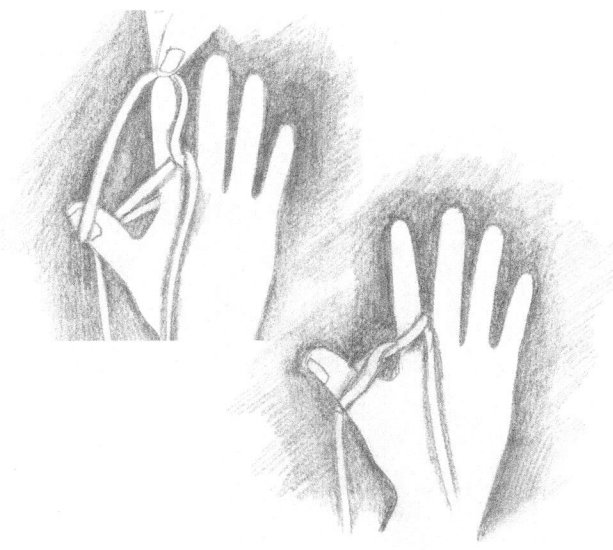

✻ You have done a leap-twist across the Thumb Notch.

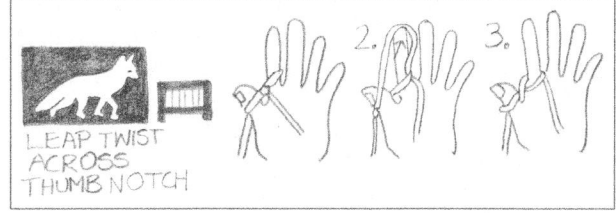

U-turn polystitch

Do a U-turn polystitch on Pointer, having the leed land on the back of the hand.

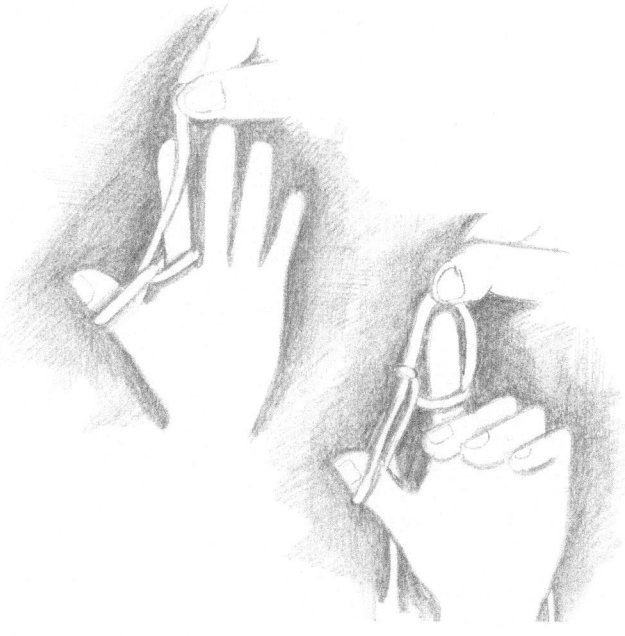

101

chapter seven

✱ You have done a U-turn leapstitch on Pointer.

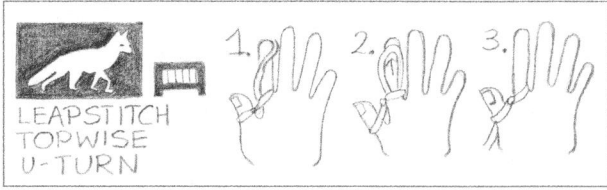

Deslack

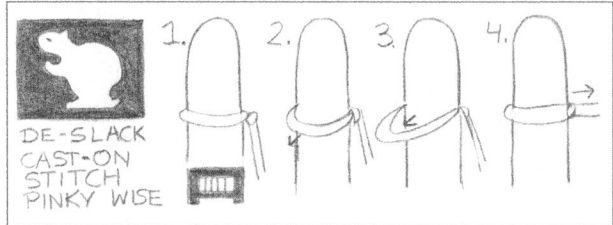

Deslack the cast-on stitch you have just completed on Pointer.

✱ You have done a cast-on polystitch across the Thumb Notch.

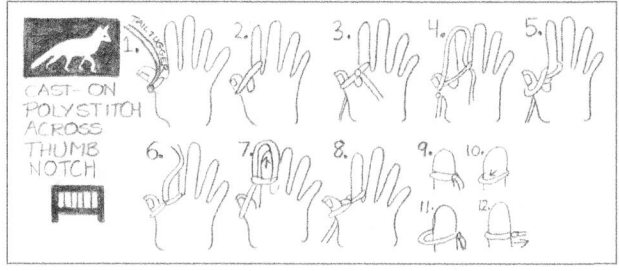

Continue cast-on

Do regular Pinkywise cast-on polystitches onto Middler, Ringa, and Pinky.

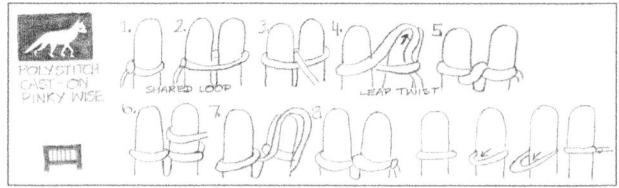

At this point, the tail will be hanging down from Thumb, and the leed is hanging off Pinky.

Work Thumbwise leapstitches on Pinky, Ringa, Middler, and Pointer to complete your return cast-on row. Leave the yarn-ring that is on Thumb out of the return row.

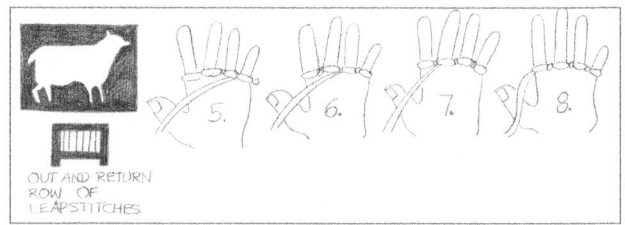

Deslack return row

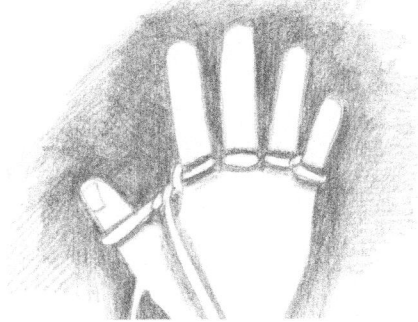

Deslack the return row Thumbwise.

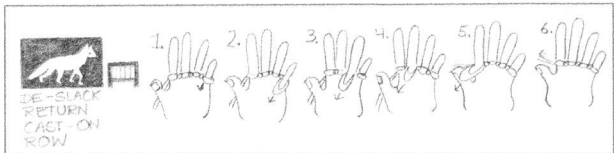

Deslack anchor

Deslack the initial tail-tugger slipknot by tugging at the tail.

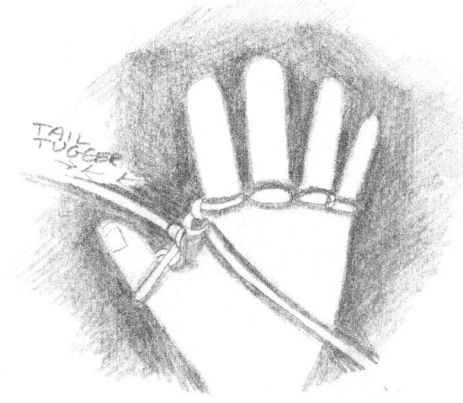

✻ You have deslacked the anchor by the tail-tugger.

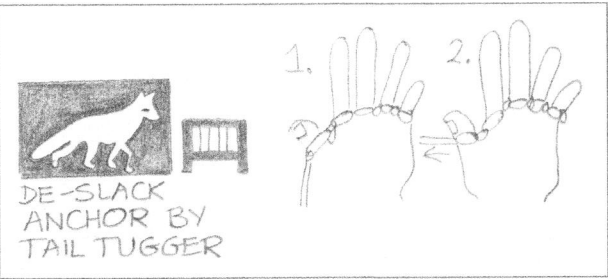

Seal the Thumb-flap

Foldback

Fold a portion of the cast-on row back over itself by lifting the yarn-rings off Pinky and Ringa and placing them upside-down onto Pointer and Middler, with the yarn-ring on Ringa ending up on Middler and the yarn-ring on Pinky ending up on Pointer.

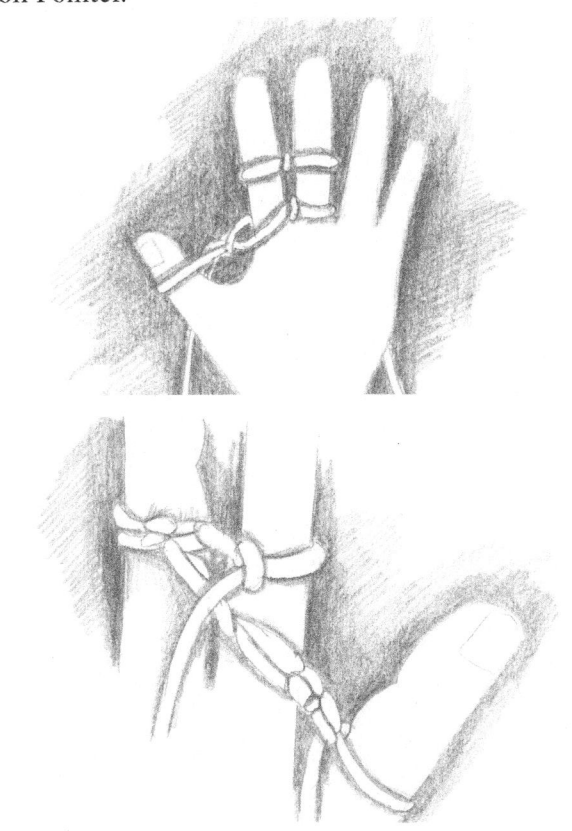

✻ You have done a two-digit *foldback*.

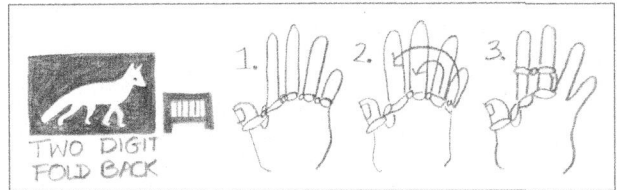

chapter seven

Flying stitch

Lift the yarn-ring on Thumb, and flipping it upside down, place it on Pointer.

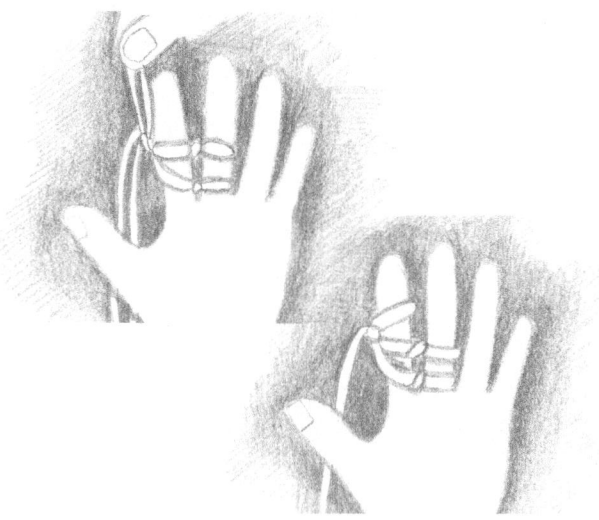

At this point, there are three yarn-rings on Pointer. Do a leap-ring on Pointer, leaping the middle ring over the top ring.

✻ You have done a leap-ring on the top layer.

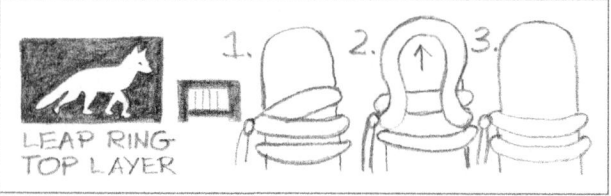

✻ You have *sealed* the Thumb-flap for the cast-on row.

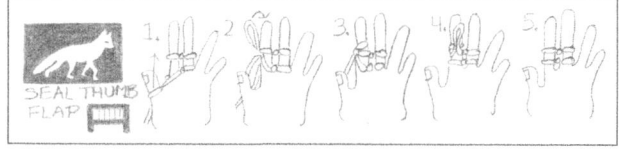

Nice, tidy rims

This action of sealing the Thumb-flap takes care of what would otherwise be a gap in your cast-on row, and gives your tunnel a continuous, tidy rim. Now only Pointer and Middler have double yarn-rings with the other fingers being bare. The leed is hanging off from Pointer.

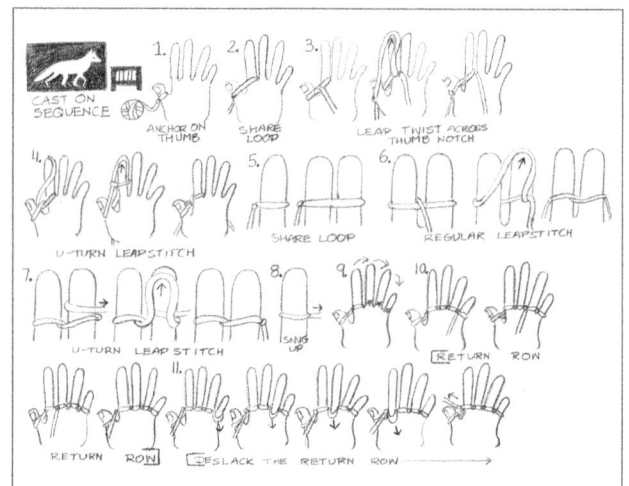

✻ You have just completed the *two-digit tunnel cast-on sequence*.

Over/under-rows

Over-rows with leapstitches

Lay the leed Pinkywise across the pads of your fingers.

Reach under this strand, pluck the upper yarn-ring on Pointer, and leapstitch it over Pointer.

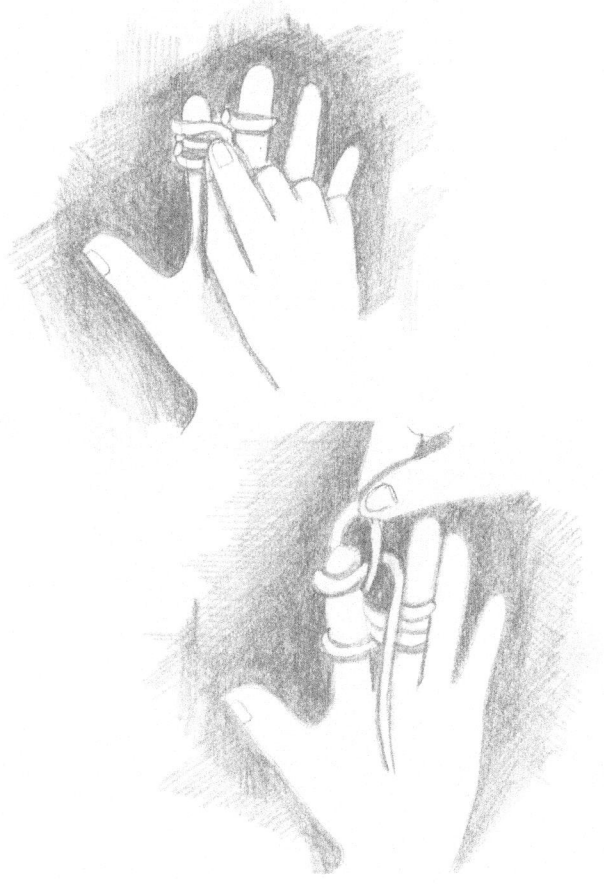

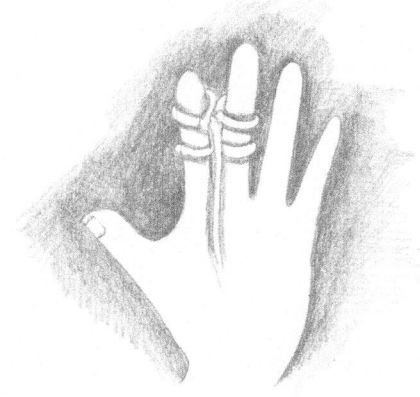

✻ You have done a Pinkywise leapstitch along the top layer.

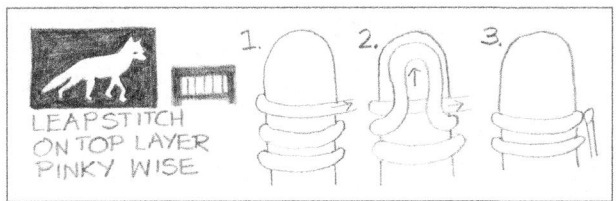

Another leapstitch

Bring the leed forward through the Arrow Notch and do a Pinkywise leapstitch with the upper yarn-ring on Middler as well.

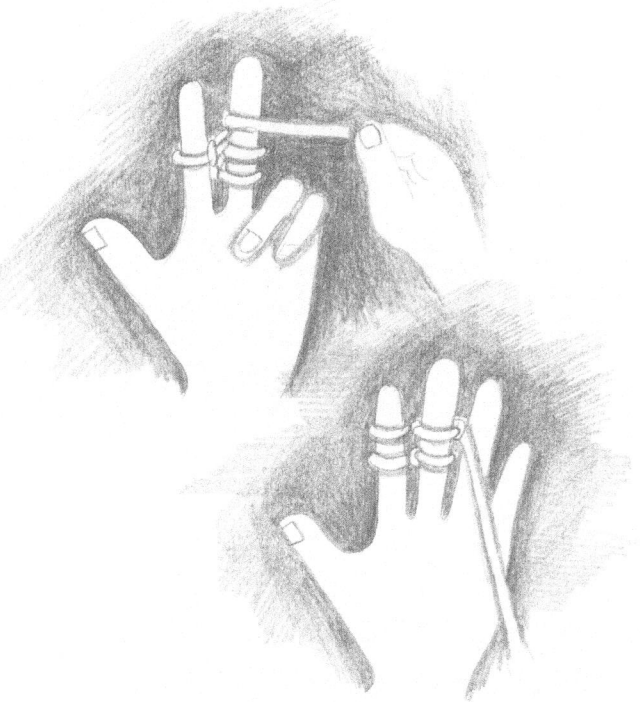

✻ This completes your first *over-row*.

chapter seven

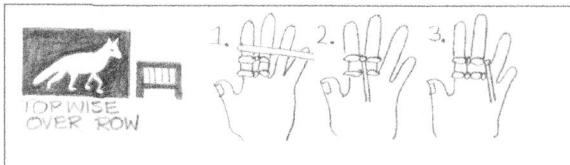

Under-rows with sneaky-fox stitch

Lay the leed Thumbwise, draping it back through the Thumb-Notch and get ready for a very special polystitch!

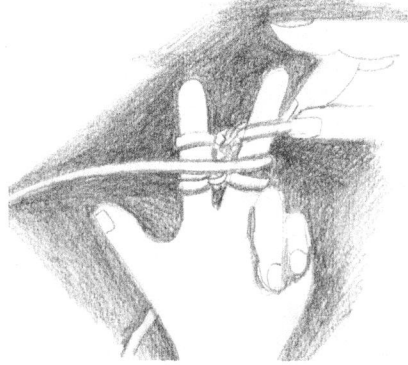

Lift and suspend

Using your Shuttle fox-pinch, temporarily lift the upper yarn-ring off Loom Middler, hooking and holding it with Shuttle Middler.

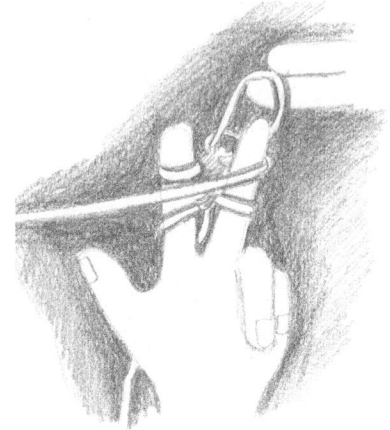

Lift over

While the top layer yarn-ring is suspended on Shuttle Middler, reach under the leed with your Shuttle bird-pinch, pluck-up the lower yarn-ring and leapstitch it over Loom Middler.

Replace ring

Now replace the top yarn-ring back onto Loom Middler, just as it was before.

✷ You have completed your first sneaky-fox stitch.

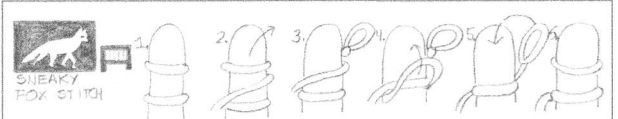

Another sneaky-fox stitch

Do another sneaky-fox stitch, this time on Pointer, as follows: Use your Shuttle fox-pinch again to temporarily lift the upper yarn-ring off Pointer, suspending in place.

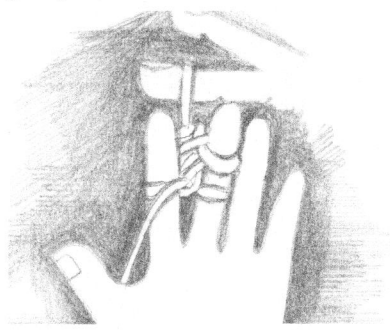

Reaching under the leed with your bird-pinch, pluck-up the lower yarn-ring and leapstitch it over Loom Middler.

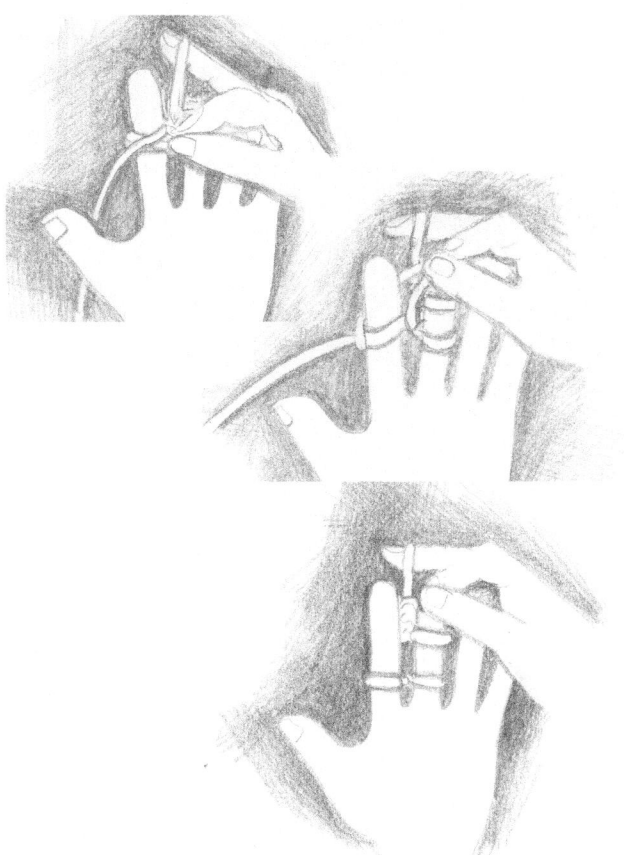

Replace the top yarn-ring back onto Loom Middler.

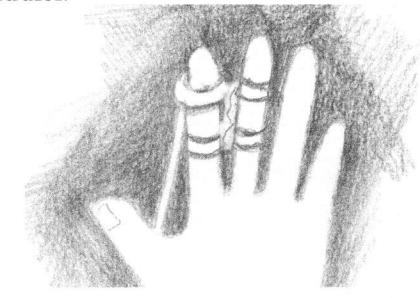

✷ You have now completed your first *under-row* of sneaky-fox stitches.

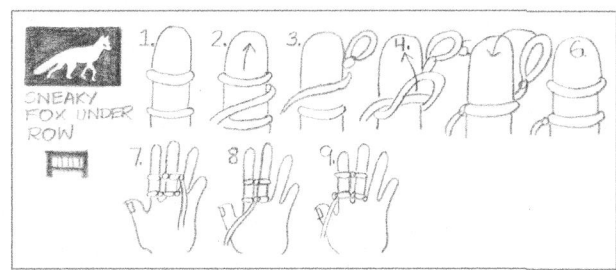

Another over-row

Lay the leed Pinkywise in preparation for the over-row.

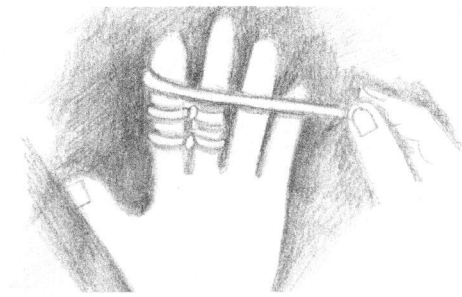

Knit an over-row of top-layer leapstitches on Pointer and Middler.

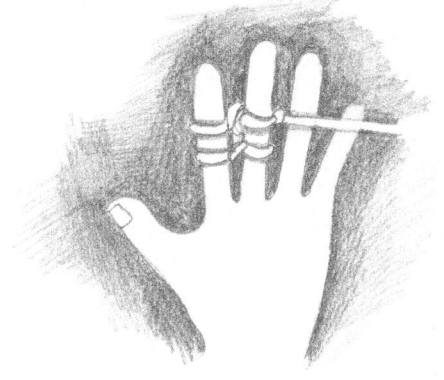

chapter seven

Another under-row

Lay the leed through the Thumb Notch in preparation for the next under-row.

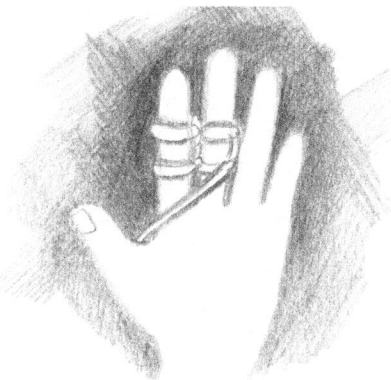

Work an under-row of sneaky-fox stitches on the bottom-layer yarn-rings on Middler and Pointer.

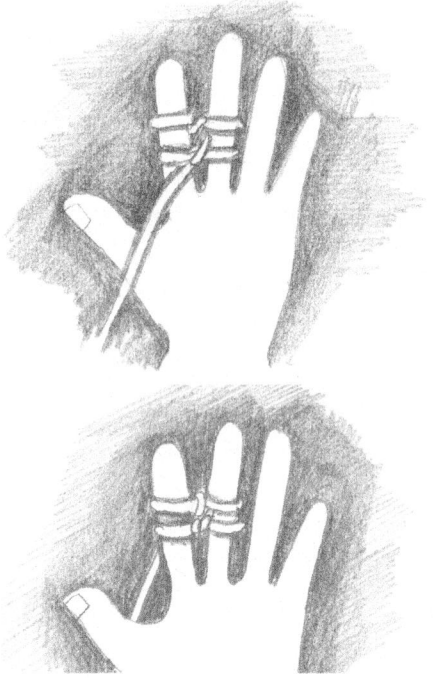

✳ You are knitting topwise over/under-rows.

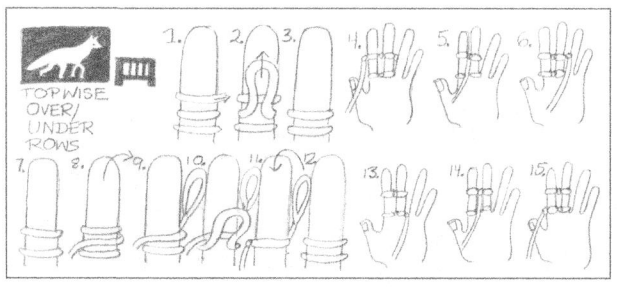

Continue tunnel-knitting. You can now see where this technique gets its name: Your knitted fabric forms a hollow flat-bottomed tube, just like a tunnel you might ride through on a train. Go ahead and poke a finger into it to check it out!

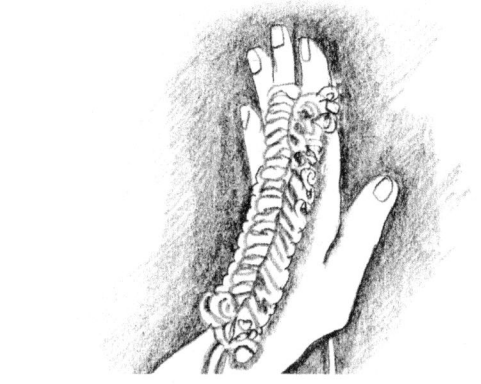

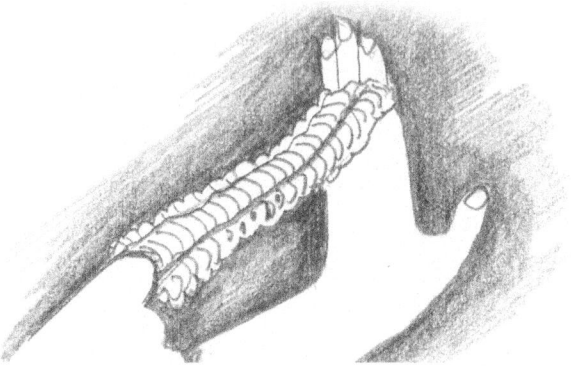

For your practice project, work around 18 over/under-rows.

Ending the row

End after completing an under-row, with the leed at the Thumb Notch.

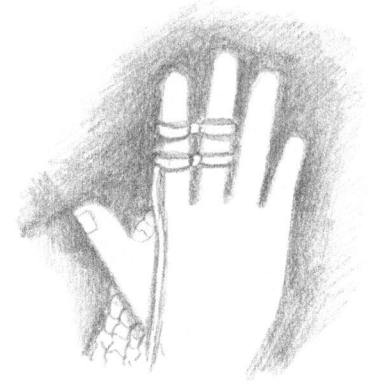

Overview of casting off over/under-rows

To cast-off from tunnel knitting, you use the same cast-off polystitch introduced in Chapter 6 on Rooted stitches. However, you now have two layers of stitches on your Loom Hand. You will begin by casting off the top layer, Pinkywise. When you have removed the over-stitch on Pointer, you will see that you now have the under-layer exposed. At this point, you will be casting off Thumbwise.

Again, this is done in exactly the same way as the Pinkywise cast-off, except that the flow is in reverse, as will be described. You will also meet with a little surprise when the stitches are rounding the bend!

Deslack to launch cast-off over-row

You ended your rows with the leed on the bottom stitch on Pointer at the Thumb-Notch.

Prepare to launch the cast-off row by deslacking the last over/under-row you knitted. To do this, begin from the top yarn-ring on Pointer and work your way, topwise, to the bottom yarn-ring on Pointer.

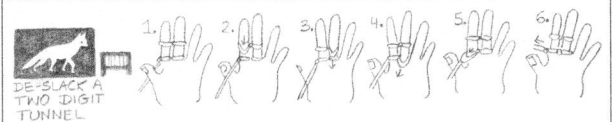

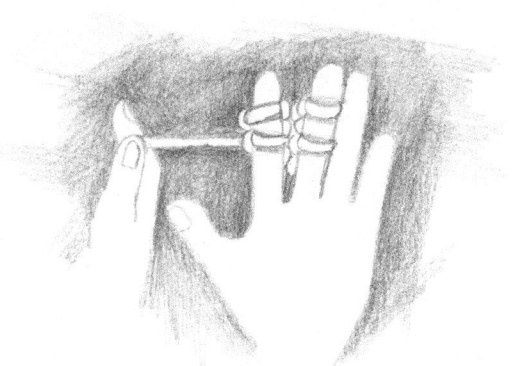

U-turn leapstitch

Do a countertopwise U-turn leapstitch on the top-layer yarn-ring on Pointer.

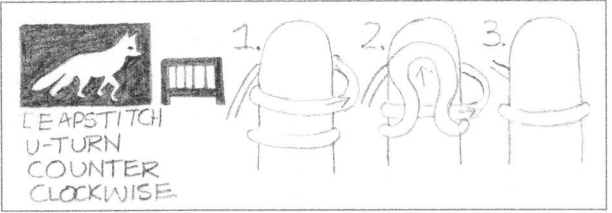

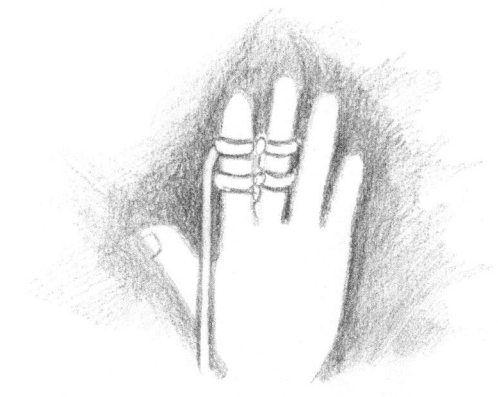

Flag with tell-tail

Place a tell-tail tie onto the top yarn-ring on Pointer using a lark's-head knot and slide it around to the back of your hand.

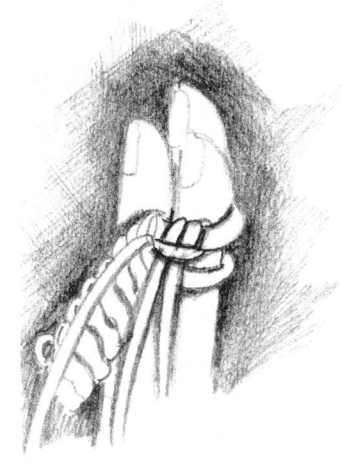

chapter seven

* You have flagged the bridge.

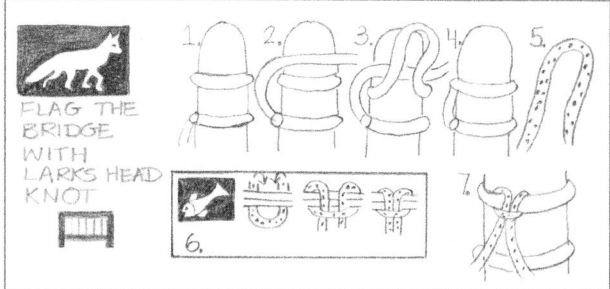

* You have launched the tunnel cast-off.

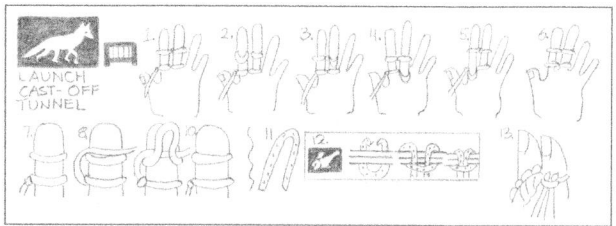

Flying stitch

Apply the cast-off polystitch to the over-row from Pointer to Middler, as follows: Do a Pinkywise flying stitch from Pointer to Middler.

* You have done a flying stitch in the top layer.

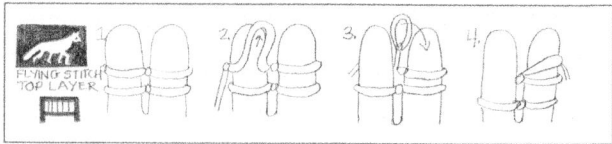

Leap-ring

Do a leap-ring on Middler. Notice that you now have three yarn-rings on Middler. (The middle-loop leaps over the top-loop.)

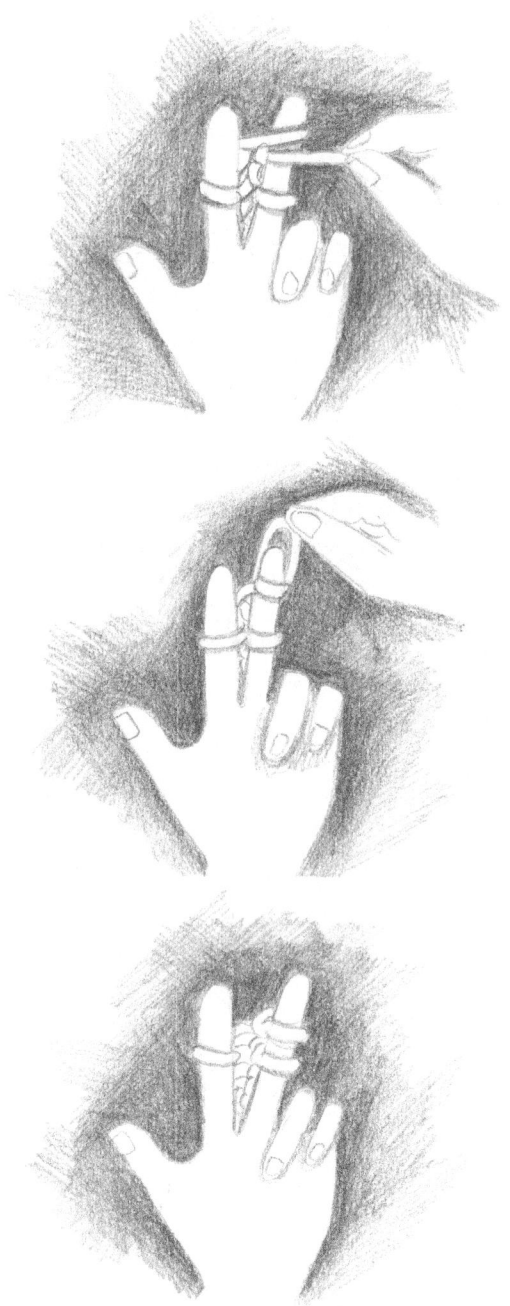

✳ You have completed a leap-ring on the top layer

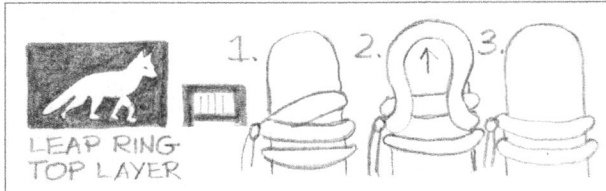

Flowwise leapstitch

Bring the leed forward through Arrow Notch and do a Pinkywise (flowwise) leapstitch on the top layer yarn-ring on Middler.

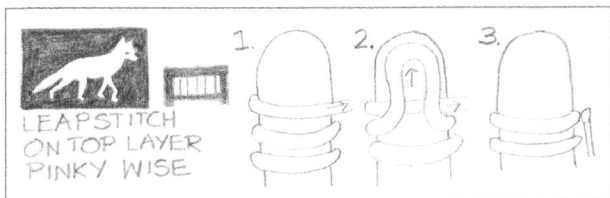

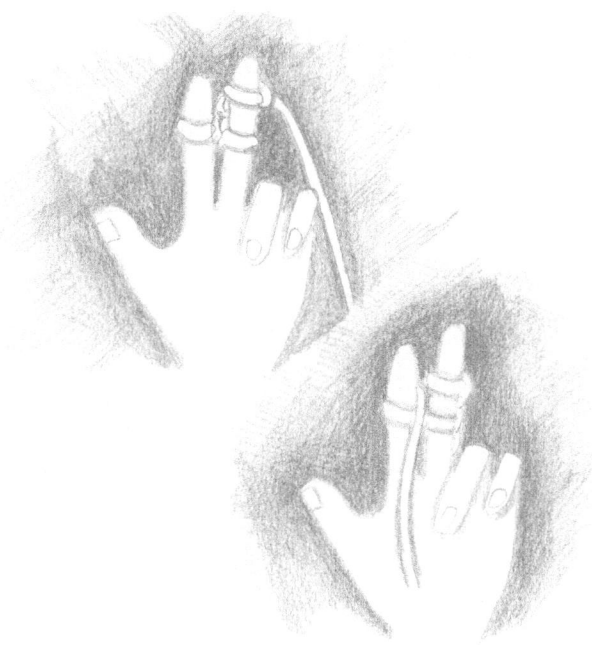

Counterflowwise leapstitch

Follow it with a Thumbwise (counterflowwise) leapstitch.

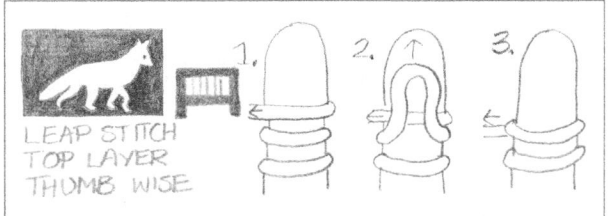

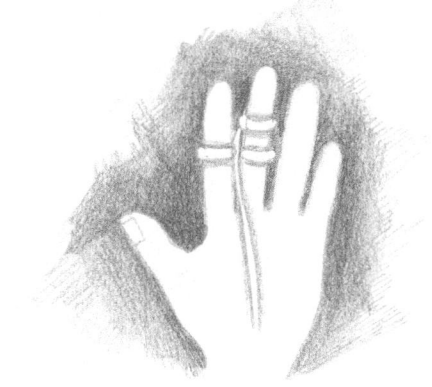

✳ You have completed a Pinkywise cast-off polystitch on the top layer.

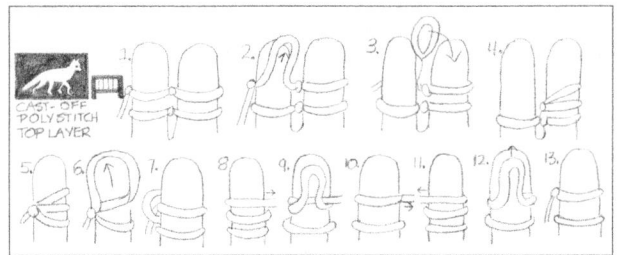

Round the bend

You have now reached the point where you must cast the upper row on Middler off onto the lower row on Middler. Here is where the surprise comes in; since the active yarn-ring is already on top of the next one to be cast-off, you will skip the flying stitch and go right to the next step of the cast-off polystitch: the leap-ring. As with any leap-ring, lift the bottom yarn-ring on Middler over the top yarn-ring on Middler.

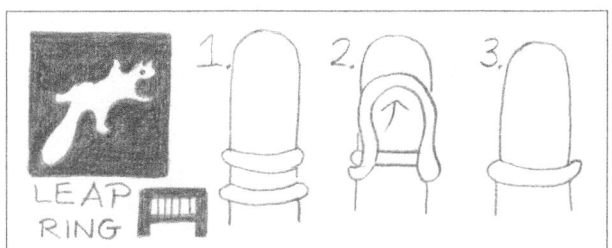

chapter seven

Flowwise leapstitch

Do a Pinkywise leapstitch on Middler.

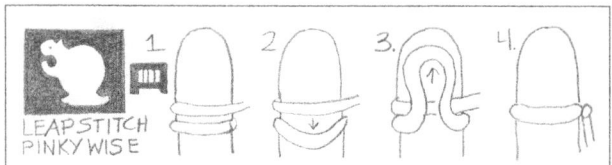

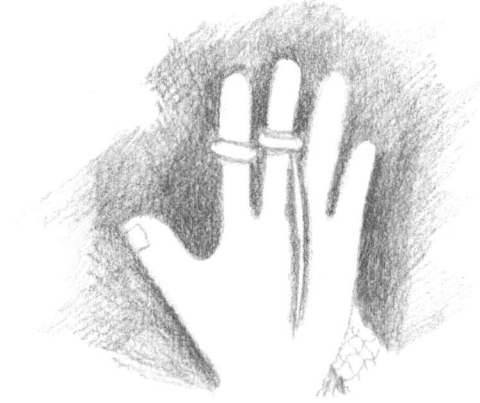

Counterflowwise leapstitch

Do a Thumbwise leapstitch on Middler.

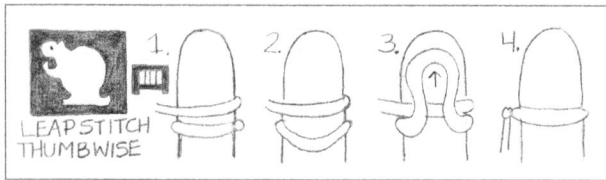

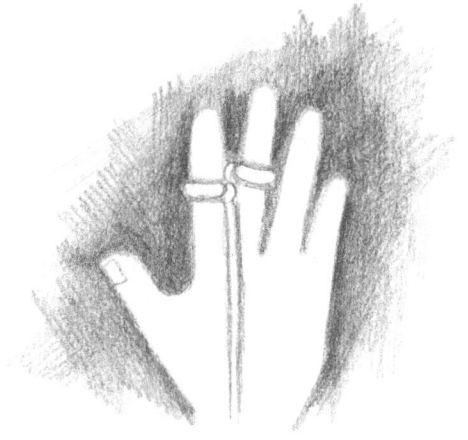

✱ You have just completed a topwise *corner cast-off polystitch*.

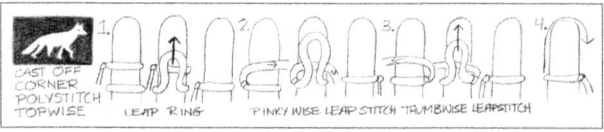

Switch direction
Rotate leed

Now that you have landed your stitch on an under-row, you'll need to reverse direction and cast-off Thumbwise. The pair of leapstitches that completes the cast-off polystitch always begins with a flowwise leapstitch followed by a counterflowwise leapstitch. To be properly set up for this, take the leed back through the Arrow Notch, tug it Pinkywise, and bring it back in through the Center Notch to switch the direction of your work, before initiating the cast-off polystitch. Now the flow of your work will be Thumbwise for the under-row.

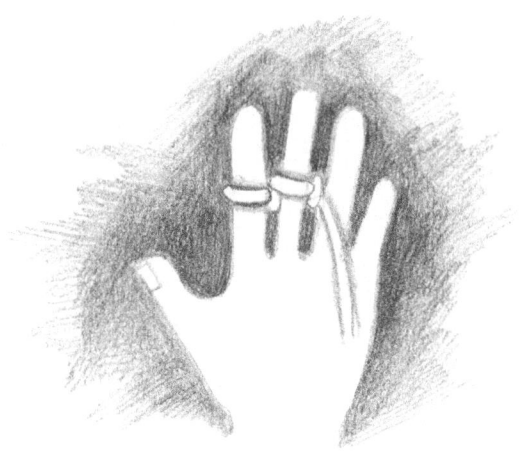

Cast-off under-row

Reverse flying stitch

Do a Thumbwise flying stitch onto Pointer.

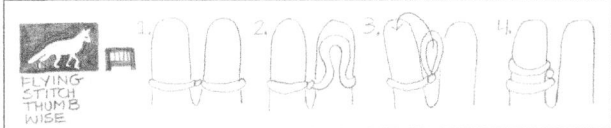

Leap-ring

Do a leap-ring on Pointer.

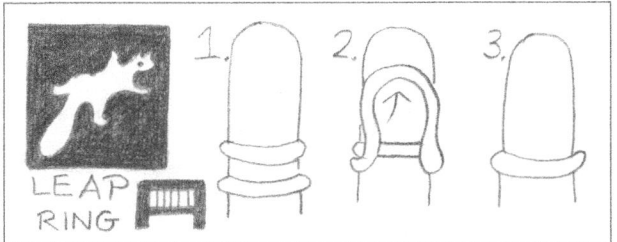

Bridge the gap

Just as you sealed the gap in the rim for the cast-on row, you will now create a smooth cast-off rim by bridging the gap.

Locate tell-tail

Locate the tell-tail flag that was used for flagging the bridge and use it to pull up the launching cast-off stitch and place it back onto Pointer.

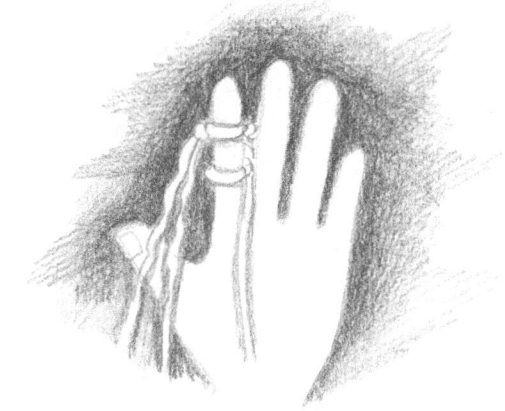

Another leap-ring

Leap-ring the bottom yarn-ring over the bridging yarn-ring that you just placed there.

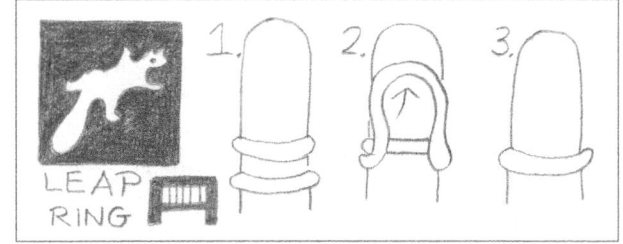

chapter seven

Remove tell-tail

At any time now, you can remove the tell-tail.

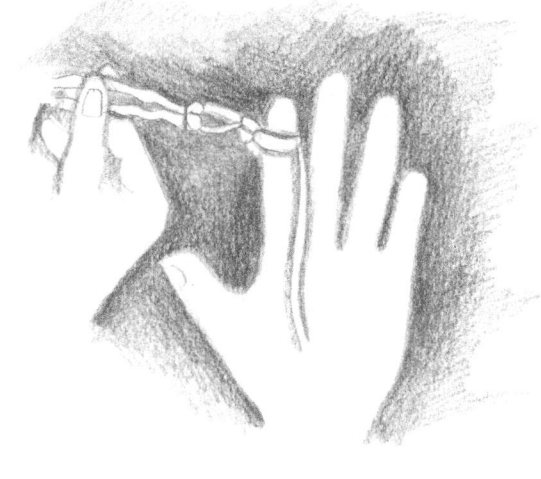

✳ You have bridged the gap for the tunnel cast-off row.

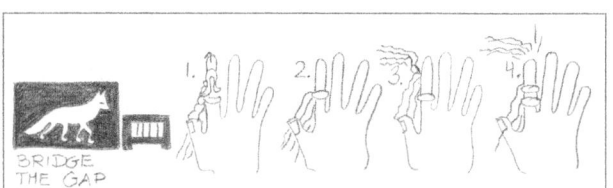

Ending the Work

Do a final leapstitch

Do a final Thumbwise leapstitch on Pointer, and tie-off.

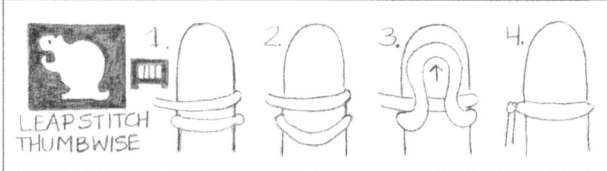

Tie off

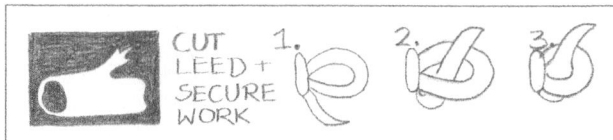

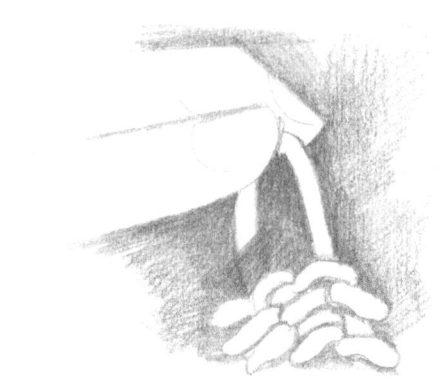

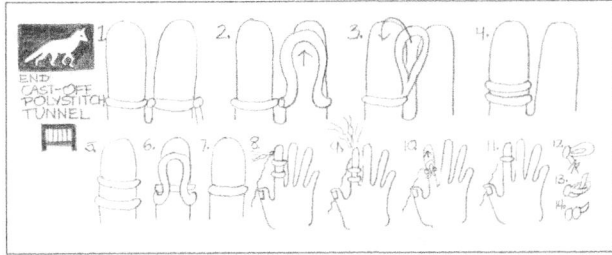

∗ You have just completed an *end cast-off polystitch for tunnel.*

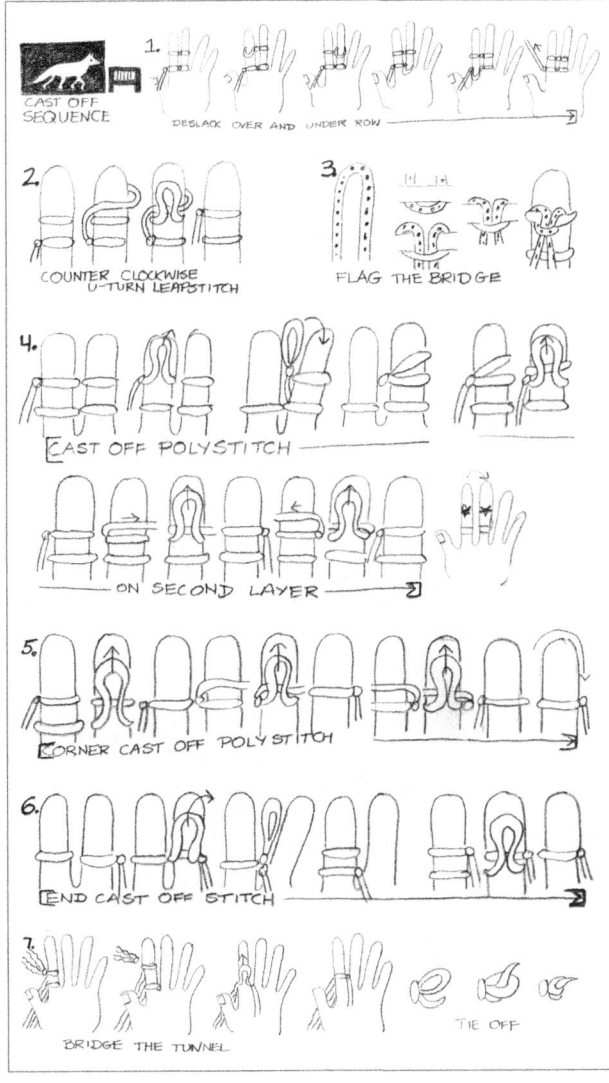

∗ You have completed the entire sequence the two-digit tunnel cast-off.

A Project with a Tunnel

Your practice-swatch may become a project, such as a scrunchie or a keychain bracelet. Make two shorter tunnels and you'll have a pair of doll leg-warmers.

Making several two-digit tunnels is a good idea for practice before taking on the wider four-digit tunnel below. As your tunnels and variations develop, many more fun projects will be within reach.

Completing a scrunchy

You are just steps away from transforming your tunnel into an adjustable hair scrunchy.

Hide ends and turn inside-out

To begin, you will want to hide the tail and dangler. Do this by tying their two ends together with a square-knot, near the midpoint of your tunnel on the outside of the work. Turn the piece inside-out to hide the ends.

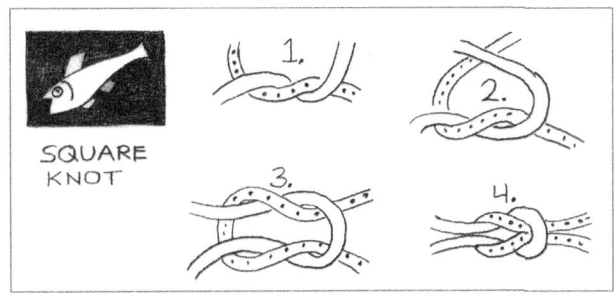

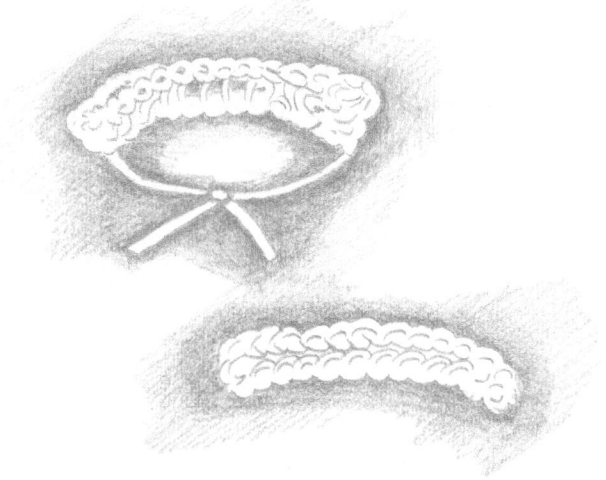

chapter seven

Knit a chain

Knit a length of chain one personal-yard long.

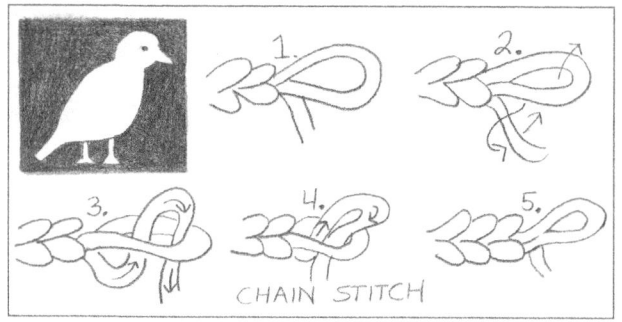

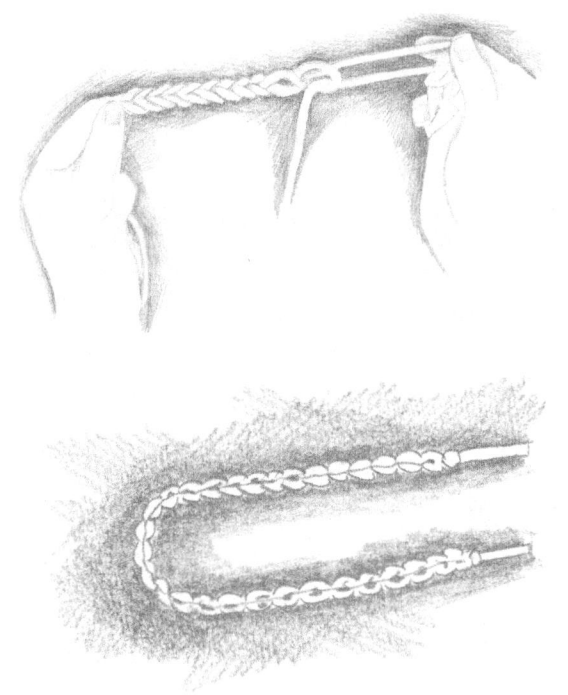

Make a tug knot

Tie an overhand tug knot in one end and pull the chain through the tube and out the opposite side.

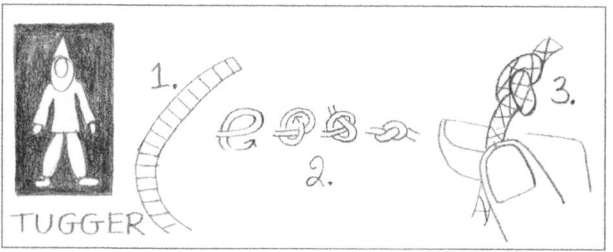

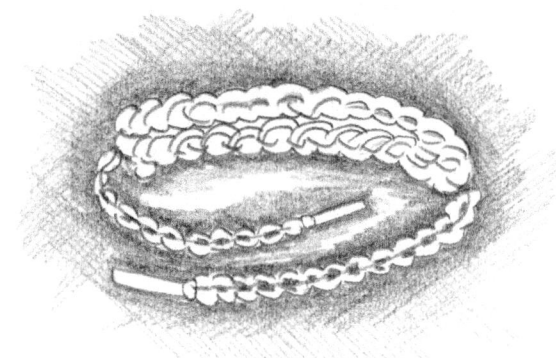

Pull to tighten

Use the knot to help pull the soft chain through a second time. To tighten the scrunchy, pull the two sides of the chain and tie them off on each other with a small bow knot.

Tunnel Knitting

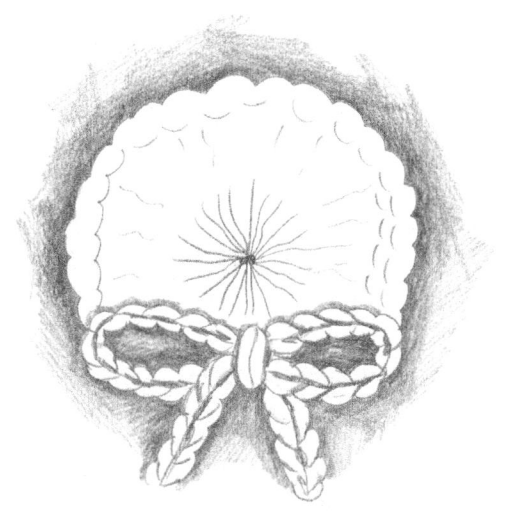

Four-digit Tunnel: Creating a Recorder Case

To make a wider tunnel, you will first cast-on to your Loom Hand in the same way as you did for the 2-fingers-wide tunnel above. But then you will meet a surprising twist waiting around the corner!

Casting on

Casting on the under-row: Create a tail-tugger slipknot.

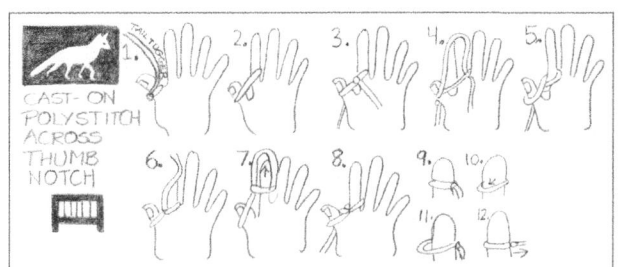

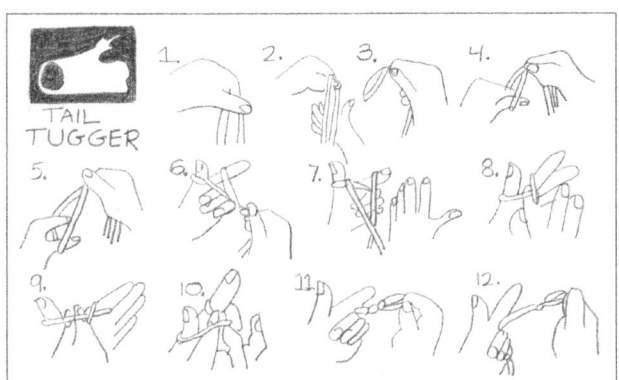

Anchor tail

Anchor the tail-tugger on Thumb; then proceed to cast-on to Pointer across the Thumb Notch.

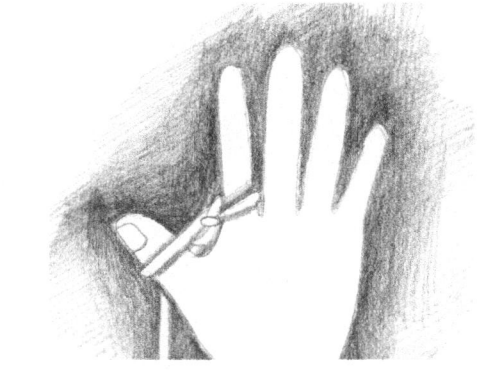

Cast-on polystitch

Do Pinkywise cast-on polystitches onto Middler, Ringa and Pinky, deslacking after each stitch.

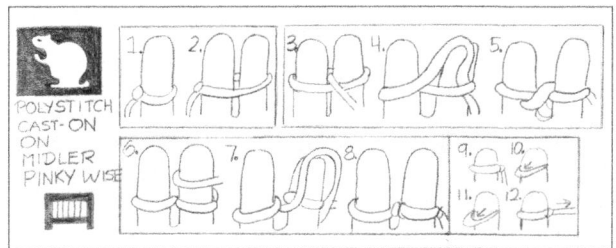

chapter seven

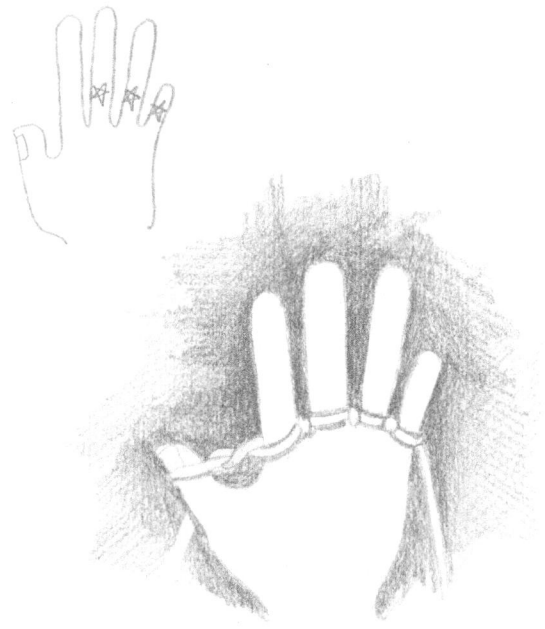

At this point, the tail is hanging down from Thumb, and the leed is hanging off Pinky.

Do not knit a return row. You will now veer off from what you've done before.

Initiate a new layer
Share loop to second layer

Pretend that you didn't just cast-on to Pinky. Go ahead and cast-on to Pinky again, as follows: Slide Pinky up through the same yarn-ring that is on Ringa.

✷ You have shared a loop with Pinky over a bottom yarn-ring on Pinky.

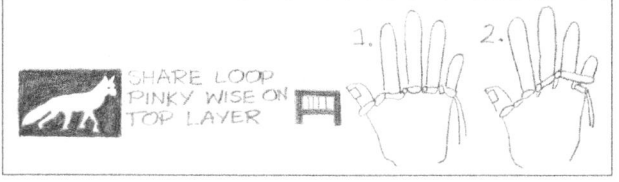

You now have two yarn-rings on Pinky and the top one is the *shared loop*.

Do a special leap-twist

Bring the leed in through your Pinky-Notch, laying it Pinkywise over the shared loop and do a leap-twist on Pinky.

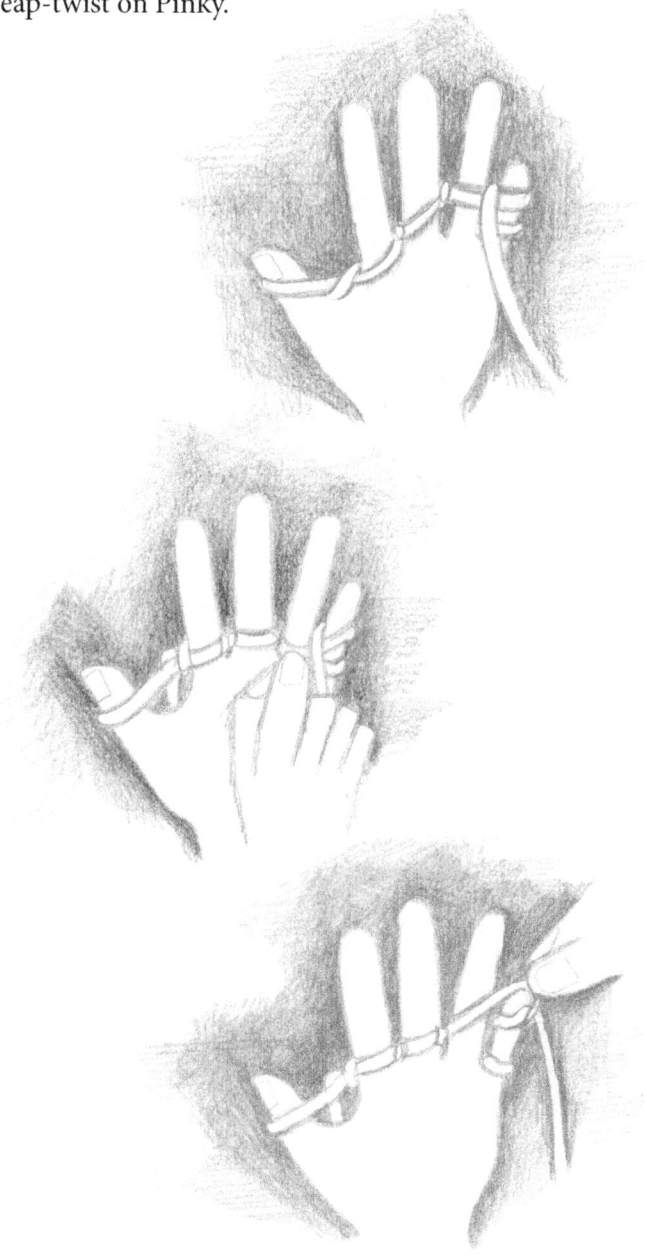

Tunnel Knitting

✷ You have done a Pinkywise leap-twist onto the top layer.

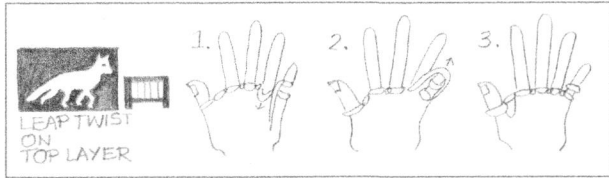

Do a special U-turn leapstitch

Do a countertopwise U-turn leapstitch on the top layer on Pinky.

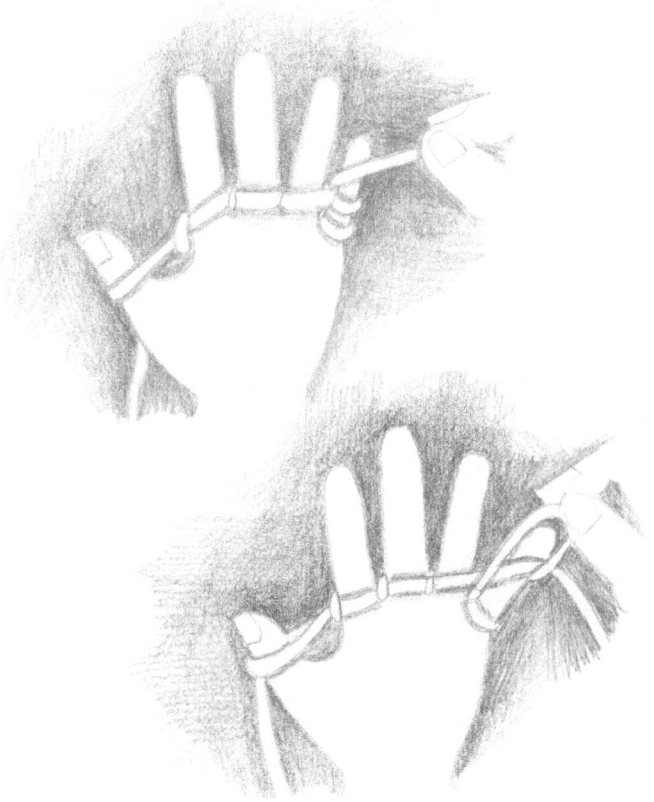

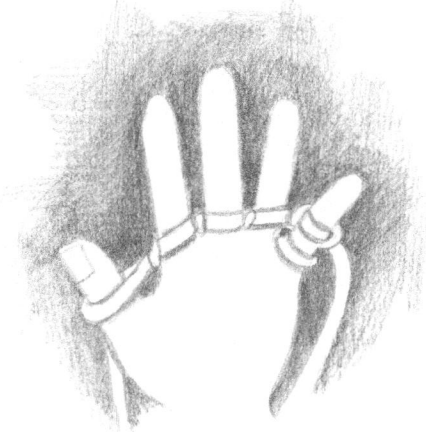

✷ You have done a U-turn leapstitch on the top layer. Surprise! With this special kind of cast-on stitch you have initiated a second level row.

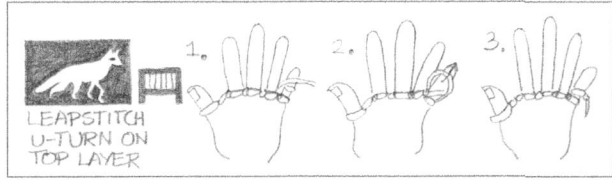

✷ You have completed your first *hitchback cast-on polystitch*, thereby initiating a new layer of stitches.

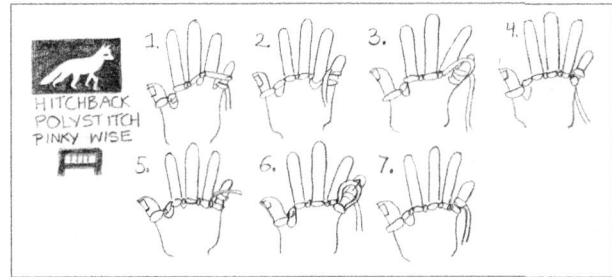

Overview for second layer cast-on

A top-layer row has been initiated on Pinky, and all that remains is to cast-on to the rest of the fingers. You know how to cast-on, but now you will be working cast-on stitches in the opposite direction, Thumbwise. This may be tricky at first—not unlike Ginger Rogers dancing "in high heels and backward." The steps are laid out as follows:

chapter seven

Share loop in reverse

Share a loop Thumbwise by slipping Ringa through the top loop on Pinky.

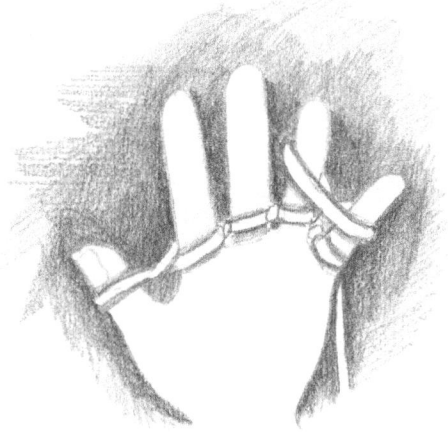

✱ You have shared a loop on the top layer, Thumbwise.

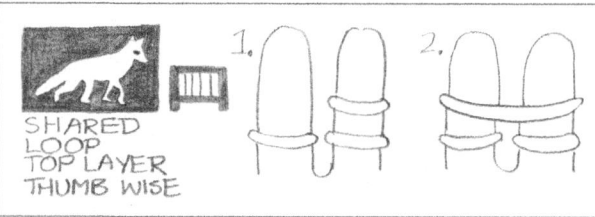

Leap-twist in reverse

Prepare for a *Thumbwise leap-twist* on Ringa by bringing the leed in through the Pinky-Notch, and letting it lie Thumbwise. It helps to lay the leed out through Thumb-Notch while you execute the stitch.

Lift the shared yarn-ring over the leed and up and over the tip of Ringa only, letting the leed land on the back of the hand.

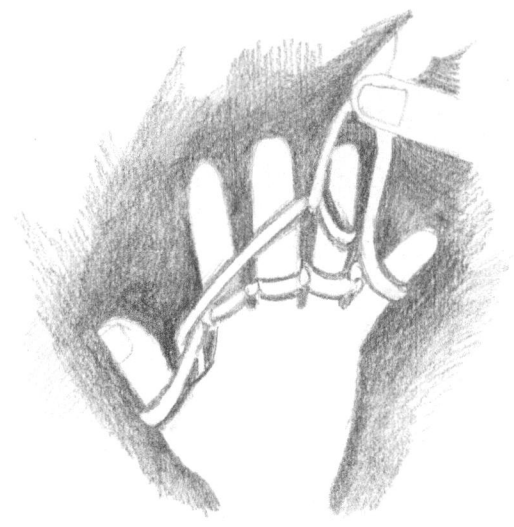

✻ You have accomplished a Thumbwise leap-twist on the top layer.

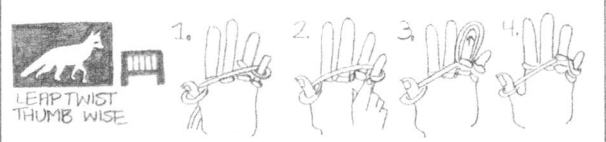

U-turn leapstitch topwise

Bring the leed forward through the Pinky-Notch and back out through the Center-Notch and do a topwise U-turn leapstitch on Ringa with the top layer only.

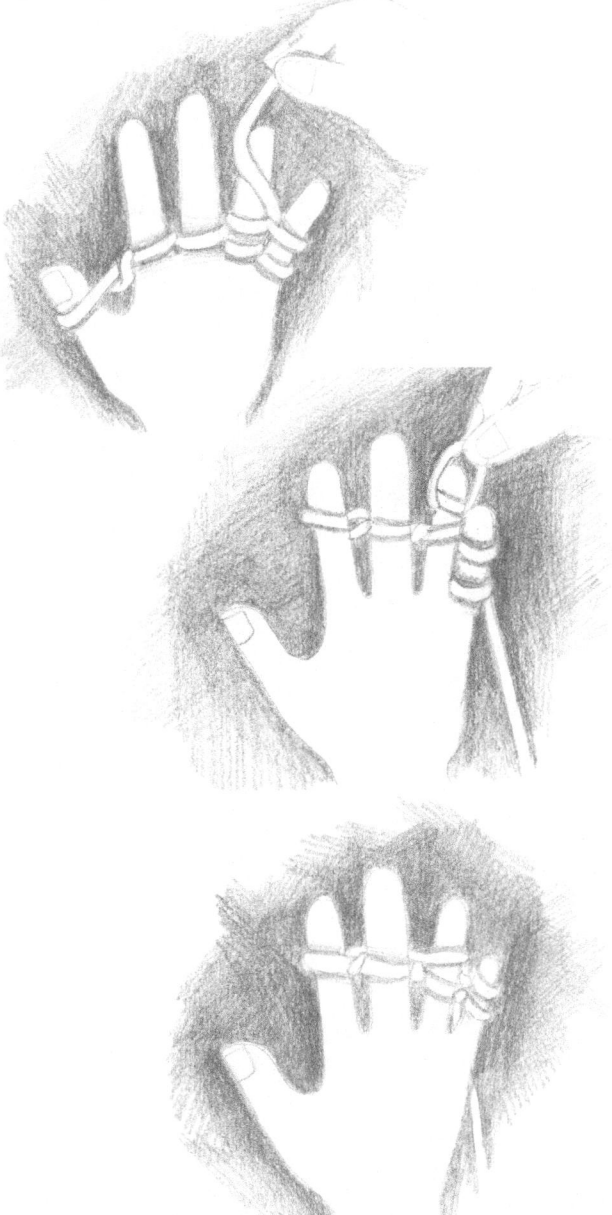

✻ You have done a *topwise U-turn leapstitch on the second layer on Ringa*.

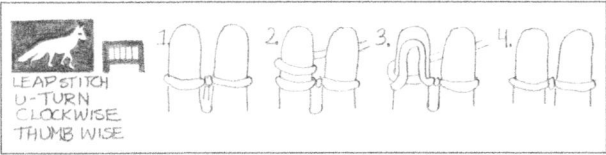

Deslack stitch

Deslack the cast-on stitch, Thumbwise.

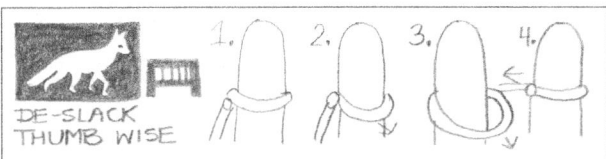

✻ This completes the *Thumbwise cast-on polystitch on the top layer*.

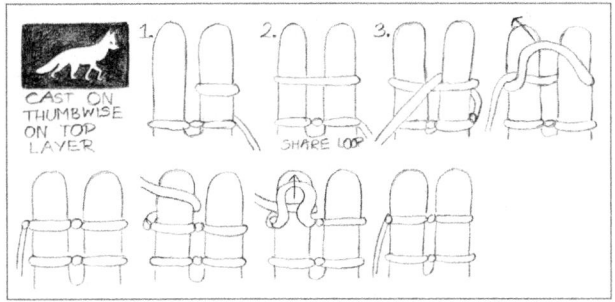

chapter seven

Continue casting on

Do a top-layer Thumbwise cast-on polystitch on Middler, and also on Pointer to complete the row.

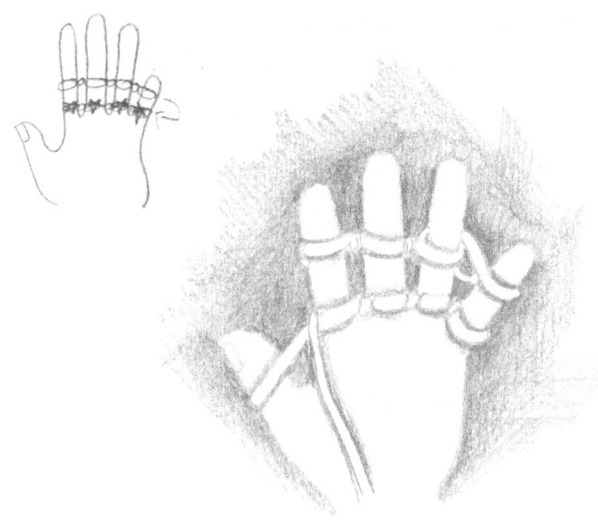

Knit a top-layer Pinkywise row of leapstitches from Pointer to Pinky.

Return cast-on rows

Over-row

Under-row

Knit a bottom-layer Thumbwise row of sneaky-fox stitches back to Pointer.

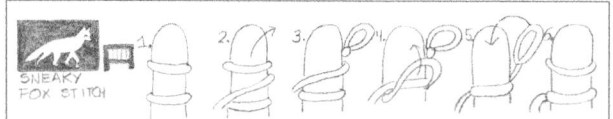

Deslack return rows

Deslack the over-row Pinkywise from Pointer's top yarn-ring to Pinky's top ring, then back Thumbwise on the under-row from Pinky's bottom ring to Pointer's bottom ring.

122

Then bring the slack from Pointer's bottom yarn-ring into the leed.

Deslack tail

Remember to also snug up the original tail-tugger slipknot as well, by tugging gently on the tail.

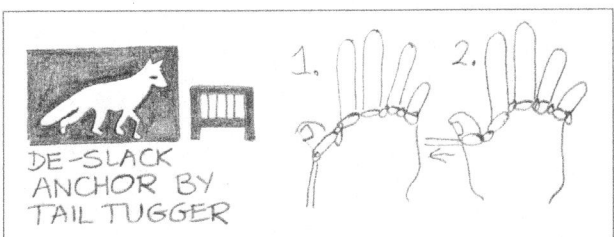

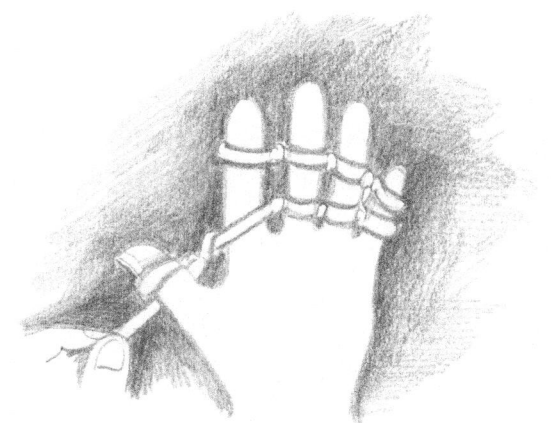

✳ You have deslacked the entire over/under-row and the anchor.

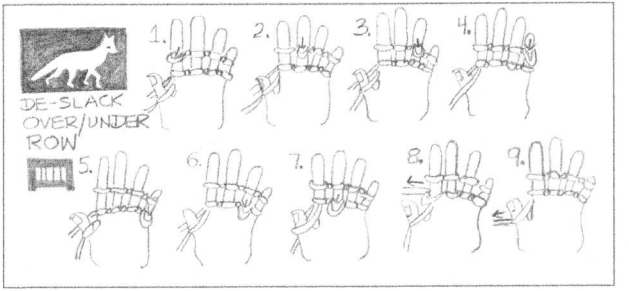

Seal the Thumb-flap

You will now seal the Thumb-flap just as you did for the two-digit tunnel.

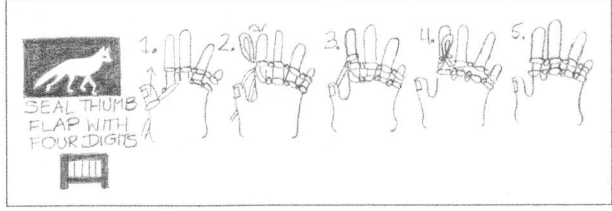

This completes the *cast-on sequence for the four-digit tunnel.*

See backside of work

Notice that without folding over the cast-on loops, you have achieved a double row of loops, just as in the two-finger cast-on method above—but this time the rows are four digits wide.

Over/under-rows

At this point proceed to knit over/under-rows exactly the same as above but using all four fingers. Work an over-row by doing leapstitches along the top layer from Pointer to Pinky.

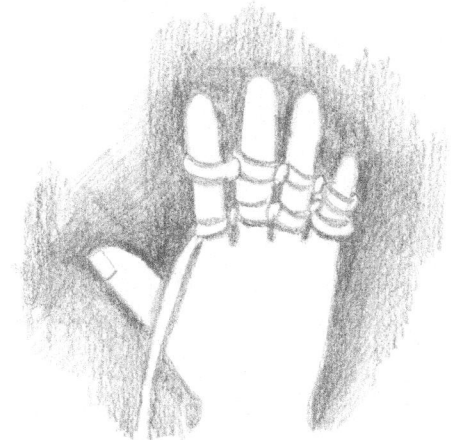

chapter seven

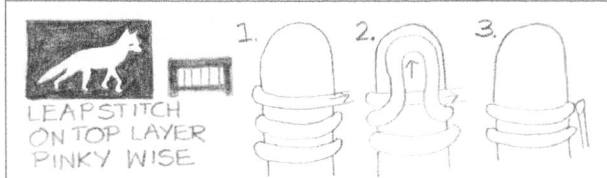

Under-row

Work an under-row of sneaky-fox stitches from Pinky back to Pointer, completing the over/under-row with the leed at the same spot where you started.

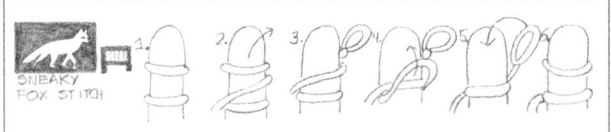

✽ This completes the sequence for *topwise four-digit over/under-rows*.

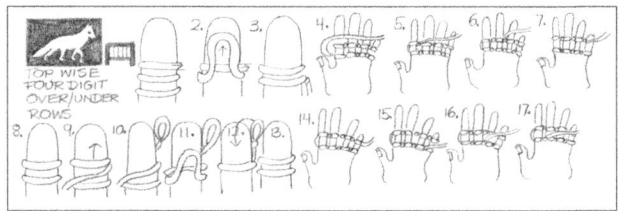

Continue rows

Continue knitting over/under-rows in a topwise rotation. You will soon see the four-digit tunnel growing from the back of your Loom Hand.

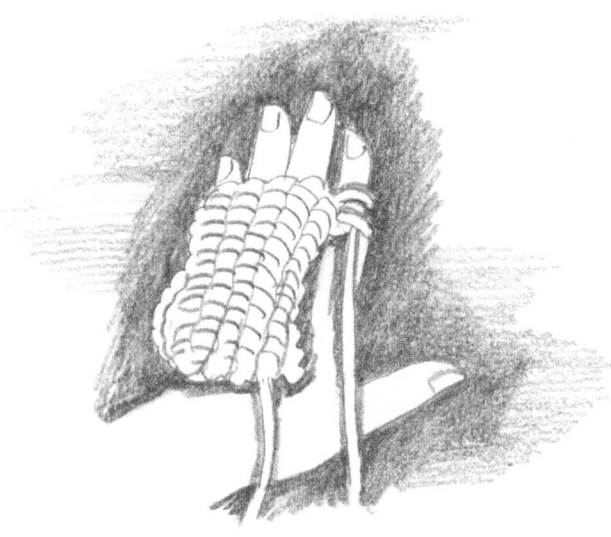

Repeat this sequence for four-digit tunnel rows for about 40 rows for your practice-swatch, ending on the completion of an under-row, with the final stitch on Pointer.

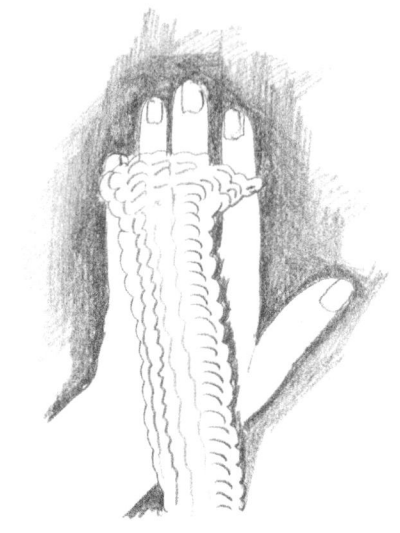

Seal the cast-off seam

For this practice project, which will have one end closed, the final complete rotation—the last under-row and over-row, must be sealed-off.

Prepare to merge

End with the leed at the Thumb-Notch.

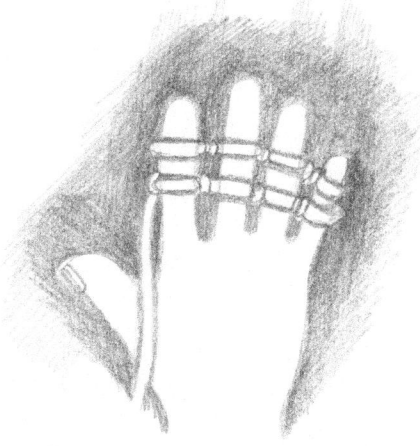

Merge rows by doing leap-rings

With the leed at the Thumb-Notch, you will now merge the final over-row and under-row into a single row of yarn-rings. Starting with Pointer, lift the bottom yarn-ring up over the top yarn-ring and over the tip of Pointer. Proceeding Pinkywise, do the same for each finger. In other words, do a leap-ring on each finger.

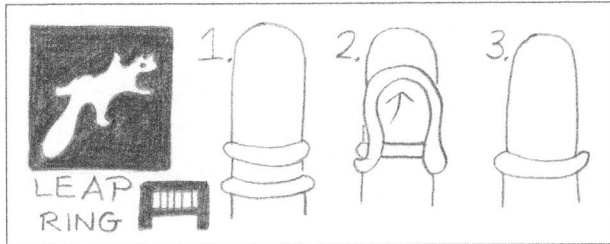

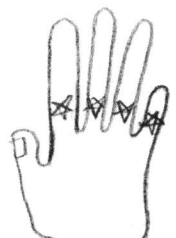

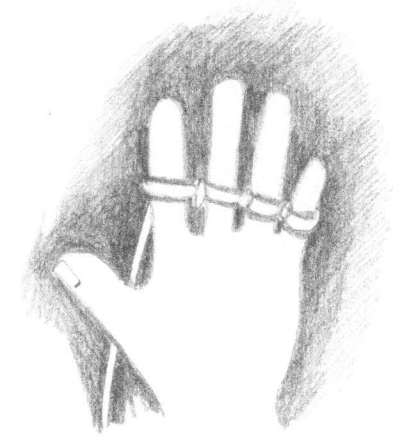

✳ You have merged the over/under-rows into a single row.

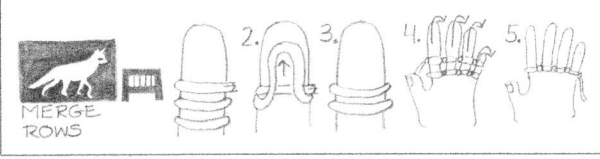

Launch cast-off

You will now cast-off Pinkywise as follows: Launch a cast-off row on Pointer with a single counter clockwise U-turn leapstitch.

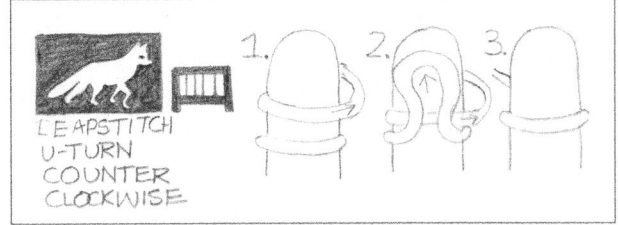

chapter seven

Continue casting off

Do a cast-off polystitch from Pointer to Middler to Ringa.

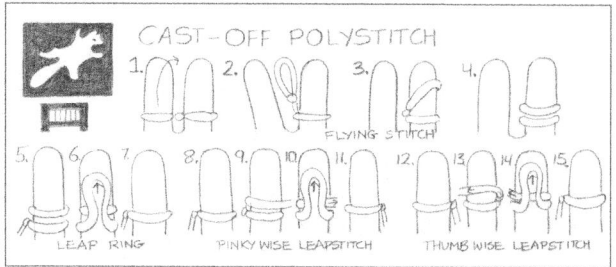

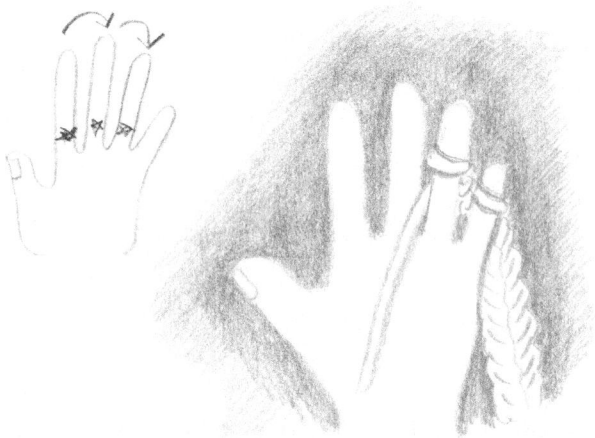

Secure the work

Work an end cast-off stitch on Pinky, cutting the leed at about a foot, leaving a slightly longer dangler than usual.

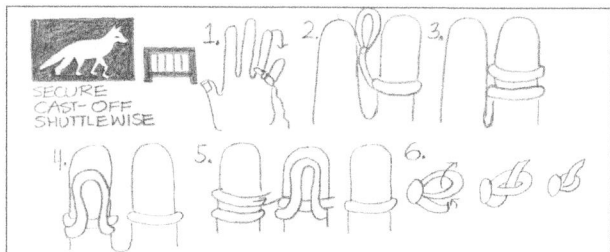

Completing the recorder case

Turn the case inside-out to hide the dangler. Use the tail for a drawstring by weaving it in and out just under the cast-on row.

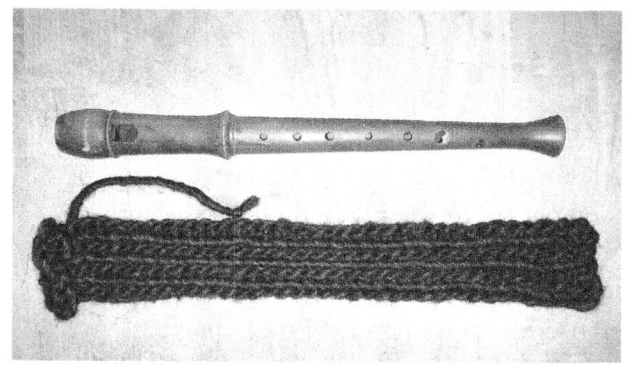

✻ You now have a seamless recorder case!

Variations

Casting off for an open tunnel

Sometimes you may want to cast-off with a knitted tunnel without sealing off one end. As with the two-digit tunnel, there are two layers of stitches to cast-off from your fingers. The sequence is the same, except that it is being applied to four fingers. Since you work your way around in the topwise direction, casting off the top layer first, the last stitch to cast-off will be the bottom yarn-ring on Pointer.

Launch and flag the cast-off over-row

Launch the cast-off row with a Pinkywise leapstitch on the top yarn-ring on Pointer and flag the bridge.

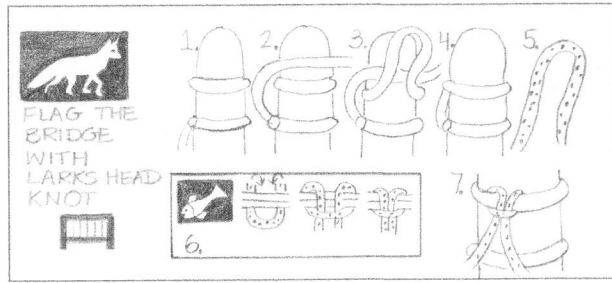

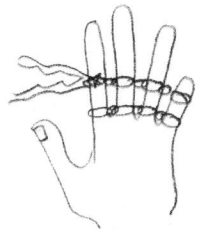

Cast-off polystitch

Do Pinkywise cast-off polystitches on the top layer on Middler, Ringa, and Pinky.

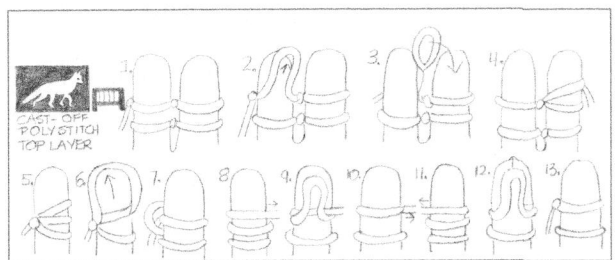

Round the bend

Do a corner cast-off stitch on Pinky (remember no flying stitch).

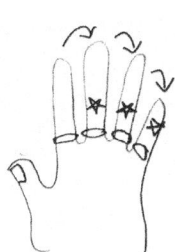

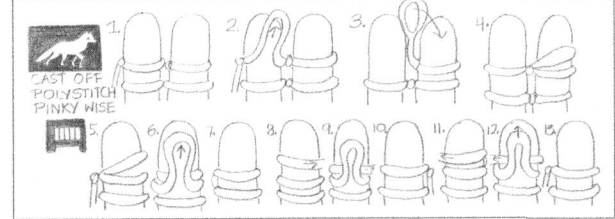

chapter seven

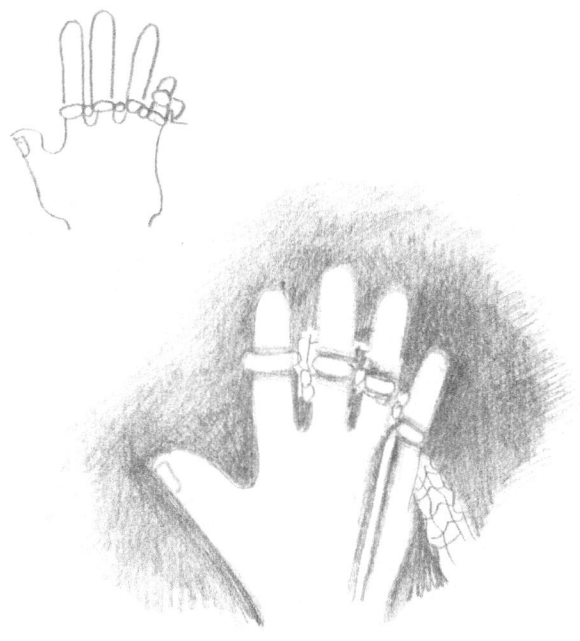

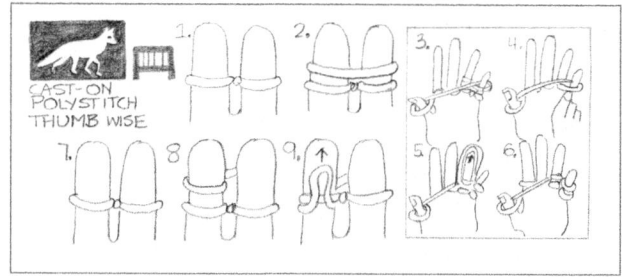

Secure work

Do a tunnel secure cast-off polystitch on Pointer.

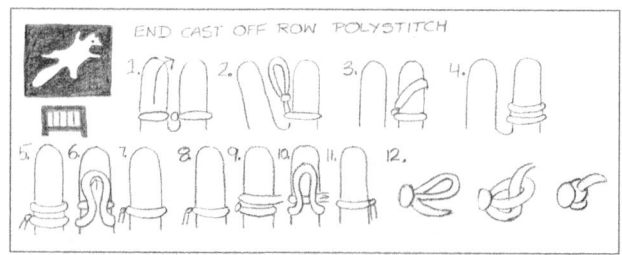

Notice that for Thumbwise cast-off polystitches, the Thumbwise leapstitch comes first, followed by the Pinkywise leapstitch, whereas with Pinkywise leapstitches, it is the opposite. (Pinkywise leapstitches are first, followed by Thumbwise.)

Explore variations

Notice that four-digit over/under Tunnel rows are just like two-digit over/under Tunnel rows, only the technique is being applied to more fingers. Work Pinkywise in the over-row and Thumbwise in the under-row. As you develop your knitting techniques you will find that countless variations on this theme are possible.

Cast-off Thumbwise

Take the leed back through the Pinky-Notch and pull it to the side, Shuttlewise, in preparation for switching direction and working the next row Thumbwise.

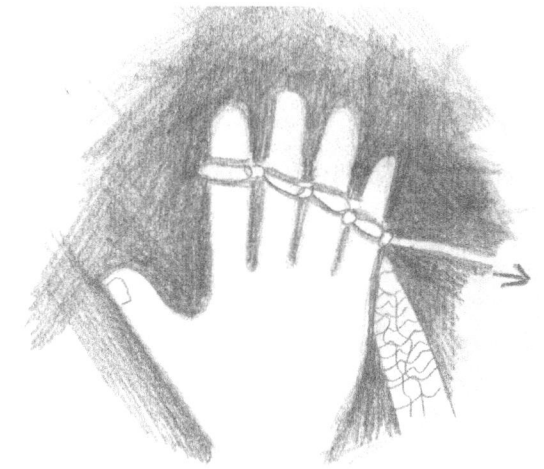

Do Thumbwise cast-off polystitches on Pinky, Ringa, and Middler.

Chapter Review for "Tunnel Knitting"

Vocabulary

corner cast-off
tunnel
foldback
over-row
under-ros
round the end

Stitches

Hitchback Polystitch Pinkywise:
- Top-layer shared loop flowwise to the most recently active digit.
- Teap-twist flowwise; countertopwise U-turn leapstitch.

Sneaky-fox Stitch:
- Lay leed workwise.
- Lift top-layer row yarn-ring with Loom fox-pinch and suspend on Middler.
- Do a leapstitch with the top yarn-ring.
- Replace the yarn-ring from Loom Middler.

Corner Cast-off Polystitch (countertopwise):
- Do a workwise leapstitch; do a counterworkwise leapstitch.
- Do a leap-ring; position the leed to middle gap in preparation for working in the opposite direction.

Sequences

Repeating Rows Sequence for Two-digit Tunnel:
- Do a Pinkywise leapstitch on the topmost yarn-ring on Pointer.
- Do a Pinkywise leapstitch on the topmost yarn-ring on Middler.
- Do a Thumbwise fox stitch on the bottom yarn-ring on Middler.
- Do a Thumbwise fox stitch on the bottom yarn-ring on Pointer.

Rows for Four-digit Tunnel on Loom Hand:
- Do a Pinkywise leapstitch on the topmost yarn-ring on Pointer.
- Do a Pinkywise leapstitch on the topmost yarn-ring on Middler.
- Do a Pinkywise leapstitch on the topmost yarn-ring on Ringa.
- Do a Pinkywise leapstitch on the topmost yarn-ring on Pinky.
- Do a Thumbwise fox stitch on the bottom yarn-ring on Pinky.
- Do a Thumbwise fox stitch on the bottom yarn-ring on Ringa.
- Do a Thumbwise fox stitch on the bottom yarn-ring on Middler.
- Do a Thumbwise fox stitch on the bottom yarn-ring on Pointer.

chapter eight

The Switchback

chapter eight

 ## About Barehand Switchback

Once you have learned to knit a tunnel, which requires two layers of stitches on your hand, there is no reason to stop at that point. Switchback is a method for creating pieces that are wider than our hands, by stacking folded layers of stitches in a zigzag pattern. This technique opens up amazing possibilities both for increased width and creative design. When you open up your first switchback project, it is as if a butterfly is emerging from its chrysalis and unfolding its wings!

The switchback method is very useful for creating beautiful, alternating patterns of ripple stitches and cornfield stitches on the face of a knitted piece. The added width renders it very useful for knitting larger items such as vests, sweaters, and shawls. Exploring variations to this three-ply approach will open the door to any number of alternating ripple and field stitch patterns, having seamless transitions on the surface of the fabric. The switchback quickly becomes familiar and fun.

Switchback rows are different from tunnel rows, in that the rows are open-ended. In other words, they do not connect unless you use a variation of the technique.

Rhyme for the switchback

To keep the eggs from Sneaky Fox,
A double latch secured the box
With an extra heavy double lid—
So this is what old Foxy did:
He brought his big coyote friend
Who lifted the lid where the ducks were penned
With his broad strong jaw and long strong legs,
While Foxy lifted out the eggs.

– A.B. and H. Akin

Creating a Wide Winter Scarf

Materials: A ball of somewhat bulky yarn of the desired color.

Anchor the cast-on

Anchor the stitch onto Loom Pointer.

Cast-on first layer

Cast-on to the four fingers of your Loom hand Pinkywise, using the Rooted cast-on technique.

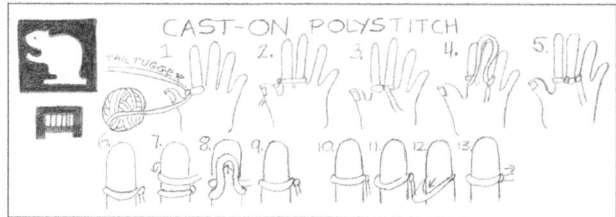

The Switchback

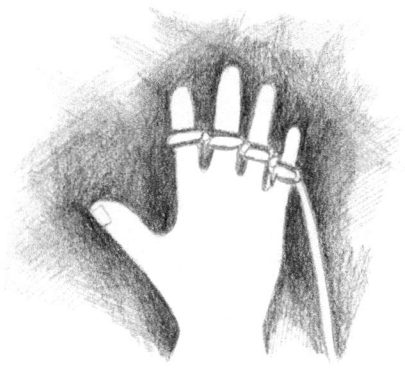

Hitchback Pinkywise to initiate a second layer

Do a hitchback cast-on polystitch Pinkywise onto Pinky, initiating a second layer of stitches.

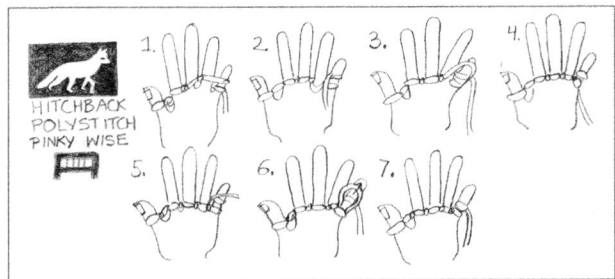

Continue casting on in reverse

Do cast-on polystitches Thumbwise onto Ringa, Middler, and Pointer to finish the second layer row.

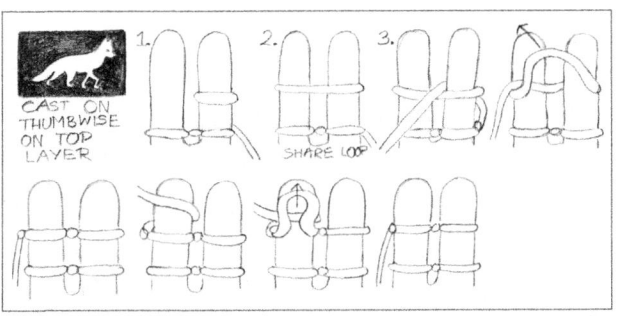

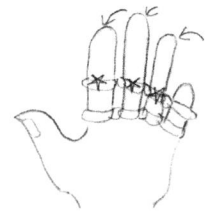

Hitchback Thumbwise to initiate third layer

Now you will start a third layer of stitches to create the top-layer row beginning with a Thumbwise hitchback.

Shared loop to third layer

Share a loop Thumbwise with Pointer.

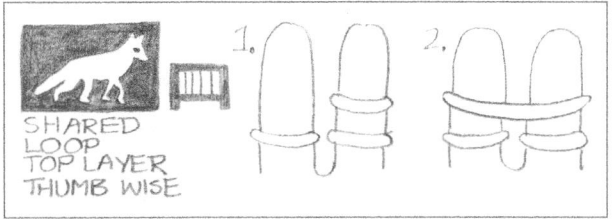

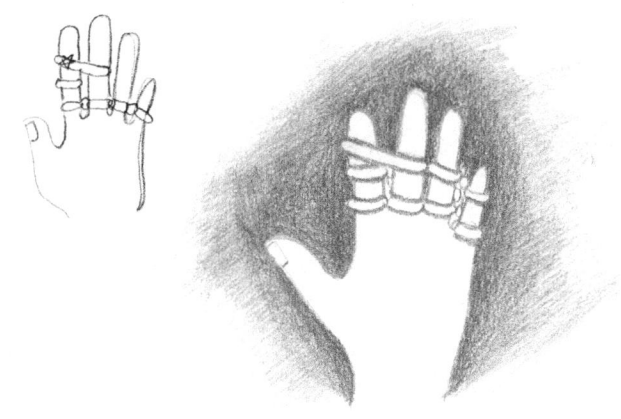

chapter eight

Thumbwise leap-twist elevated

This is just as you have learned to do onto Pinky, only the stitch will be done Thumbwise, as follows:

Do a leap-twist on the top-layer shared yarn-ring on Pointer Thumbwise just as you have learned previously only this time elevating to a third layer.

✻ This is a leap-twist elevated.

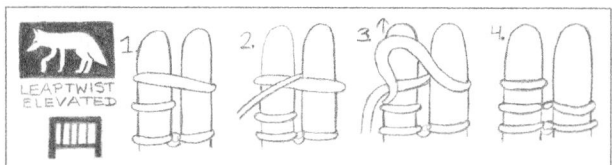

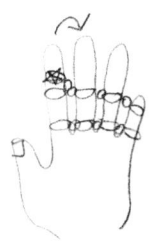

Do a U-turn leapstitch topwise on the top yarn-ring on Pointer on the top layer just as you have learned previously—only this time elevating to a third layer.

✻ This is the leap-twist elevated.

U-turn leapstitch

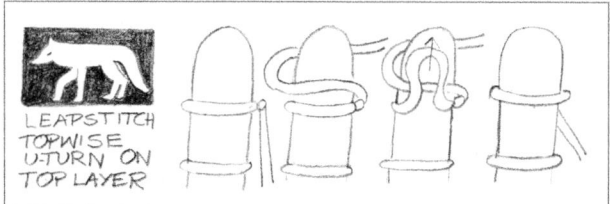

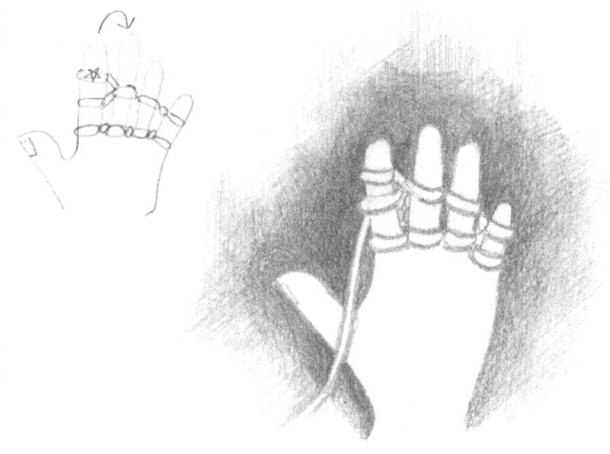

✻ You have completed a hitch-back polystitch, Thumbwise from Middler's middle layer to Pointer, initiating a top layer of stitches on Pointer.

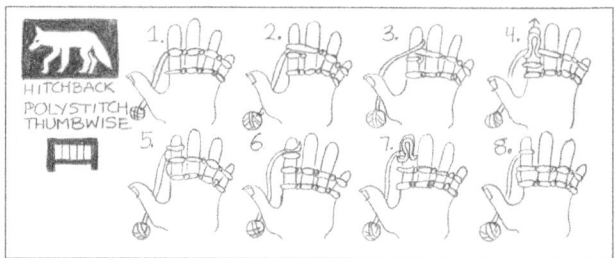

Continue to cast-on third layer

Work cast-on polystitches Pinkywise, on Middler, Ringa, and Pinky, creating a third layer of yarn-rings.

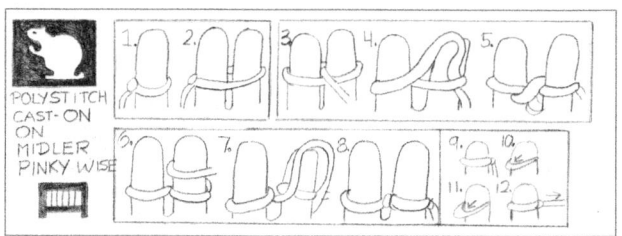

The Switchback

Return cast-on row

Note: On completing the switchback cast-on sequence, the leed is coming from the top yarn-ring on Pinky and the tail is on the bottom yarn-ring on Pointer. Now, in preparation for the return row, take a moment to consider: A single 12-digit row is laid down, zigzag fashion on your Loom Hand in three layers. When you knit rows, each layer will require a different type of polystitch.

Top layer leapstitches

Begin the return cast-on row by laying the leed Thumbwise in preparation for a Thumbwise row.

Do Leapstitches along the top layer from Pinky to Pointer.

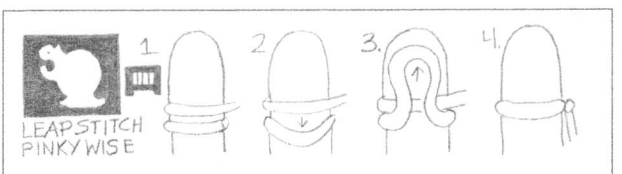

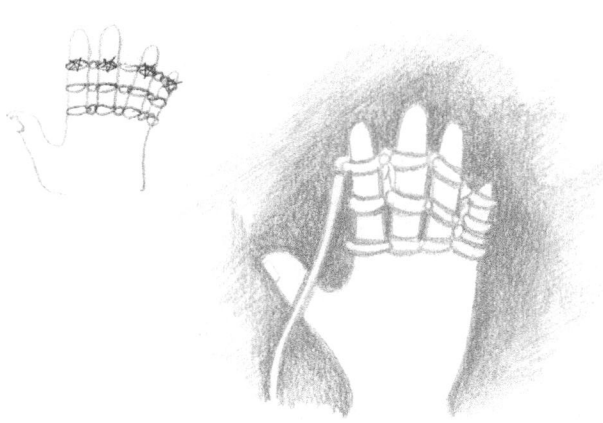

Switch direction for second layer of sneaky-fox stitches

At this point, switch the direction of your flow to do a Pinkywise row of sneaky-fox stitches, from Pointer to Pinky. Up until now your sneaky-fox stitches were worked Thumbwise and to a bottom layer stitch, but now, applying the stitch to a middle layer stitch, you will do a sneaky-fox in the opposite direction (Pinkywise) as follows:

Lay the leed Pinkywise.

Pinch and suspend

Do a sneaky-fox stitch:

With Shuttle fox-pinch, lift the upper yarn-ring off active digit, suspending it from Shuttle Middler.

chapter eight

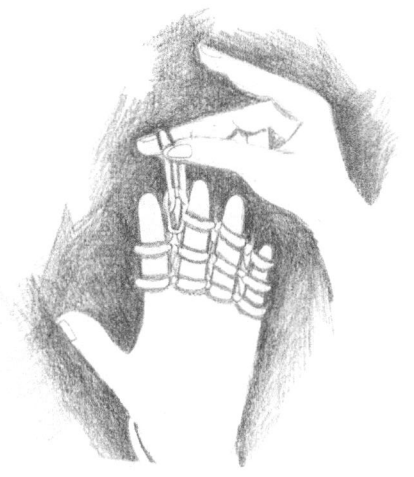

With bird-pinch, pluck up the lower yarn-ring and leapstitch it over the active digit.

Lift up and over

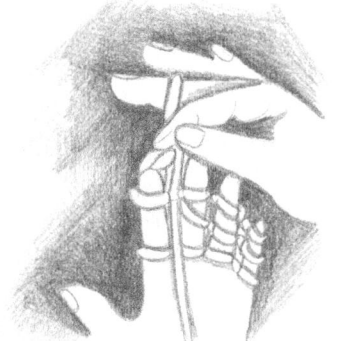

Replace top layer

Place the top-layer yarn-ring back on Pointer.

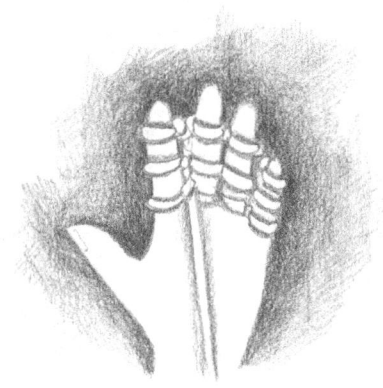

✻ You have done a sneaky-fox stitch Pinkywise on the middle layer on Pointer.

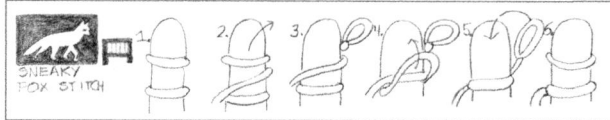

More sneaky-fox stitches

Do sneaky-fox stitches Pinkywise with the middle layer yarn-rings on Middler, Ringa, and Pinky.

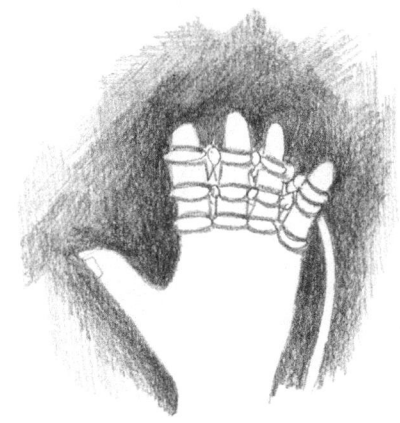

Switch direction for first layer coyote stitches

Note: Here is where we meet something altogether new. The maneuver called for here is similar to the fox stitch, except that you lift two yarn-rings from each finger, using your coyote-pinch, instead of the fox-pinch.

Lay the leed

First, lay the leed Thumbwise and begin on Pinky…

Lift and suspend

… lift the top two yarn-rings from that finger with your Shuttle coyote-pinch.

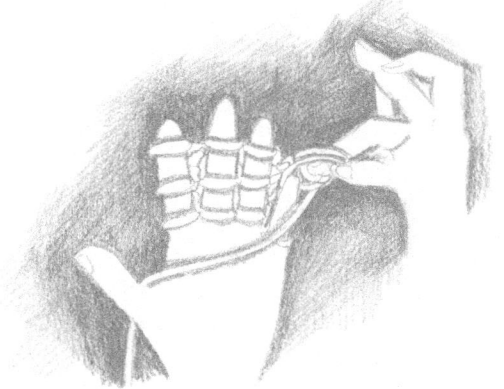

Suspend the yarn-rings on Shuttle Ringa, as your Shuttle fox-pinch plucks the bottom yarn-ring up over the leed and over the top of Pinky.

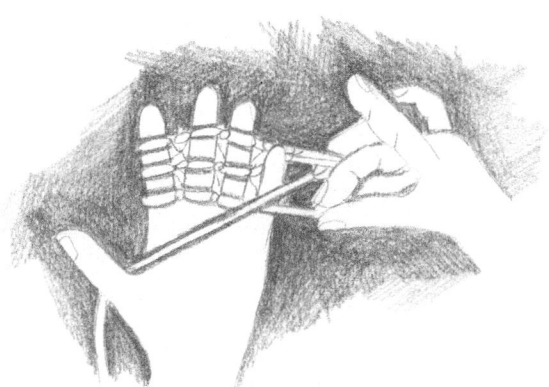

Return rings

Return the two upper rings to Pinky by sliding them back off Ringa.

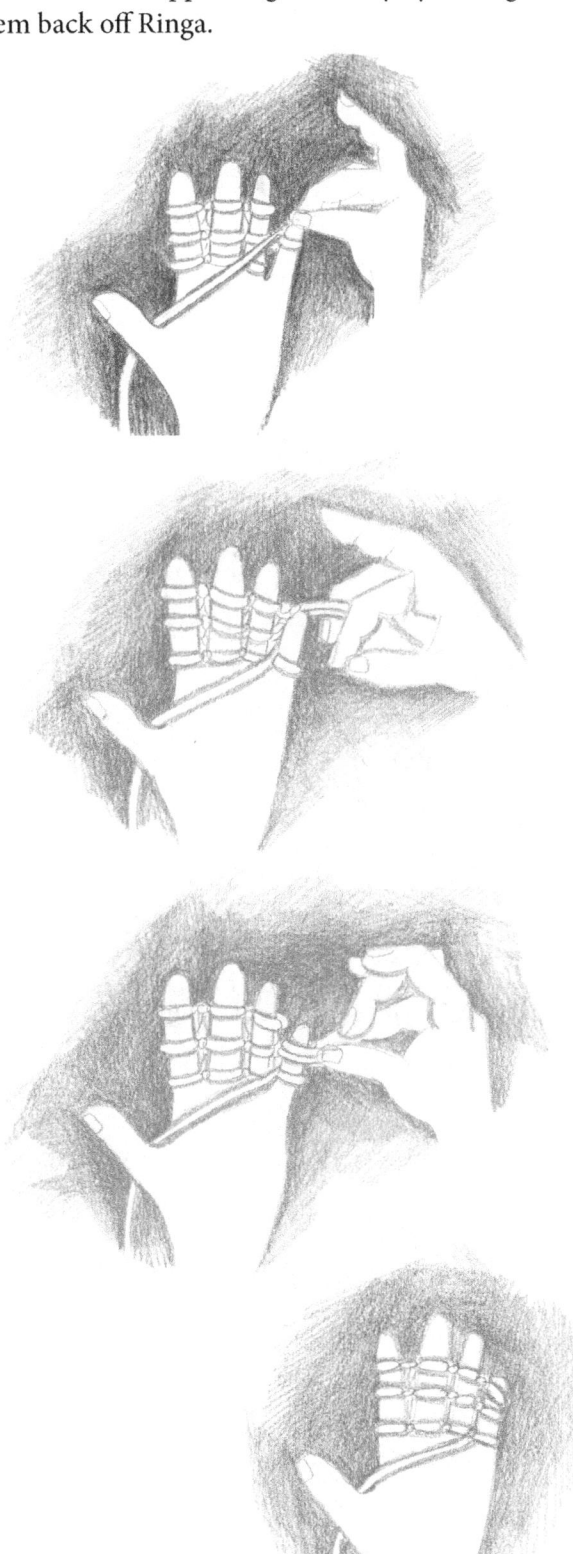

chapter eight

* You have just completed your first clever-coyote stitch Thumbwise (coyote stitch for short).

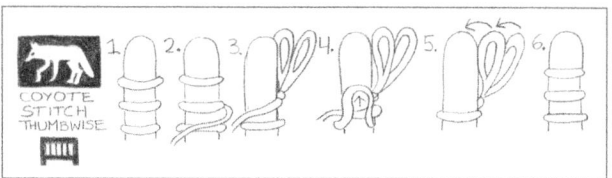

Continue coyote stitches

Do coyote stitches Thumbwise on Ringa, Middler, and Pointer.

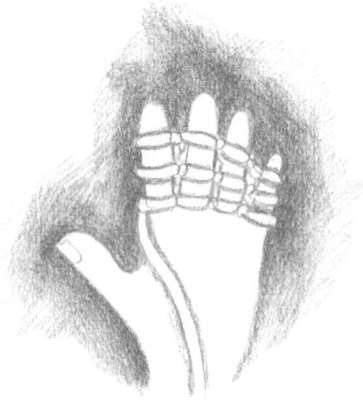

Deslack layers

Deslack the entire switchback row from the top yarn-ring on Pinky to the bottom yarn-ring on Pointer, as follows:

Deslack the top layer of stitches Thumbwise.

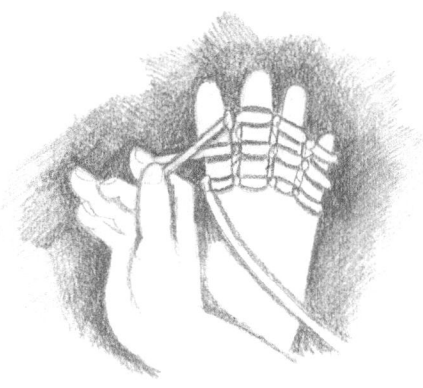

Deslack the middle layer of stitches Pinkywise.

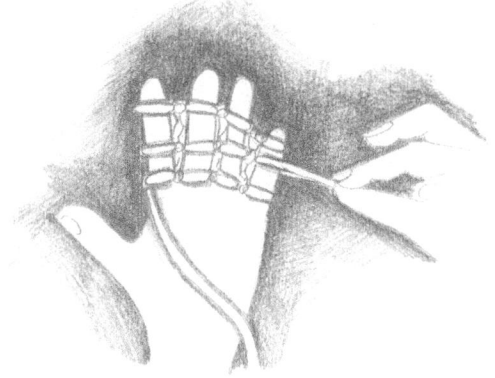

Deslack the bottom layer of stitches Thumbwise, bringing the slack into the leed.

* You have deslacked down the S-line of a switchback return row.

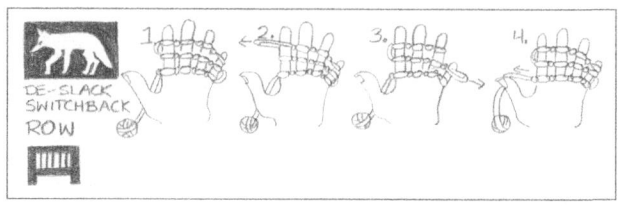

View the back of the hand

Take a look at the back of your hand and observe your switchback cast-on row. Notice which corners connect and where they are free. Trace your fingers along them, familiarizing yourself with this shape.

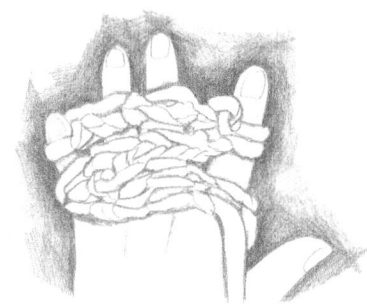

Keywords Reminder
For the switchback cast-on

Anchor and cast-on bottom layer: Anchor the cast-on row on Pointer and work cast-on stitches Pinkywise to Middler, Ringa, and Pinky.

Middle layer: Do a hitchback polystitch to the next level on Pinky and work Thumbwise cast-on Polystitches on Middler, Ringa, and Pinky to create a middle layer.

Top layer: Do a hitchback polystitch onto Pointer Thumbwise and work cast-on Polystitches Pinkywise on to Middler, Ringa, and Pinky.

Knit return row: Thumbwise leapstitches along the top layer, Pinky wise stitches along the middle layer, and Thumbwise coyote stitches along the bottom layer.

Deslack: Remove the slack from the top, middle, and bottom layer of the return cast-off row.

Switchback rows

Knit your first regular out row by doing everything you just learned, only in the reverse, working your way back up the S-shape on your hand.

Bottom row of Pinkywise coyote stitches

You have already learned to do sneaky-fox stitches Thumbwise and Pinkywise. Soon you will be doing coyote stitches in both directions as well. As you work your way back up the switchback, take note that the only difference is the direction of your leed.

Out row on first layer

Switch the direction of your flow by laying the leed Pinkywise and do a coyote stitch on Pointer. Lift the top two yarn-rings from Pointer with your Shuttle coyote-pinch.

Suspend the yarn-rings on Shuttle Ringa, as your Shuttle fox-pinch plucks the bottom yarn-ring up over the leed and over the top of Pinky.

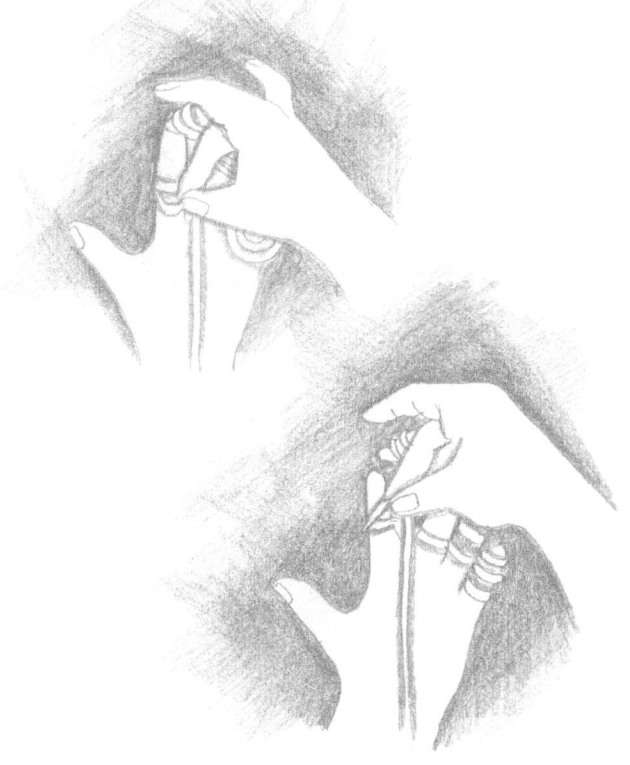

The Switchback

chapter eight

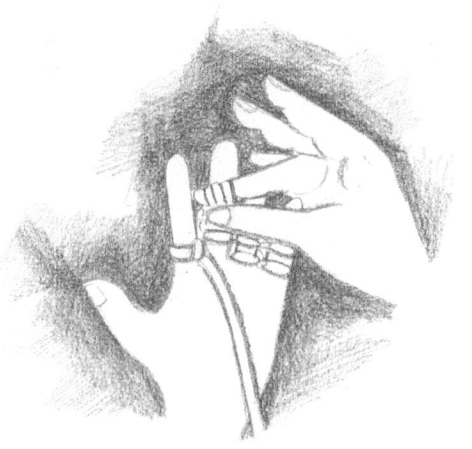

Return the two upper rings to Pinky, sliding them back off of Ringa.

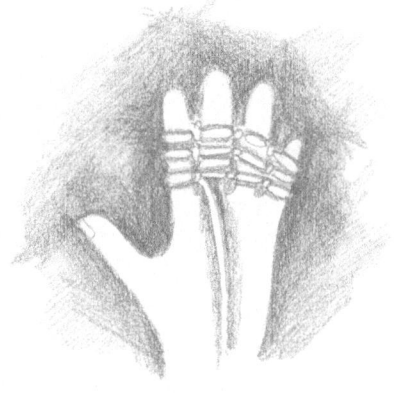

✷ You have just completed your first coyote stitch, Pinkywise.

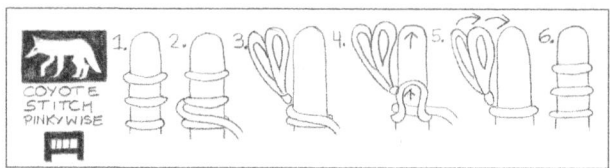

Complete bottom layer of out row

Complete the out row by doing coyote stitches Pinkywise along the first level row, on Middler, Ringa, and Pinky.

Middle layer of out row

Switch flow with the sneaky-fox stitch

Switch the direction of your flow back Thumbwise and do sneaky-fox stitches along the middle row, on Pinky, Ringa, Middler, and Pointer.

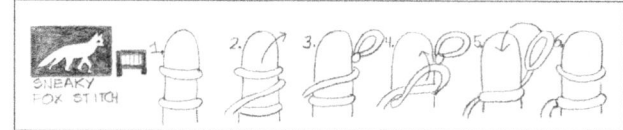

Top layer of out row

Switch flow with leapstitches

Switch the direction of your flow Pinkywise again and do a row of leapstitches along the top row from Pointer to Pinky.

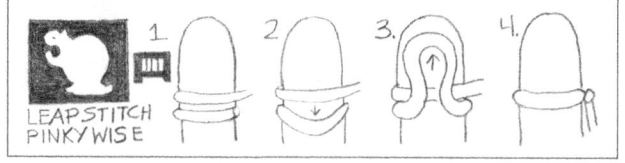

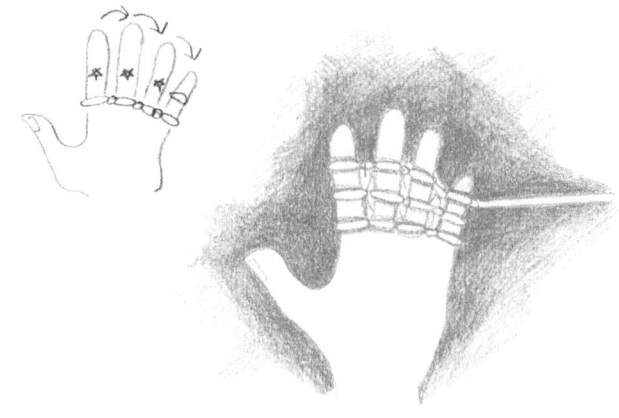

140

Return switchback row

It is time to knit another return row back down along the S-line. This is done in the same way as was done for the return cast-on row. Below is a review.

Thumbwise on top layer

Knit a Thumbwise layer of leapstitches along the third layer—the top.

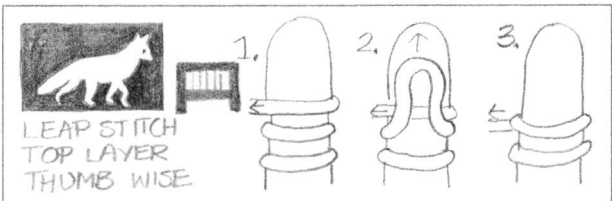

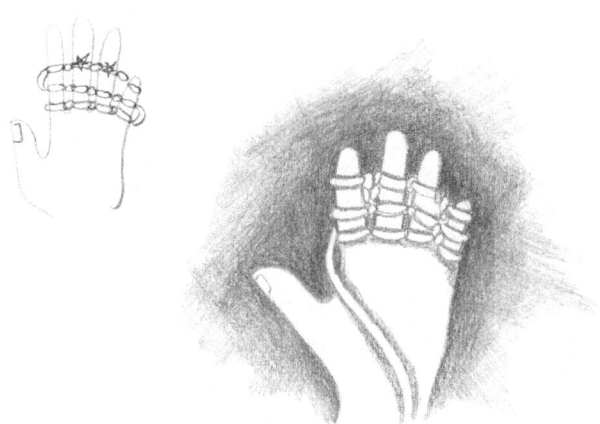

Pinkywise on middle layer

Knit a Pinkywise layer of fox stitches along the second layer—the middle row.

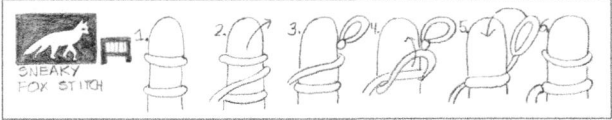

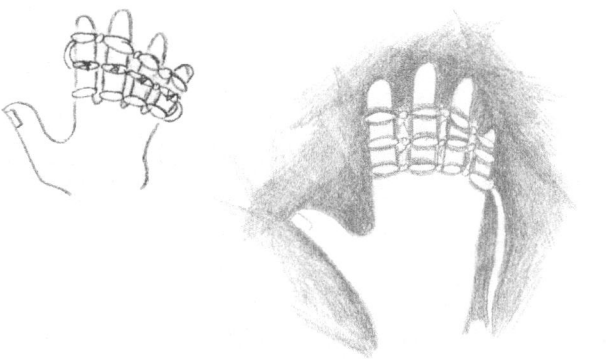

Thumbwise on bottom layer

Knit another row of coyote stitches, Thumbwise, along the first layer—the bottom row.

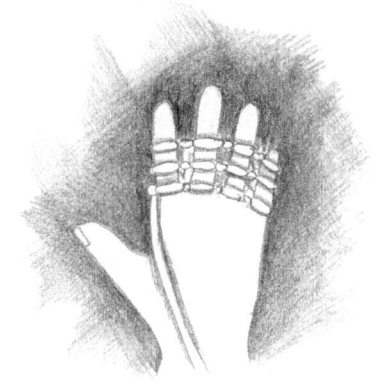

✻ You have completed the repeating rows sequence for the switchback.

Review of repeating rows sequence

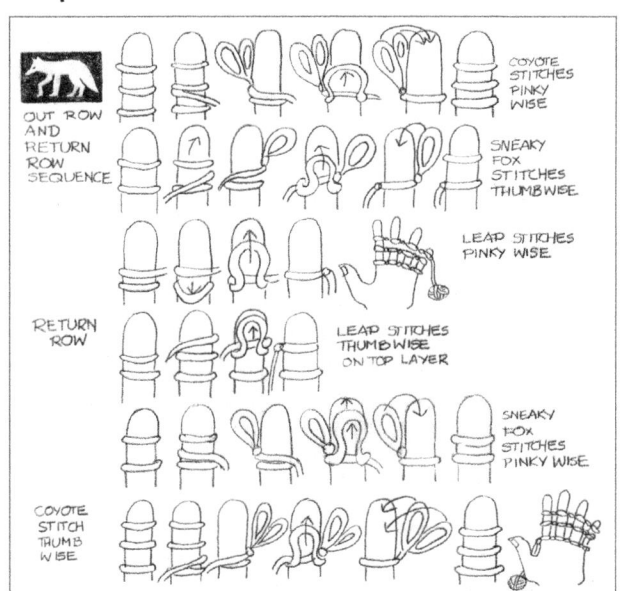

Continue knitting rows

Continue to knit switchback rows and watch as the three-fold swath of knitted fabric grows from the back of your hand.

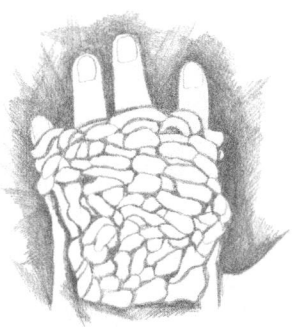

chapter eight

Keeping track of the direction of your rows

The pattern of stitches looks like a letter Z from behind, even though on the face of your hand it is in the shape of an S.

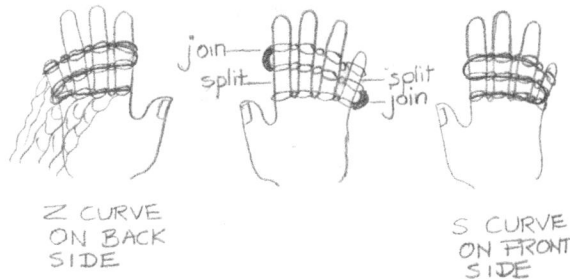

You will need to continue along this S-line as you knit your rows. If you lose track of direction, just look at the work along the edge-digits to see where you round a bend and where you simply turn around.

Troubleshooting

If you accidentally round a bend in the wrong spot—for example from the top layer to the middle layer on Pinky, instead of on Pointer—or, on the other hand, if you switch direction ending a row on the bottom row on Pinky instead of Pointer, you will attach the work where it is not supposed to connect and will be unable to open-out your switchback fabric when finished. Even one such mistake will be a big problem. The work will have to be taken out to correct it. To avoid having to take out large amounts, you should check your work often, running your fingers between the layered rows to be sure nothing went wrong.

It is important to understand the difference between layers and rows. *Your first three layers make only a single row that is folded back and forth across the fingers of your Loom Hand.* The out row goes Pinkywise-Thumbwise-Pinkywise, whereas the return row goes Thumbwise-Pinkywise-Thumbwise. You can practice by tracing an S-shape up and down along

the switchback layers on the face of your fingers with the tip of Shuttle Pointer. So keep up the S-uper effort!

Check your rows

Along the back side of your hand you can separate out the folds in your work to be sure everything is running smoothly. On the back side you will find that the edge assumes a Z-shape.

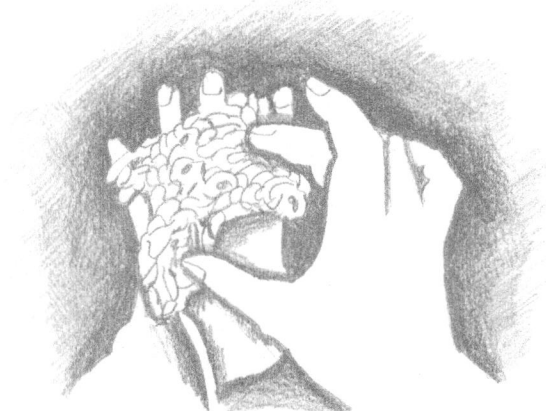

Finish the rows

Knit until the piece is as long as you want it to be. End on an out row with your leed coming from the top yarn-ring on Pinky. For our practice project, a winter scarf, you will want around 75 out-and-return rows. Remember that your work will elongate once stretched out.

Cast-off

You can choose to cast-off anytime at the completion of an out row—that is, after you have done leapstitches across the top layer, from Pointer to Pinky.

The Switchback

Overview of switchback cast-off

For casting off, we use the same flying-squirrel cast-off polystitch that we learned previously. Because the cast-off sequence moves in the direction of a return row, the flow moves Thumbwise on the top row, Pinkywise on the middle row, and Thumbwise on the bottom row.

Launch switchback cast-off

Deslack rows
Launch the cast-off by deslacking the last out row, moving up the S-line: Deslack Pinkywise along the bottom layer, Thumbwise along the middle layer, and Pinkywise along the top layer.

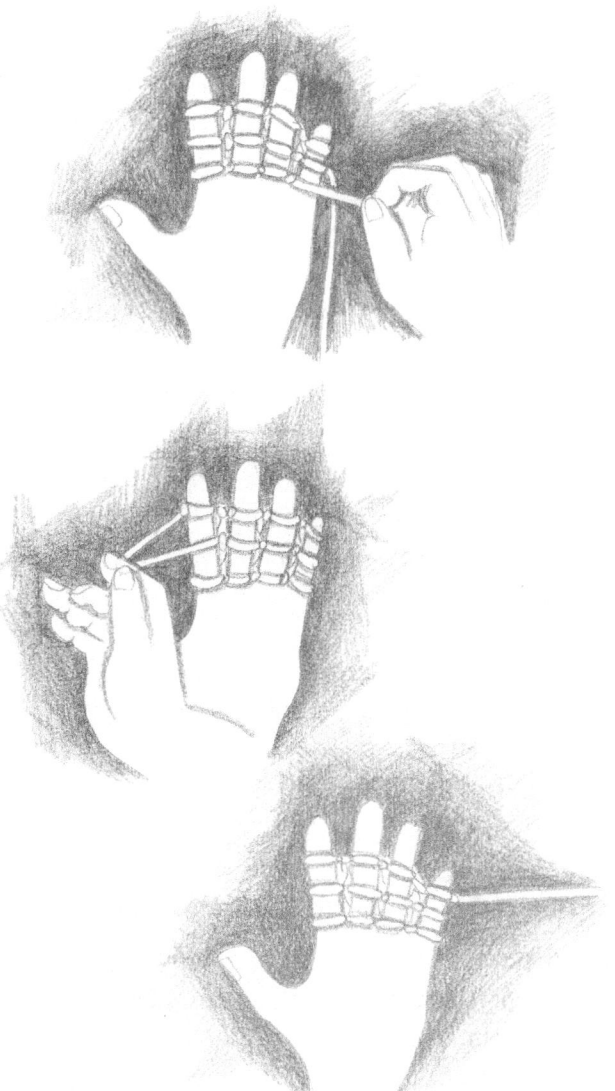

∗ You have deslacked up the S-line of a switchback row.

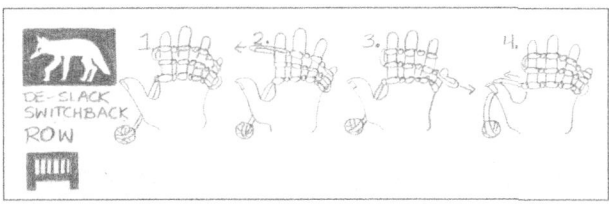

U-turn leapstitch

Do a topwise U-turn leapstitch on the top yarn-ring on Pinky.

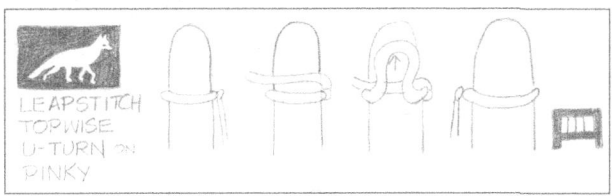

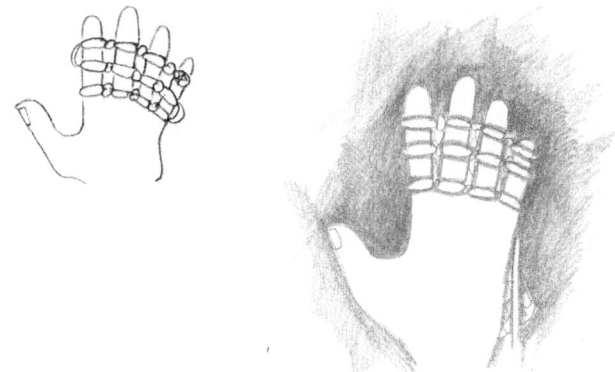

∗ You have launched the switchback cast-off row.

Cast-off top layer Thumbwise

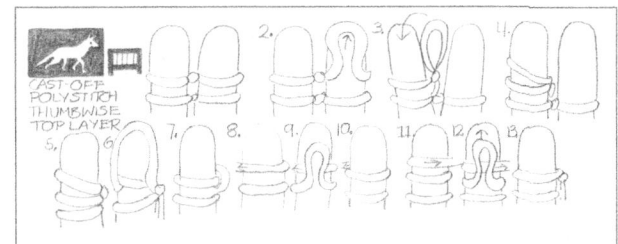

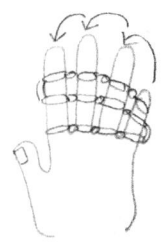 Do cast-off polystitches to the top layer yarn-rings, Thumbwise from Ringa to Middler and from Middler to Pointer.

chapter eight

Round the bend

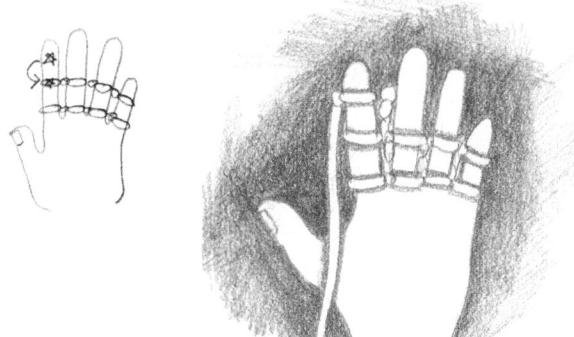

Do a corner cast-off polystitch from the top yarn-ring to the middle yarn-ring on Pointer.

Do a countertopwise corner cast-off stitch on Pointer, Thumbwise.

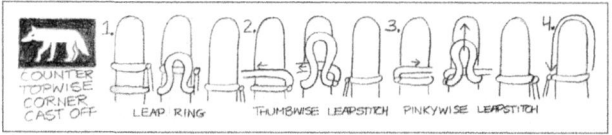

Work flow is now Pinkywise

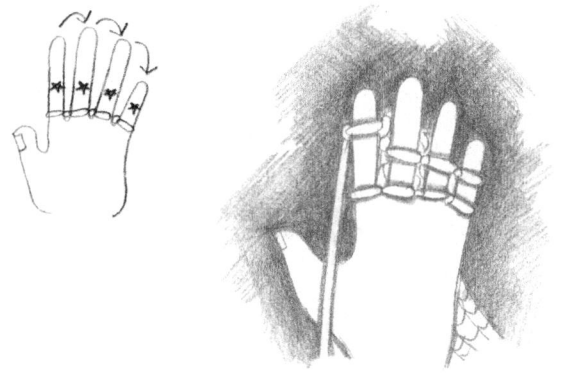

Lay the leed Pinkywise and do a row of cast-off stitches on the top layer from Pointer to Pinky.

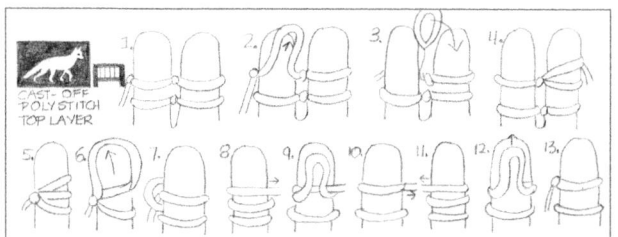

Rounding the bend

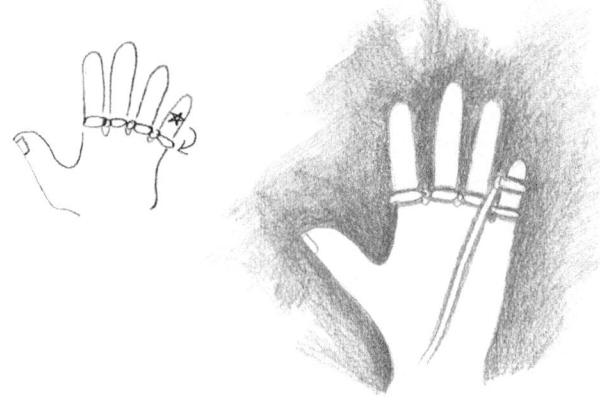

Do a corner cast-off polystitch, countertopwise.

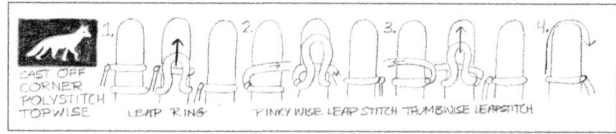

The last step of the corner cast-off stitch that you just completed brought the leed to the center notch, which switches the flow of the work.

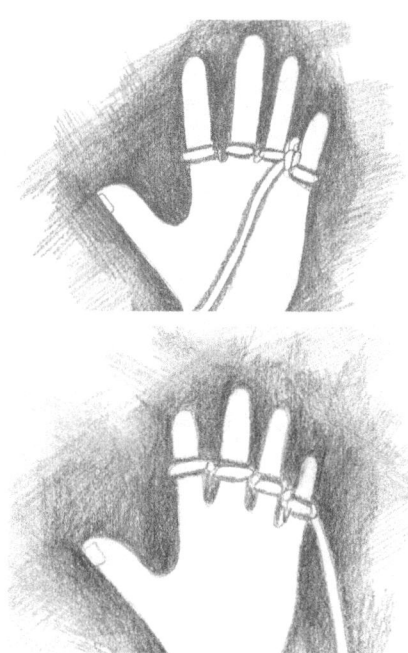

Work flow is now Thumbwise

Now that the leed has been brought back around to the Center Notch to switch direction, lay the leed back Thumbwise and do cast-off stitches from Pinky and Ringa.

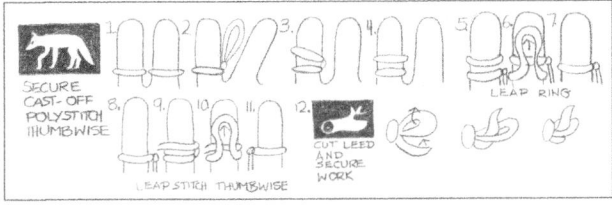

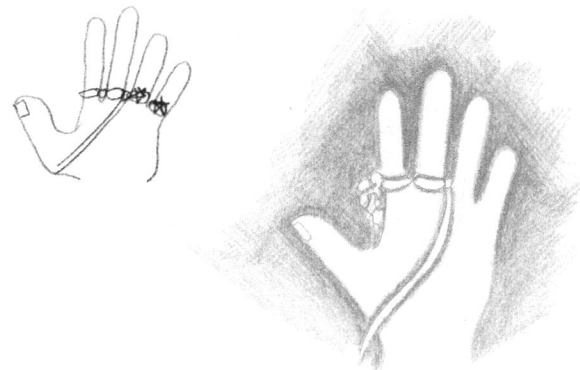

Do a securing cast-off polystitch from Middler to Pointer and then off from Pointer, Thumbwise.

✽ This is the secure Thumbwise cast-off polystitch.

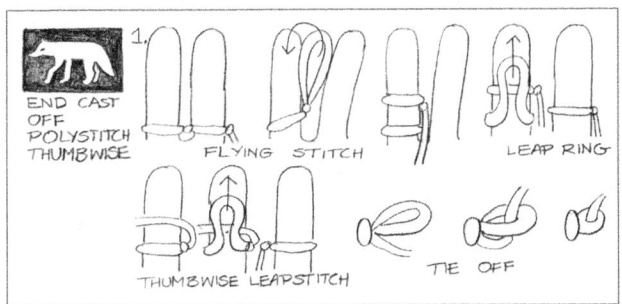

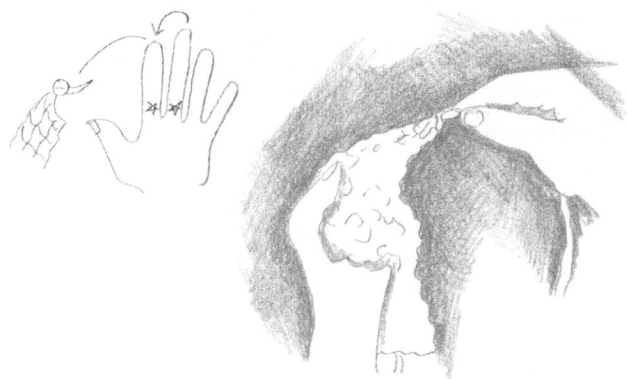

✽ This completes the entire switchback cast-off sequence.

Keywords Reminder
For the switchback cast-off
- Launch the cast-off row.
- Do Thumbwise cast-off polystitches on Ringa, Middler and Pointer.
- Do a countertopwise corner cast-off stitch on Pointer.
- Do Pinkywise cast-off stitches on Pointer, Middler, Ringa, and Pinky.
- Do a topwise corner cast-off stitch on Pinky.
- Do Thumbwise cast-off stitches on Pinky, Ringa and Middler.
- Do securing cast-off polystitch on Pointer.

Full Block and Let Dry

Until you learn the Spruce technique for making seamless ends to your knitted garments, it is a good idea to felt down the edges of your scarf to give them a flat curvy artistic edge. Full your garment and block it out to dry for 24 hours.

chapter eight

Setting Your Work Aside

When you have three layers of knitting on your hand and you suddenly have to tend to something on the stove or answer the door, what do you do? Fortunately, setting aside and resuming work can be done quickly and in an orderly manner.

Fold back leed

To do this, first fold a few feet of leed back on itself and take up the bight with your Shuttle bird-pinch.

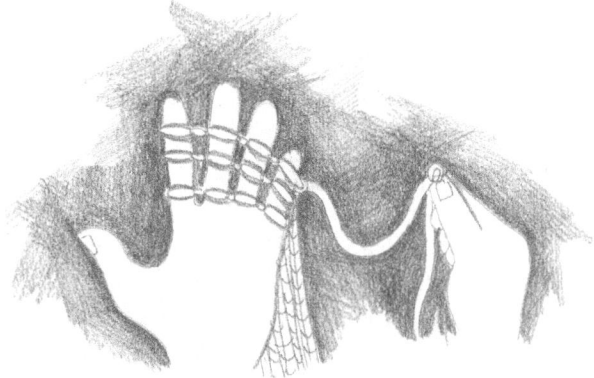

Pinch rings and push bight through

Pinch the three yarn-rings on Pinky and push the bight up under these rings, pulling the two ply section of leed right up through them.

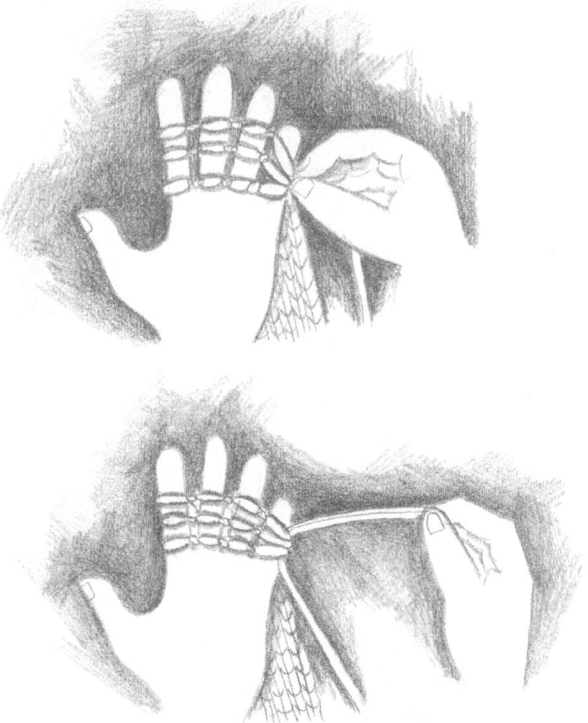

Repeat on all fingers

Do the same on Ringa, Middler, and Pointer.

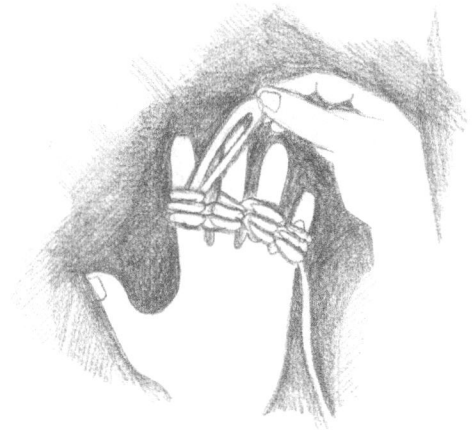

Secure leed

Tie the leed off on itself in a loose square knot.

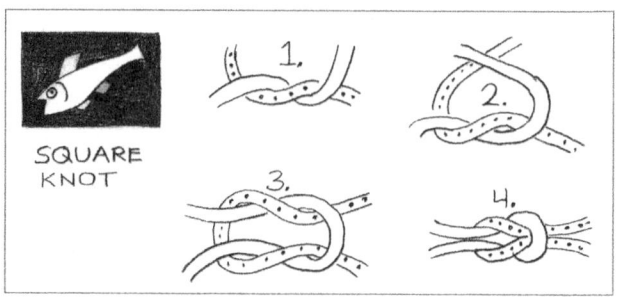

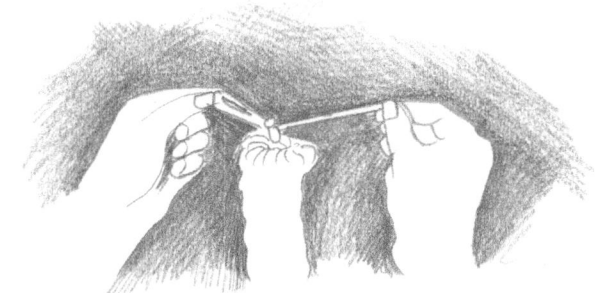

Resuming Work

Release the leed
Untie the loose square knot in the leed. When you are ready to replace the knitting onto your fingers and resume work, hold the fabric with ripple stitches uppermost and field stitches down.

Push up and pull out
Push Loom Pointer up through its own column of yarn-rings.

Remove leed from column
Pull the folded-over section of leed from out of the columns of yarn-ring on Pointer.

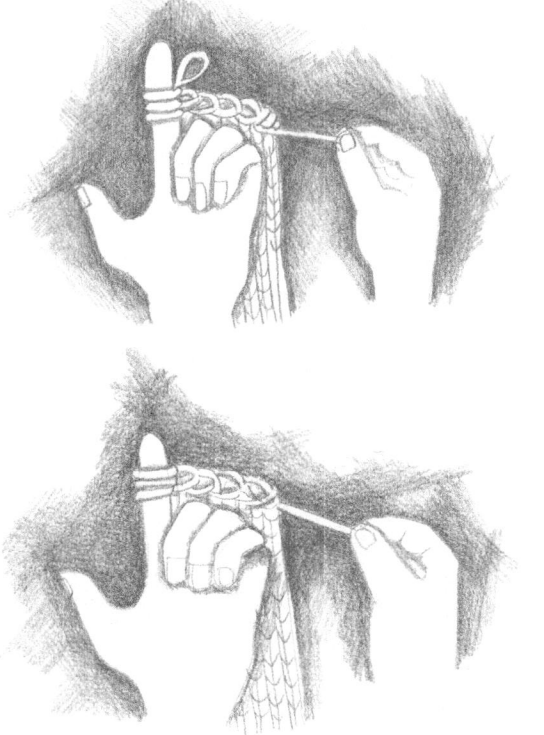

Repeat for other fingers
Do the same with Middler, Ringa, and Pinky.

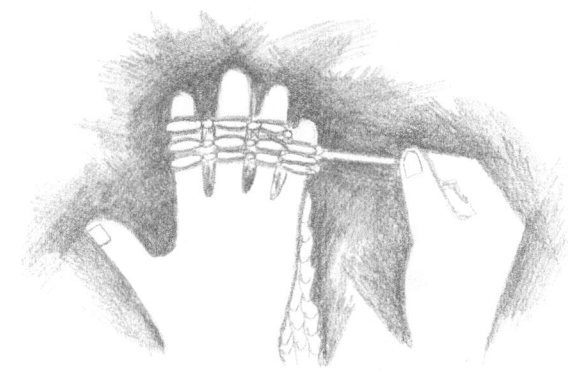

Now that you have learned to secure your work with a fold of the leed, you can apply this technique for setting your work aside to any of your knitting projects.

Creating a split

To create a garment with a selvaged split, incorporate a layer of cast-off stitches followed by a layer of cast-on stitches, as described below in the Doll's Vest project.

chapter eight

Practice Project: Doll's Vest

Knit 17 rows (adjust for the length of the doll or gnome that will be wearing the vest by adding or subtracting four of the rows.)

Pause with the leed on an out row, with the leed coming from the middle yarn-ring on Pointer.

Suspend the top row.

Slip the top layer of yarn-rings to the corresponding finger of the Shuttle Hand to temporarily have them out of the way.

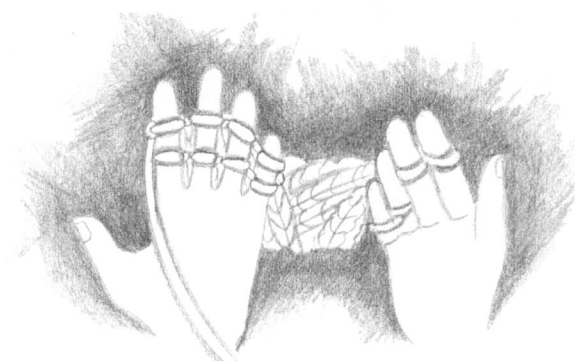

✳ You have put-up a row of stitches on the corresponding fingers of your Loom Hand.

Cast-off row

Cast-off Pinkywise from Pointer to Middler to Ringa to Pinky. Do not cast-off from Pinky.

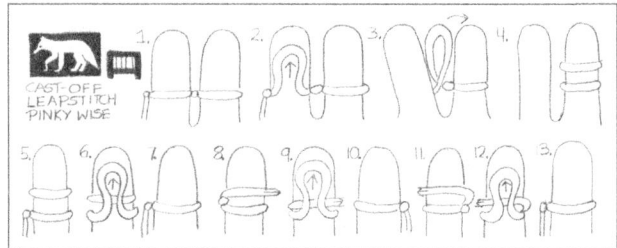

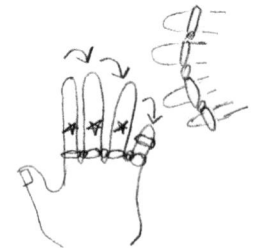

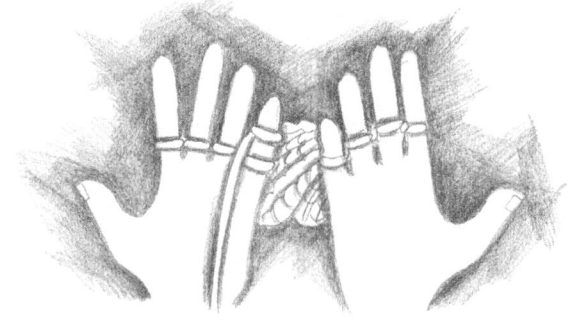

Hang up Pinky's ring

Do not cast-off from Pinky. Instead, put-up the middle yarn-ring on Shuttle Pinky, Leave it there, along with the other hung-up stitches.

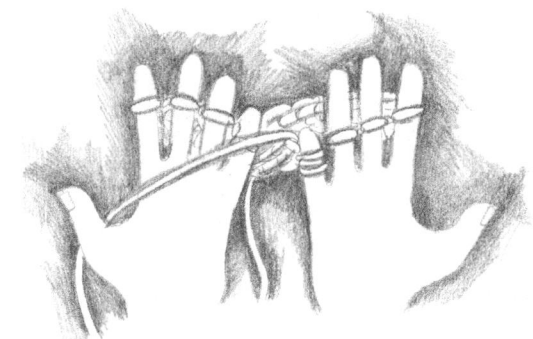

Knit a row to Pointer and back

Do a Thumbwise row of stitches from Pinky to Pointer. (Since the above yarn-rings are already removed, these stitches are leapstitches.)

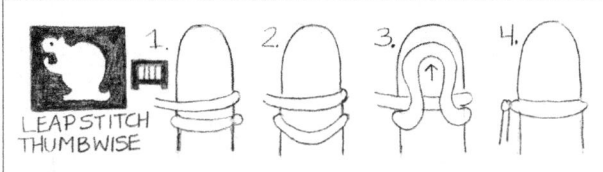

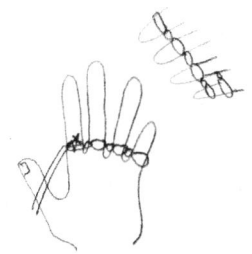

Do leapstitches back to Pinky again.

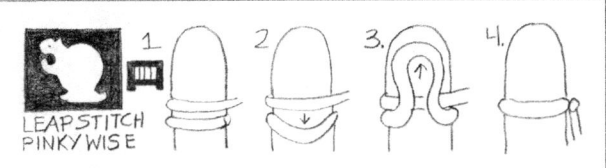

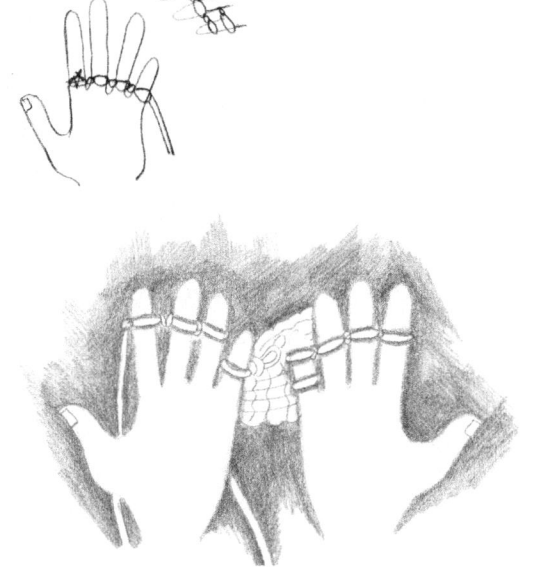

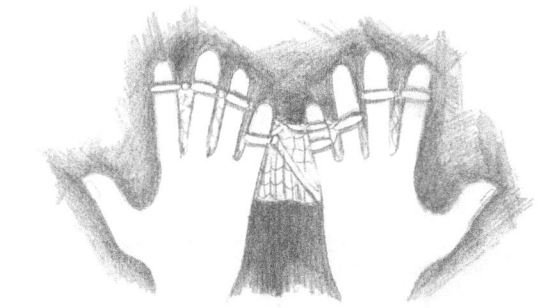

Replace yarn-ring

Having completed an out-and-return row of leapstitches along the underlayer, replace Loom Pinky's middle yarn-ring, taking it back from Shuttle Pinky.

✳ You now have put-back a stitch on Pinky.

Cast-on row to end the split

Do a row of Thumbwise cast-on stitches to Ringa, Middler, and Pointer, replacing the middle layer of your Switchback row.

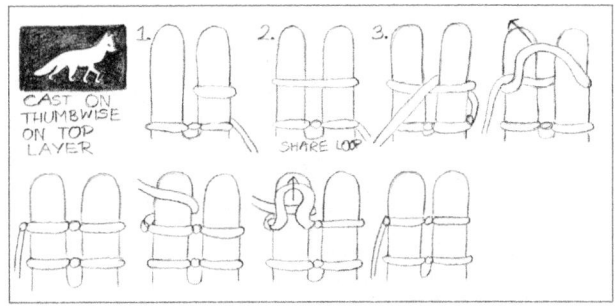

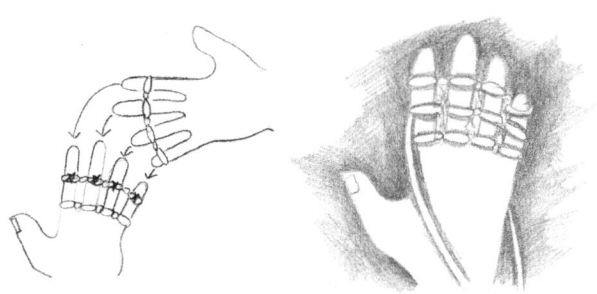

Put back the top row yarn-rings that had been hung up.

chapter eight

Resume rows

Now you are back where you began when you initiated the split. Complete the top layer of your switchback out row and resume knitting rows until you have completed 17 more rows and cast-off.

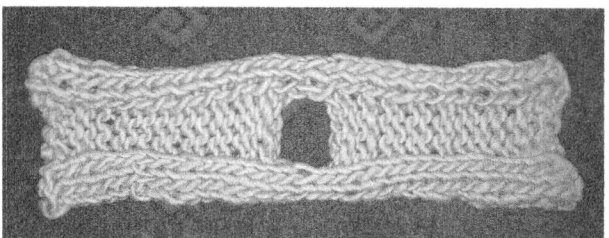

✳ You have created a selvaged split in your work along the middle layer of your switchback row.

You now have a piece of fabric with a horizontal split down the center of the midline of the fabric.

Sew sides of vest

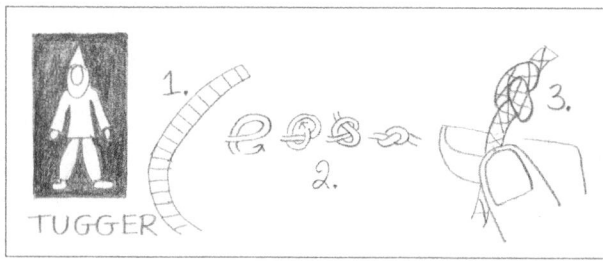

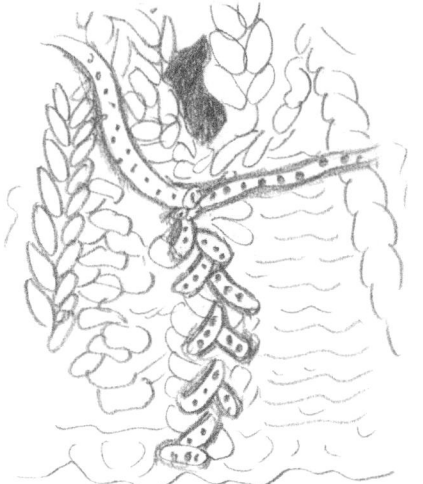

✳ You have created a nice little vest.

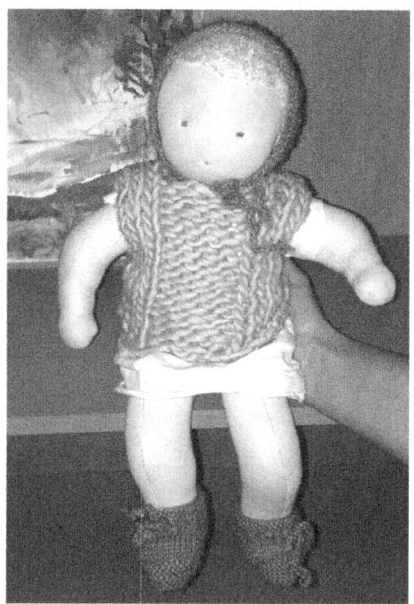

Enjoy creating your own doll clothes designs using the techniques you have learned thus far.

Variations

In the chapter for Combined Projects, discover Folded Wing Technique, which makes it possible to add width and volume to a three-dimensional piece by combining the Switchback with the Tunnel.

Chapter Review for "The Switchback"

Vocabulary

top layer
middle layer
bottom layer
switchback rows
out-and-return rows
S-line
bight
selvaged split

Stitches

Sneaky-fox stitch on middle layer:
- Lay leed workwise.
- Lift top layer row yarn-ring with Loom fox-pinch and suspend on Middler.
- Do a leapstitch with the middle yarn-ring.
- Replace the yarn-ring from Loom Middler.

Clever-coyote stitch Pinkywise:
- Lay leed Pinkywise.
- Lift top and middle layer row yarn-ring with Loom coyote-pinch and suspend them on Ringa.
- Do a leapstitch with the middle yarn-ring.
- Replace the yarn-ring from Loom Ringa.

Clever-coyote stitch Thumbwise:
- Lay leed Thumbwise,
- Lift top and middle layer row yarn-ring with Loom coyote-pinch and suspend them on Ringa.
- Do a leapstitch with the middle yarn-ring.
- Replace the yarn-ring from Loom Ringa.

Repeating rows sequence for switchback rows:
(Out-and-Return Switchback Rows)

For the out row:
- Work a Pinkywise row of leapstitches along bottom row,
- followed by a Thumbwise row of leapstitches along the middle row,
- followed by a Pinkywise row of leapstitches along the top row,
- reverse direction and work in the opposite direction.

For the return row:
- With a Thumbwise row of leapstitches along the top row,
- followed by a Pinkywise row of leapstitches along the middle row,
- followed by a Thumbwise row of leapstitches along the bottom row.

chapter nine

Tapering

chapter nine

Widen and Narrow the Fabric

Tapering gives you a strategy for adding or taking away a stitch in any given row, resulting in a widening or narrowing of the work in progress, that can be utilized for any variety of interesting, sculptured-looking projects.

Although the tapering method is introduced using pylon rows it can also be adapted for doubleback rows. (See explanation of doubleback and pylon rows in Chapter 6, page 95.)

Rhyme for tapering

Thumbkin the gnome lives by the sea
Beneath the roots of an old hollow tree;
He makes magic cloth for the Mermaid Queen
With moonwashed fleece from Aberdeen.
The spry gnome spins and leaps and twirls
For shipwreck gold and mermaids' pearls
His neighbor, Pointer, ducks through the door
Says, "The Mermaid Queen needs much, much more!"

So the gnomes work together side-by-side
Making magic cloth that's twice as wide.
Each gnome leaps and twists and twirls
For shipwreck gold and mermaids' pearls
Their neighbor, Middler, ducks through the door
Says, "The Mermaid Queen needs much, much more!"

So the gnomes work together side-by-side
Making magic cloth three times as wide.
Each gnome leaps and twists and twirls
For shipwreck gold and mermaids' pearls.
Their neighbor Ringa ducks through the door,
Says, "The Mermaid Queen needs much, much more!"

So the gnomes work together side-by-side
Making magic cloth four times as wide.
Each gnome leaps and twists and twirls
For shipwreck gold and mermaids' pearls.
Their neighbor Pinky ducks through the door;
Says, "The Mermaid Queen needs a little bit more."

So the gnomes work together side-by-side
Making magic cloth five times as wide.
Each gnome leaps and twists and twirls
For shipwreck gold and mermaids' pearls.
The Queen receives her cloth with pleasure
And showers the gnomes with deep-sea treasure.

– H. Akin

Creating a Gnome Hat

Set-up: Choose a medium- to bulky-weight wool yarn while you are learning. Find a comfortable place to sit and place the yarn-ball in a basket to your Loom side. Create a tail-tugger slipknot and anchor it on Thumb.

Take up the leed and wind a single countertopwise loop around Thumb, above the slipknot loop. Then, pick up the bottom yarn-ring on Thumb, and leapstitch it over the loop and the top of your Thumb.

✽ You have just completed your first topwise full-turn leapstitch on Thumb.

Snugging up your stitches

After each stitch, you'll want to snug up your work by deslacking the stitches as you go. For the single digit row this is accomplished by tugging slightly at the tail while bracing the leed against your Palm with Loom Middler.

Again, wind the leed once, topwise, around your Thumb, above the yarn-ring that is already there, doing a topwise full-turn leapstitch, and snug it up. Keep doing single-digit rows in this sequence:

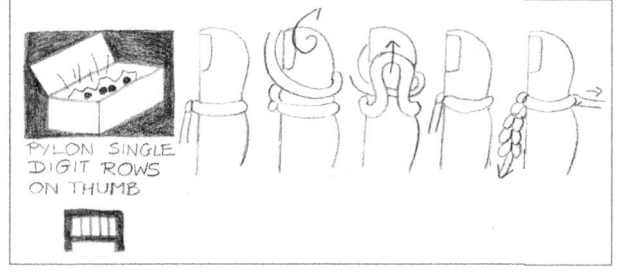

✽ You are knitting pylon single-digit rows.

chapter nine

Continue one-digit rows

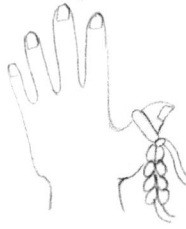

For your practice swatch, do another 9 or 10 topwise full-turn leapstitches as the length of chain grows down from the back of your Thumb.

Expanding the Width of the Fabric

Following each section of rows, you will widen the work by one digit and continue this pattern until the project calls for narrowing the work again. For the practice swatch, you will gradually increase the number of columns to a five-digit width before it narrows again.

Tapering out

Increase to Double Digits

Let both your work and your leed fall back behind the Thumb Notch.

Cast-on across the Thumb Notch to Pointer.

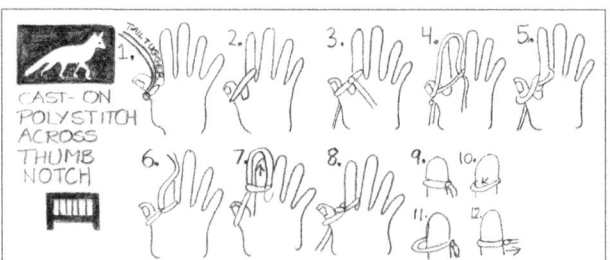

Bring the leed forward through the Thumb Notch.

✳ You have expanded your width by one digit, Pinkywise.

Smoothing tensions

Since tensions can be peculiar around the Thumb Notch it is a good idea to "shake out" the work in progress after each stitch that is on or near the Thumb. This is done by wiggling Thumb and Pointer and giving a little tug to both ends—a tug on the tail end of the work, and a tug on the leed. A sort of "wiggle-wiggle, tug-tug." This deslacking move is necessary to snug up and even out the tension as you go.

✳ You have done a shake out.

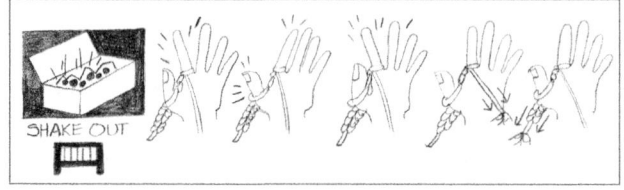

Now that you have tapered out, you will resume knitting rows.

Two-digit rows

Since Pointer, just like Thumb, is at this point holding the stitches of the pylon rows along the selvage of the pylon rows, both will take special pylon style leapstitches. You will wrap the leed around Pointer—only counterclockwise. To complete the stitch, lift the yarn-ring on Pointer up and over the leed and Pointer, as is done with any sort of leapstitch.

156

Tapering

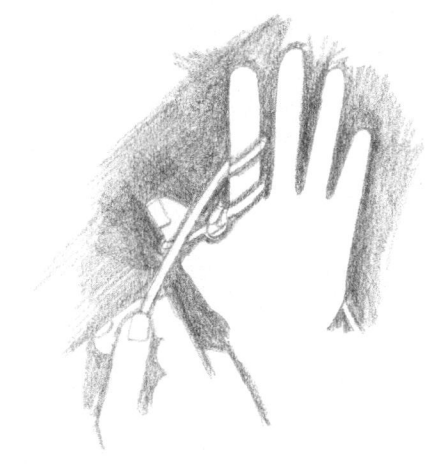

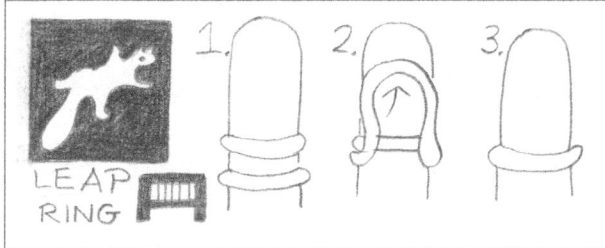

∗ You have done a countertopwise full-turn leapstitch on Pointer.

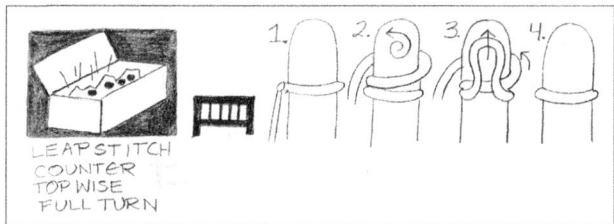

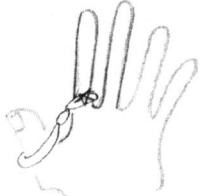

Wrap the leed clockwise around Thumb and do a full-turn leapstitch on Thumb.

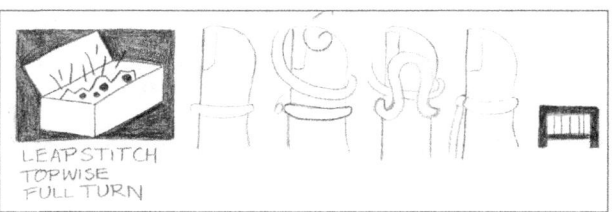

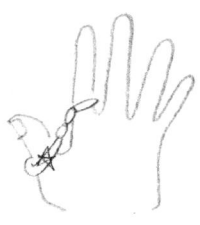

∗ You have completed the repeating rows sequence for pylon two-digit rows.

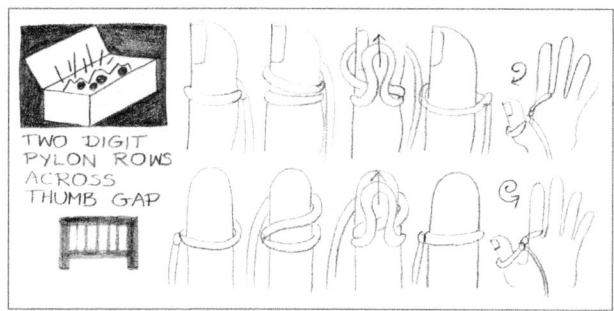

Each repetition of the above sequence completes one out-and-return pylon two-digit row.

Work twelve two-digit rows for your practice project, ending on the final element of the sequence, the countertopwise full-turn leapstitch on Pointer.

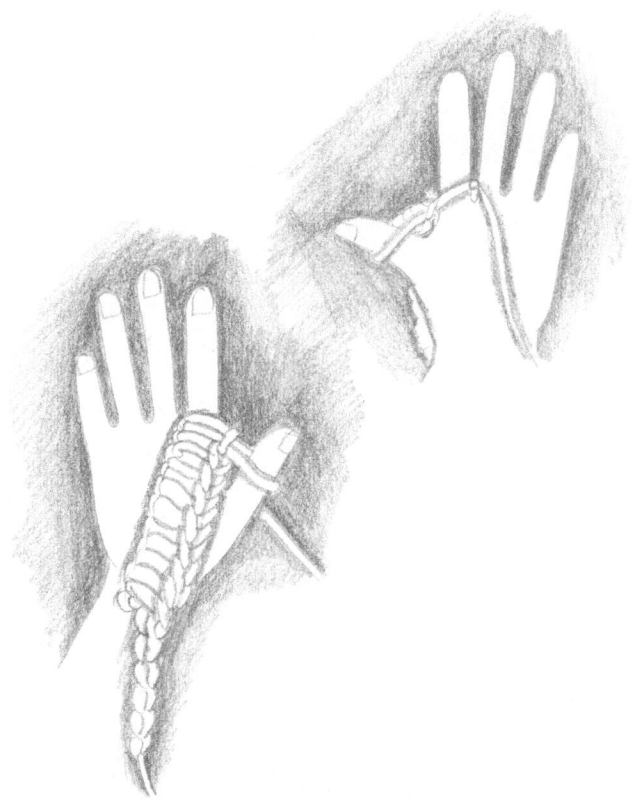

chapter nine

Work to three digits

Expand by one digit Pinkywise to Middler.

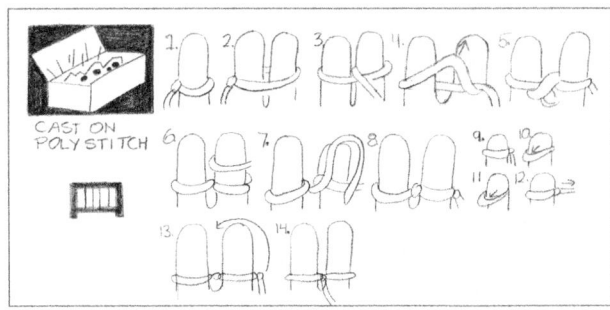

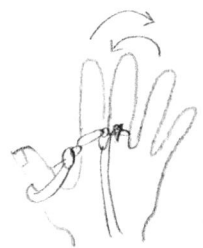

Resume knitting rows as follows:

Work a Thumbwise leapstitch on Pointer.

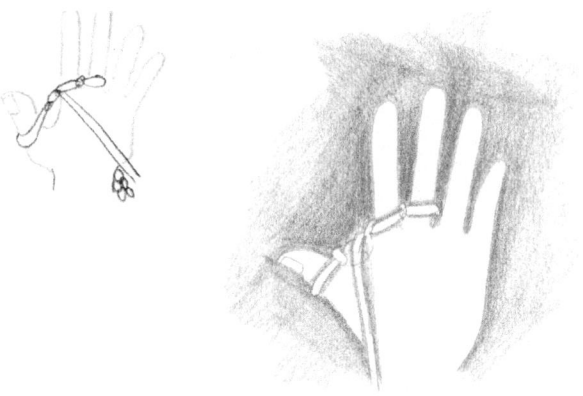

Knit a clockwise full-turn leapstitch on Thumb.

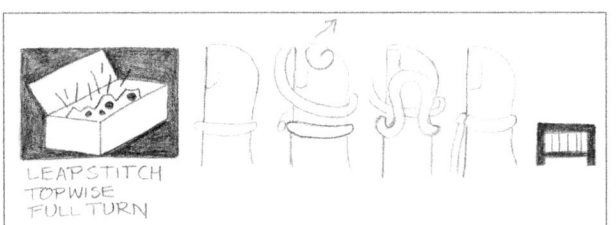

Knit a Pinkywise leapstitch on Pointer.

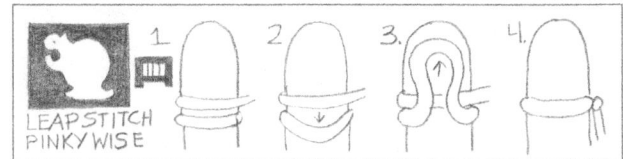

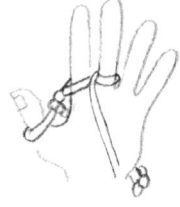

Work a countertopwise full-turn leapstitch on Middler.

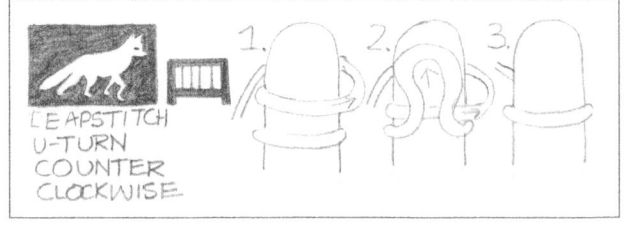

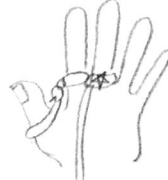 Note: You will notice that Thumb and Middler, because they mark the edges of the cloth at this point, are given full-turn leapstitches, while Pointer—being in the center of this short row—takes only a simple leapstitch, be it Pinkywise or Thumbwise.

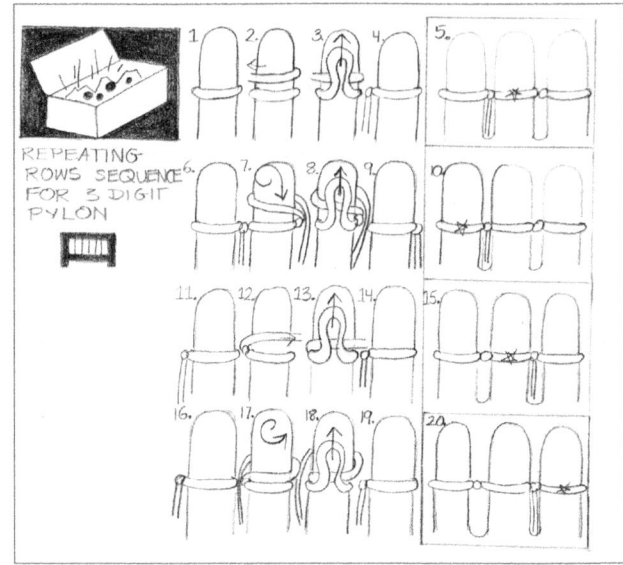

158

Tapering

* You have completed the repeating rows sequence for the three-digit pylon row.

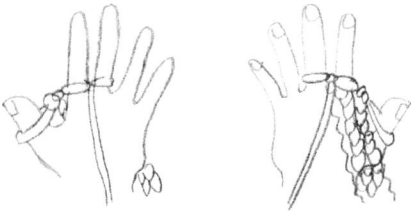

After you have done this series 12 times, adding twelve three-digit rows for your practice swatch, end on the next-to-the-last element of the sequence: the countertopwise full-turn leapstitch on Middler.

Increase to four-digit rows

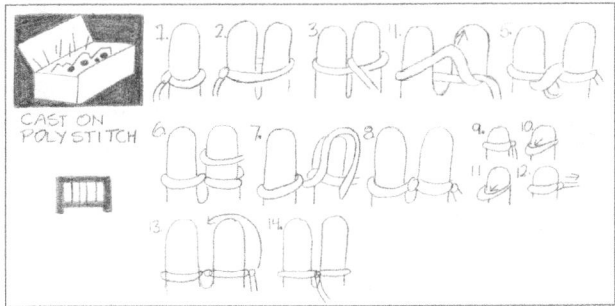

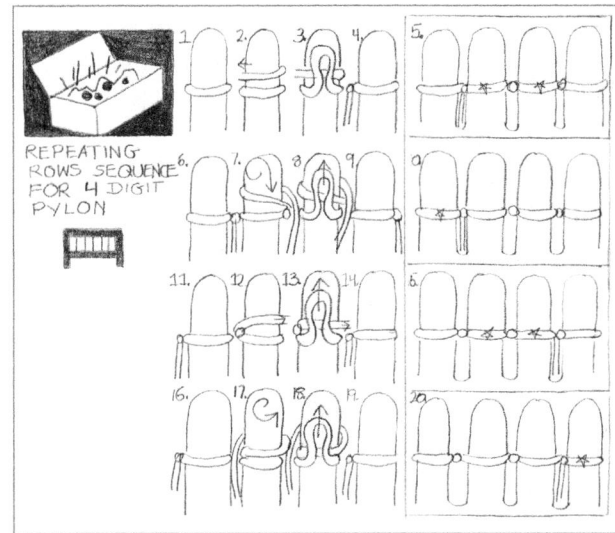

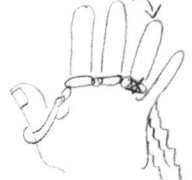

Expand by one digit Pinkywise to Ringa.

Beginning with a Thumbwise leapstitch on Middler, resume knitting out-and-return rows, only this time on four fingers. And remember to use pylon stitches on the edge digits as is done with all pylon rows.

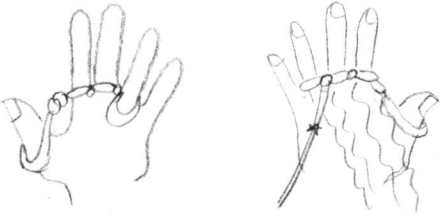

After you have done this sequence six times, giving you 12 rows for your practice swatch, end on the last step in the sequence, with a countertopwise full-turn leapstitch on Ringa.

Widen to five digits

Expand by one digit Pinkywise to Pinky.

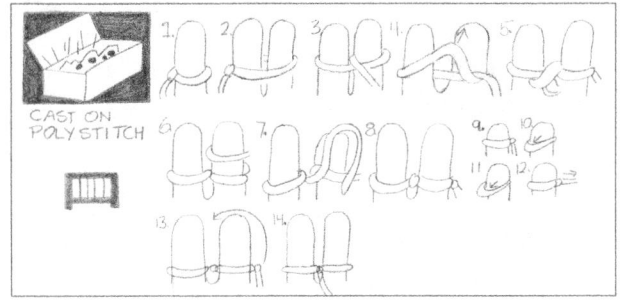

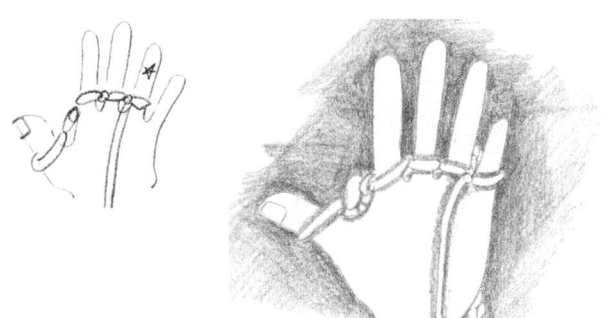

159

chapter nine

Resume knitting rows, beginning with a Thumbwise leapstitch on Pointer and continue knitting your five-digit rows until you have completed 12 rows on your practice swatch, ending on the final element of the sequence: the countertopwise full-turn leapstitch on Pinky.

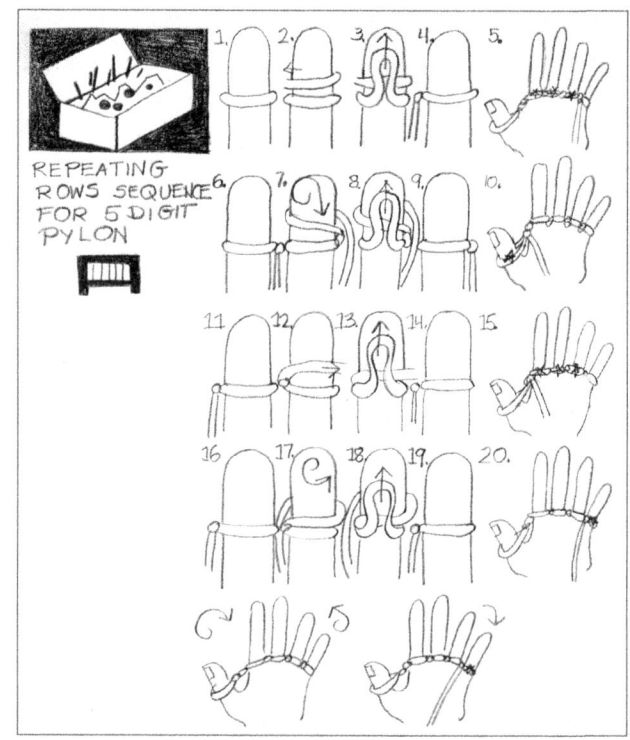

Narrowing the Width of the Fabric

Backside view of five-digit work

Just as you lengthened each succeeding segment to widen the fabric, now you will begin the process of gradually making your work narrow, until it is reduced back down to a one-digit width, and finally casting off. This process is called "reefing-in," based on the nautical verb to "reef," which means to roll-up and tie-off a portion of a sail to make the sail-area smaller.

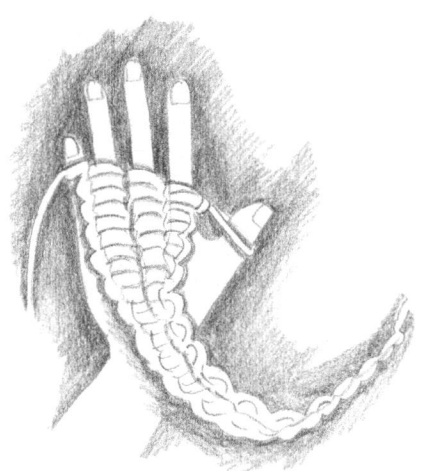

Narrow to four digits

Continue with the practice swatch, leaving the yarn on your Loom Hand, with the leed coming out from Pinky. What you will do now is basically the same as a flying stitch, except that the loop on the resting finger flips over to land upside-down on the active finger, as follows.

From Pinky to Ringa: Lift the yarn-ring off Pinky and carefully fold it over onto Ringa, like gently closing the lid of a treasure chest or a clam closing its shell. In this example, Pinky is the resting finger and Ringa is the active finger.

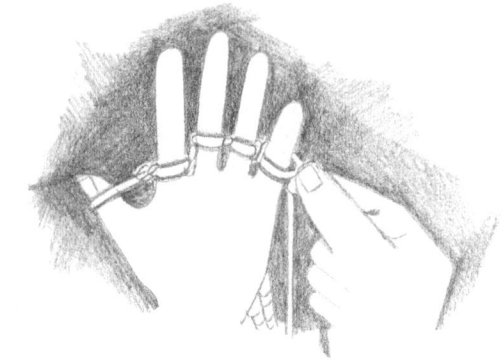

Tapering

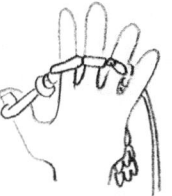

Bring the leed in through your Center Notch in preparation for resuming rows.

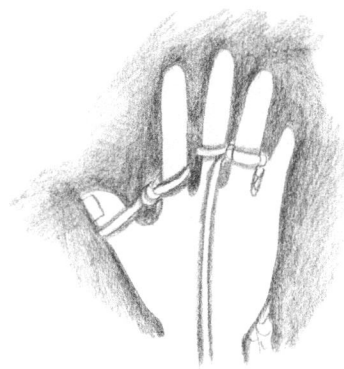

✶ You have now completed your first Thumbwise reef-in polystitch. The first step of the reef stitch is a flying stitch, followed by leap-ring stitch.

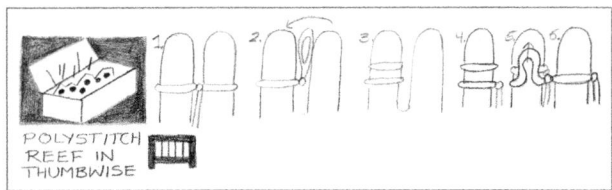

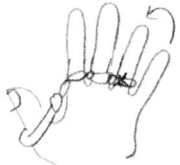

✶ You have flipped down a stitch.

Secure off your reduction, with a leap-ring on Ringa.

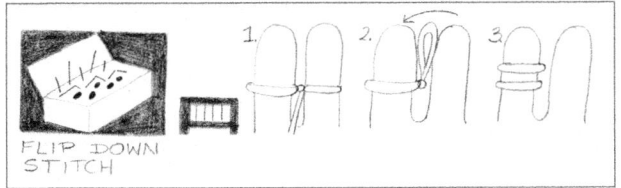

Do a leap-ring on Ringa.

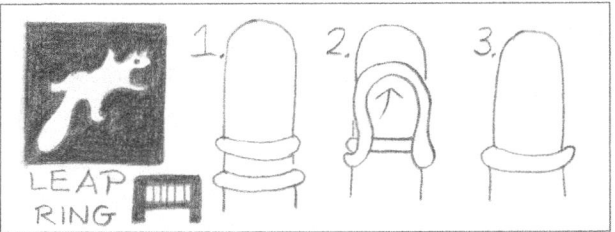

Resume knitting four-digit rows. Repeat this sequence six times on your practice swatch, giving you 12 rows of four-digit-wide fabric. When you are ready to narrow your work again, end this sequence on the 4th element: the countertopwise full-turn leapstitch on Ringa.

chapter nine

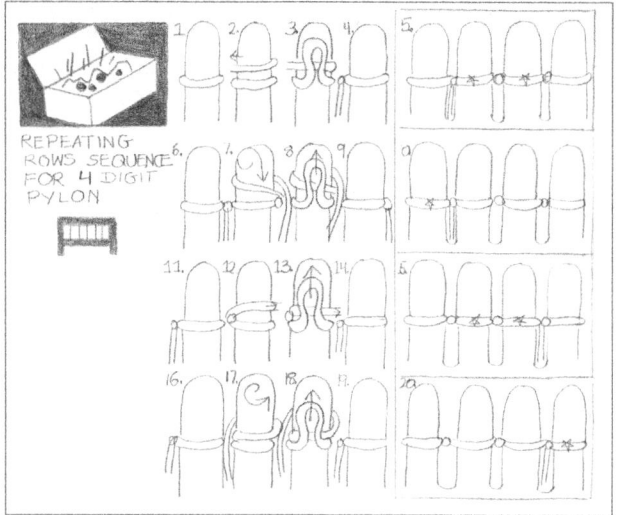

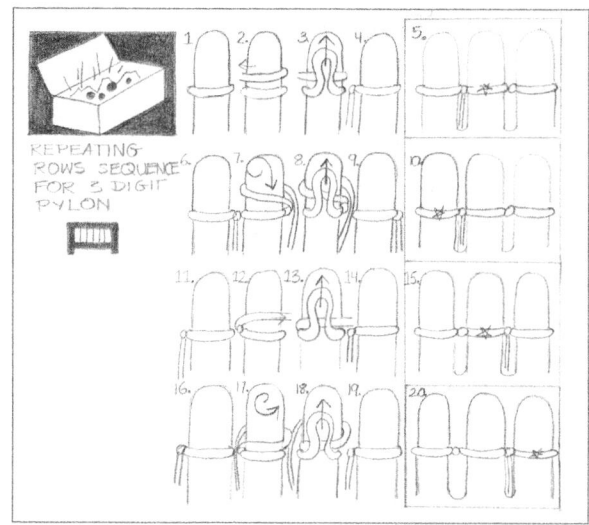

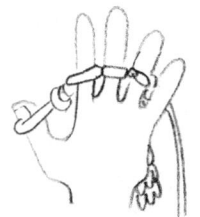

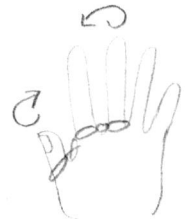

Narrow to three digits

Do a reef-in polystitch from Ringa to Middler.

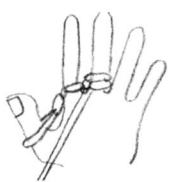

Work three-digit rows, in keeping with the rows sequence: Repeat this sequence six times on your practice swatch, giving you 12 rows of three-digit-wide fabric. When you are ready to narrow your work, end with the next-to-the-last element, a countertopwise full-turn leapstitch on Middler.

Backside view of three-digit work

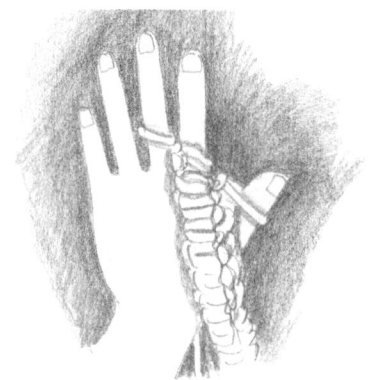

Narrow to two digits

Do a Thumbwise reef-in polystitch from Middler to Pointer.

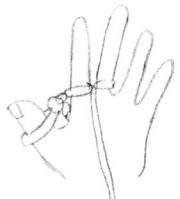

Knit two-digit rows

Work two-digit rows in keeping with the two-digit rows sequence, as follows: Repeat this series six times on your practice swatch, giving you 12 rows of two-digit-wide fabric. End on the last element of the sequence, the countertopwise full-turn leapstitch on Pointer.

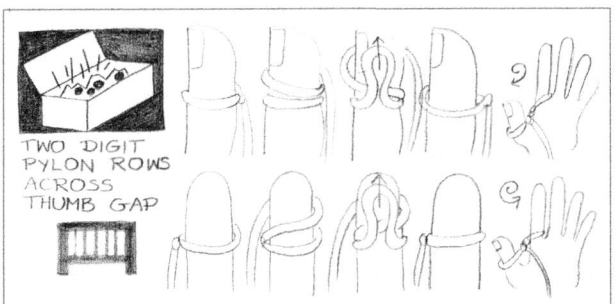

Backside view of two-digit work

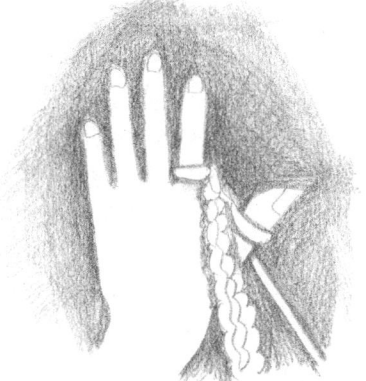

Narrow to one digit

Bring the the leed in through your Thumb Notch and do a Thumbwise reef-in from Pointer to Thumb.

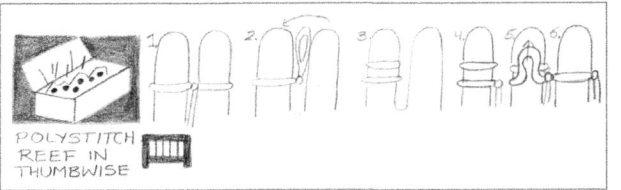

Resume knitting single-digit rows on your Thumb, and repeat this series 12 times on your practice swatch, giving you 12 rows of one-digit-wide fabric.

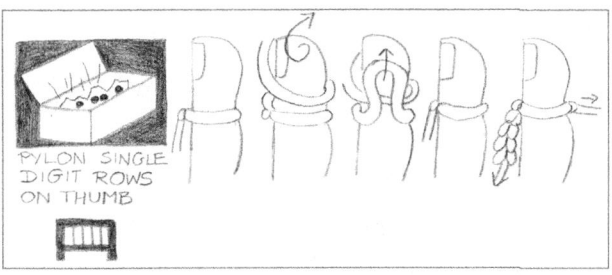

Remove the last loop from Thumb and tie-off.

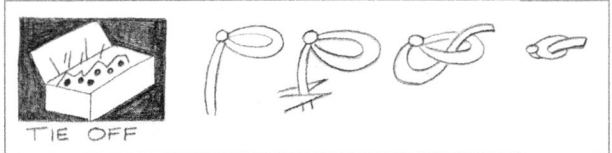

Stitch up a gnome hat

Place a tug knot into yarn of a lighter shade than the color of your hat piece and begin to stitch along the inner selvage of the hat.

You will now stitch the spiral together from the middle, working in pieces (two into one) into the outer most selvage (the selvage closest to the base of the hat) as you go.

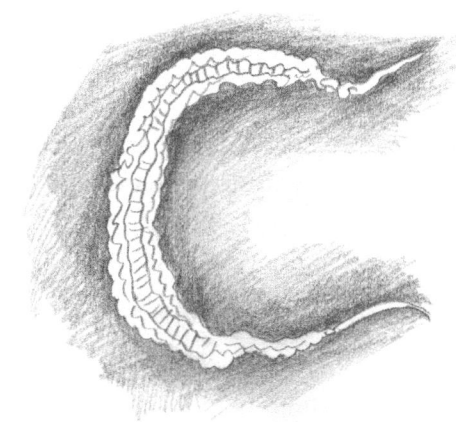

chapter nine

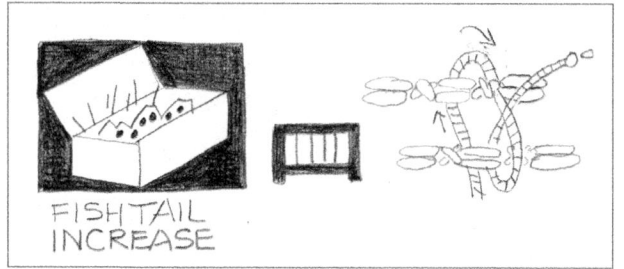

The pattern of increases

Spiraling row #1 – work stitches under only fishlips of the inner selvage and under fishlips and fishtails of outer selvage;

Spiraling row #2 – work stitches only fishlips of inner selvage and under fishlips and every other fishtail of outer selvage;

Spiraling row #3 – whip-stitch under fishlips on the inner selvage and under fishlips and every third fishtail of outer selvage;

Spiraling row #4 – work stitches under fishlips on the inner selvage and fishlips and every fourth fishtail of the outer selvage;

Spiraling row #5 – work stitches under fishlips on the inner selvage and fishlips and every fifth fishtail of the outer selvage.

Spiraling row #6 – work stitches under fishlips on the inner selvage and fishlips and every sixth fishtail of the outer selvage. Continue this pattern of expansion for any number of rows.

Snip the stitching-yarn, tie off and weave in the ends.

(Step-by-step instructions for whip-stitching are outlined in *Bare Hand Knitting* Book I, Chapter 7.)

Increasing hat size

Make a gnome hat of any size by reducing the width of your piece and the length of each segment.

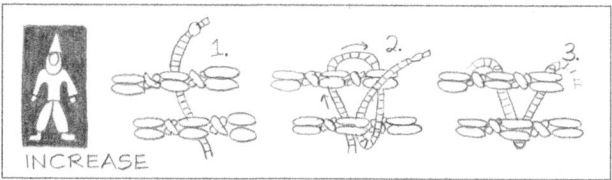

Be creative with tapering

For different projects you can create countless variations to this sequence. For example, you can start and end on any finger during a given knitting project. Try using these techniques to create reductions or breaks in your work at any point in any project, be it flat or three-dimensional. In addition, practice tapering with both pylon and doubleback rows (see page 95, Chapter 6, Rooted Stitches).

Also note that it is possible to taper in or out in either a Thumbwise direction or a Pinkywise direction.

Pattern for Making a Barehand Indoor Ball

Materials
- One skein of bulky yarn
- One half skein of stitching-yarn, preferably in a slightly lighter color.

Taper out (expand)

<u>Knit 6 one-digit rows</u>
Place a tail-tugger slipknot on Pointer and knit 6 single digit pylon rows.

<u>Knit 12 two-digit rows</u>
Expand by one digit to Middler and knit 12 two-digit out-and-return pylon rows on Pointer and Middler.

<u>Knit 18 three-digit rows</u>
Expand by one digit to Ringa and knit 18 out-and-return three-digit pylon rows on Pointer and Middler, and Ringa.

<u>Knit 35 four-digit rows</u>
Expand by one digit to Pinky and knit 35 four-digit pylon rows on Pointer, Middler, Ringa and Pinky.

Flag halfway point

Place a tell-tale onto Middler's yarn rung, on the 35th row and knit 35 more four-digit pylon rows on Pointer, Middler, Ringa, and Pinky.

Reef in

<u>Knit 18 three-digit rows</u>
Reef in by one digit, Pinkywise from Pointer to Middler and knit 18 three-digit pylon rows on Middler and Ringa and Pinky.

<u>Knit 12 two-digit rows</u>
Reef in Pinkywise, from Middler to Ringa and knit 12 two-digit switchback rows on Ringa and Pinky.

<u>Knit 6 one-digit rows</u>
Reef in Pinkywise, from Ringa to Pinky, and knit 6 single-digit pylon rows on Pinky and tie off.

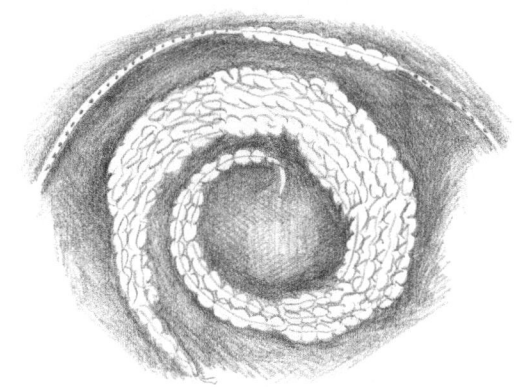

Whip-stitching the ball

<u>Measure out two stitching-yarn</u>
Measure out your stitching-yarn to three times the length of the knitted fabric along one selvage. Cut the stitching-yarn in half, giving you two stitching threads of equal length.

<u>Create a tug knot</u>
Tie two overhand knots on one end and one overhand knot on the other end of each stitching thread.

<u>Shrink stitching thread</u>
You will let out stitching-yarn length as you go, as needed.

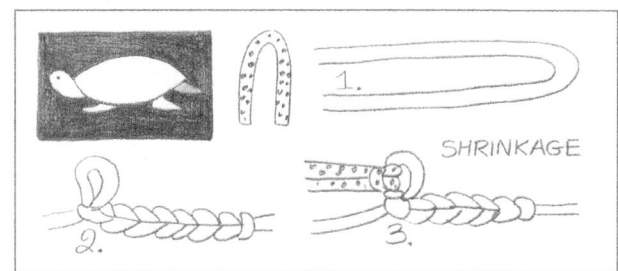

<u>Loosely chain knit the yarn</u>
to reduce its length for stitching, leaving about 18 inches unknitted on the finishing end of the chain. Secure the last chain stitch with a tell-tail, about a yard from the dangler. Tie a knot in the tip of the starting end of the chain.

chapter nine

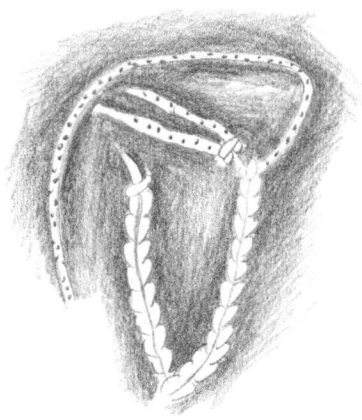

Stitching the spiral

Lay out the work
In preparation for stitching, lay out the knitted fabric for the ball so that the end to your Loom side has the tapered selvage away from you.

One end at a time
Begin on one or the other end of the knitted fabric, knowing that you will be doing the same thing on both sides, only spiraling in the opposite direction.

Push a bight through
On either end of the knitted fabric, push the bight of the folded stitching thread through the sixth single-digit row of the work. Fold over the tail end of the stitching thread at about six inches.

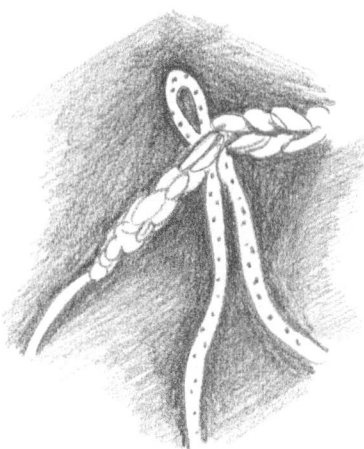

Weave in tail of stitching thread
Weave the stitching thread in and out of the single-digit stitches till you reach the end of the work.

Pull the tail gently until the loop shrinks up a bit but do not snug it up yet. Just as you save the tightening of the loop till last when we crochet a hat, this will be a final step when the ball is stitched up. Keeping it loose will help make the next steps easier to accomplish.

Shrink up the spiral
You should now have a loose circle in the end of your knitted fabric.

Bend the loose circle around countertopwise so that it begins to coil into the knitted fabric. Bend the rest of the fabric around topwise and feed the stitching-thread back through the loop and cinch it up lightly, creating a circle of knitting that will be the center of the spiral.

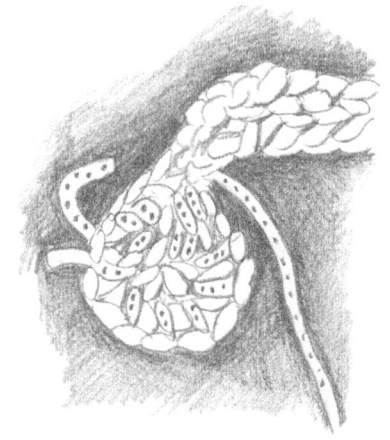

Stitching pattern

Increasing the work

You will stitch this side into a spiral, rolling it in as you go in a topwise direction. A pattern is given below for the disbursement of increase stitches along the seam to join the inner and outer selvages of the spiral. Stitch the selvage of the outer layer of the spiral to the inner selvage, until you have reached the tell-tail that marks the center of the knitted fabric, then stop.

Stitch the second side

Lay the other end of the fabric before you with the tapered selvage away from you. At this point, stitch up the other side of the knitted fabric into a spiral, in exactly the same way; only working in the opposite direction, countertopwise stitch until this side has also reached the tell-tail that marks the center of the knitted fabric.

Pattern for spiral increase

All of the increases in this pattern are inward pointing toward the middle of the spiral.

Note: When we crochet a flat circle, we start with six stitches for the first orbiting row and work that number, plus an additional six stitches into each orbiting row that follows. We will follow the same pattern here using whip-stitches to connect orbiting rows.

<u>Selvage of two-digit width to inner selvage:</u> Stitch two fishlips into one. (In other words, work only inward-pointing increase stitches.)

<u>Selvage of three-digit width to inner selvage:</u> single stitch, followed by an inward-pointing increase stitch.

<u>Selvage of four-digit width to inner selvage:</u> single stitch, followed by a single stitch, followed by an increase.

The knitted fabric now forms a figure eight. Once the two sides are stitched and the ball is stuffed, you will stitch the two sides of the ball together.

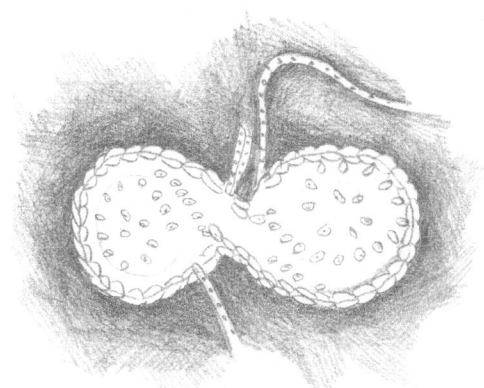

Prepare your ball of roving for stuffing the ball

Synch the ends

Snug up the initial orbiting rows on each side of your ball, tie off the tail of the stitching-yarn to the tail of the knitted fabric, and tuck the dangling ends into what will be the inside of the ball (the ripple-stitch side). Go back and gently snug up enough of your whip-stitches to even out the tensions of your stitches and to work out any additional slack. Tug at the tail of each stitching thread to do this.

Create a snug ball of roving by winding it around and around as if you were winding a ball of yarn, until it is about the size of a cantaloupe or small pumpkin. In other words, you will wind up a large ball of wool roving in the same way that you would wind a ball of yarn, only with a wider swath of fiber. Wind until it is large enough to fit into the slightly stretched cover of your knitted ball.

Sandwich the roving between the ball covers before stitching the two halves of the ball together.

Stitch the center seam

The last seam cuts right down the middle of the ball and is stitched with single stitches only. Begin stitching using either stitching thread from the place where you left off.

chapter nine

You have reached the end of the three-digits wide section of the knitted fabric. At this point stop and do the same thing to the other side of the knitted fabric, only coiling it in the opposite direction, so that you end up with a figure of eight form.

Closing the gap

Before you stitch up the middle seam of the ball, check to be sure you have the same number of fishlips along the top and bottom selvages of what will become the seam. If they do not match up evenly, work an extra increase pointing to the selvage with the least stitches for every missing stitch of the shorter side and then continue stitching.

Variations

Fulling your ball

You also have the option to "full" the ball to snug it up a bit. To do this, wet the ball thoroughly in warm soapy water and place it in a very large mixing bowl and get it whirling around and around until it is felted down a bit, giving it a slightly different look. In the photo below the ball on the right has been felted and the one on the left has not.

Wet felting the stuffing

For an even harder ball you can wet-felt the roving stuffing into a hard-felt ball before placing it inside. Instructions for wet felting a ball were introduced in *Bare Hand Knitting* Book I.

Chapter Review for "Tapering"

Vocabulary

digit   expand   narrow   reef-in

Rows

Expand by one:
- Cast-on to neighboring digit
- Bring leed forward through the notch of the finger just cast-on to, workwise.

Repeating sequence for one-digit pylon rows:
- Topwise full-turn leapstitch on Thumb
- Snug up work.

Repeating sequence for two-digit pylon rows:
- Clockwise around Thumb
- Shake out
- Counterclockwise around Pointer
- Snug up work.

Repeating sequence for three-digit pylon rows:
- Topwise full-turn leapstitch on Thumb
- Shake out
- Pinkywise leapstitch on Pointer
- Countertopwise full-turn leapstitch on Middler
- Thumbwise leapstitch on Pointer.

Repeating sequence for four-digit pylon rows:
- Topwise full-turn leapstitch on Thumb
- Shake out
- Pinkywise leapstitch on Pointer
- Pinkywise leapstitch on Middler
- Countertopwise full-turn leapstitch on Ringa
- Thumbwise leapstitch on Middler
- Thumbwise leapstitch on Pointer
- Countertopwise full-turn leapstitch on Ringa
- Thumbwise leapstitch on Middler
- Thumbwise leapstitch on Pointer.

chapter ten

Spruce

chapter ten

Sprucing It Up!

Normally, barehand knitting produces a smooth, flowing fabric in the body of a panel, but the starting and ending rows just don't quite blend in. Fingers are thicker than knitting needles, thus the challenge. In order to progress onto projects that call for separate panels of knitted fabric to be stitched together, it is necessary to have a system for creating sharper edges and uniformity on all sides of the work. It is important to have start and finish edges that can be joined across a seam between two panels to form a single smooth surface.

The Spruce cast-on and cast-off method removes the first and last rows of your work—no scissors needed. It treats the initial row as a sort of launching pad or scaffold, for the work. The scaffold is then removed, leaving the more orderly part of the work, to become the actual edge.

For knitting projects large and small, you will appreciate the crisp edges produced by this "cutting-edge" technique.

Props

The only equipment, or props, that are needed, you will make yourself out of yarn. The first such prop is a small length of yarn called the *pilot*, and the second, is an even shorter length of yarn called a *lanyard*. Additionally, two small lengths of knitted chain, called *mooring* are used to hold the panels of knitted fabric. Eventually, the pilot, lanyard and moorings are set aside for future projects and only the work itself will remain.

Once this little skill set has been learned by heart and hand, it is a bit like adding a little magic to your bag of barehand tricks.

Poem for spruce edges

The Viking King, for his queen, Hildegard,
Ordered a boat from the Royal Shipyard;
They first built a scaffold, and then built the boat,
The Queen pulled a lanyard and set it afloat.

– H. Akin

Creating a Viking treasure pouch

Preparing your materials and props

Use three different colors for the working yarn, the pilot, and the lanyard. Use different colors for the two moorings.

Yarn: A ball from half an average-size skein (roughly 75 yards) of bulky yarn. Having two different shades of this color for an optional color-change can be nice. This yarn will become your knitted fabric.

Drawstring: For this particular project you will also need a length of yarn for a knitted chain in a color that goes nicely with the pouch.

Pilot: A 1½ personal yard length of yarn will be the pilot. Make it red for the practice project.

Lanyard: One personal yard length of yarn with an overhand knot placed on one end. Make it yellow for the practice project.

Moorings: Two four-yard lengths of yarn in differing colors, finger-knitted down into two knitted chains that are each roughly one yard in length. For clarity, we will call these mooring #1 and mooring #2 (you decide which color is which). Chain-knit the moorings from yarn of a slightly thinner size than that of the working yarn for a given project. Leave 6-inch tails and danglers with an overhand knot at the end of each mooring.

(For larger projects than those in this chapter, the moorings will need to be longer.)

String: Any scrap piece of string or yarn about one yard in length for securing the knitted fabric in place for stitching.

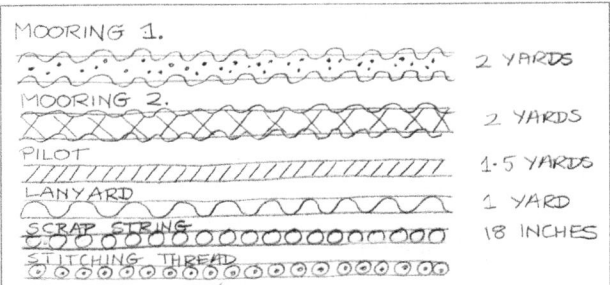

Launch the knitting

Take up the red pilot and weave-on, slalom style, onto your Loom Hand, ending with the securing leapstitch on Pointer.

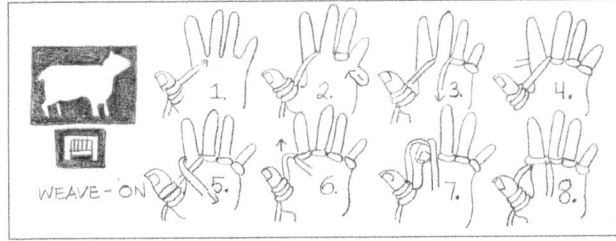

Drape the lanyard

Pick up the yellow lanyard and drape it along your Finger Palm Crease, so that the end with the knot hangs down the Thumb Notch.

✳ You have draped the lanyard over your Loom Hand.

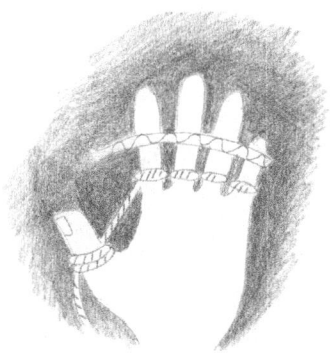

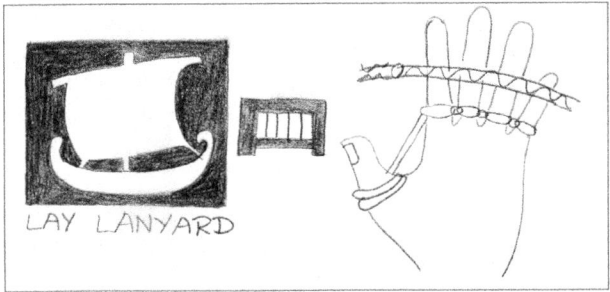

Leapstitch over lanyard

Do one Pinkywise out row of leapstitches onto the yellow lanyard, just as if the lanyard was an ordinary leed and, for the moment, leave the ends of the knitted-over lanyard hanging from either side of your Loom Hand.

At any time, you can remove the yarn from your Thumb.

Mark tail of leed

Take up the leed from the ball of working yarn and place two overhand knots near the end. These two knots are markers, so you can later identify the start end of your panel (which, on occasion, can be helpful to know—for example, when repairing mistakes).

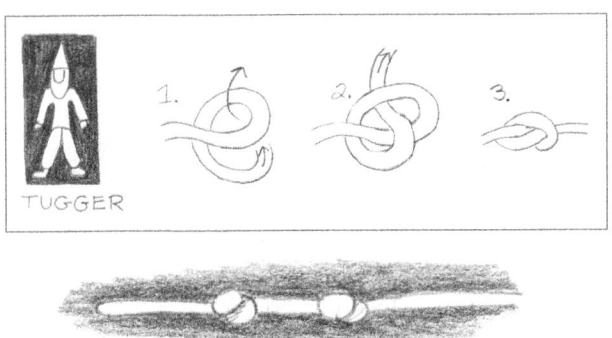

chapter ten

Lay the leed

Lay the leed so that the tail hangs through the Thumb Gap so the flow will move Pinkywise.

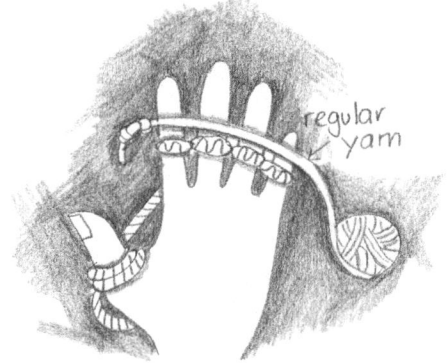

✳ You have laid the leed Pinkywise.

Knit rows

Begin your repeating rows sequence for regular pylon rows Pinkywise. Knit an out-and-return row, (the border row) followed by another single out row (steps 1 through 4 in the code below) and stop.

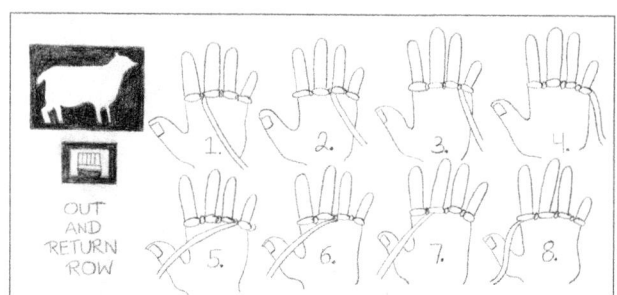

Find the teardrop

Look closely and you will see a teardrop-shaped loop on Pointer with a line of yarn going through it.

Take up a line of mooring

Take up mooring #1, and lift up the teardrop-shaped loop to poke the knot down through it. (It is possible to place a tug knot just near the tip of each mooring to help with the threading-through.)

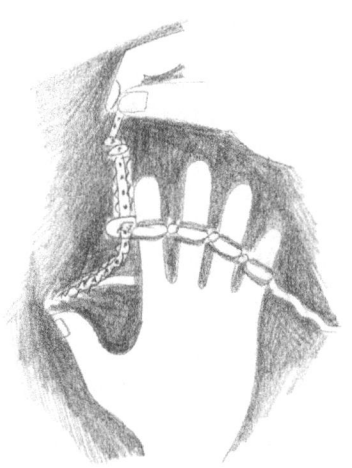

Secure mooring rings

Continue to poke the overhand tug knot of mooring number 1 up through each of the first four stitches formed of the actual leed that poke up through the lanyard, along the knuckle side of your hand, thus securing them.

Once you have the four original leed rings on the mooring chain, draw them toward the middle of the chain.

Spruce

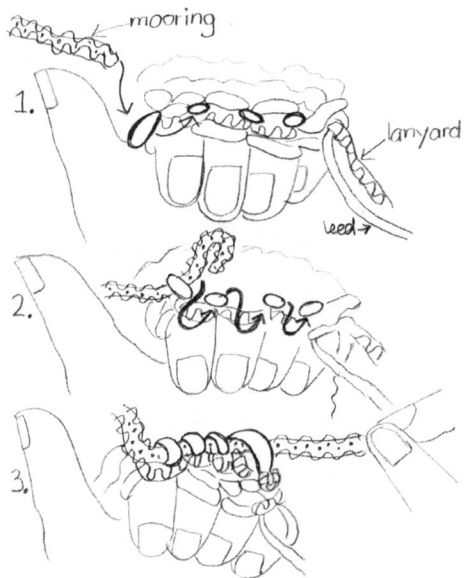

Lanyard sloughs off

Note: There may be some bits of the pilot still poking through the work, preventing it from fully detaching but you can just give the pilot a nudge and it will slough off from your work altogether, if it hasn't already. Set the pilot aside in a visible spot, as you will need it for starting off each new column.

✳ You have released the lanyard.

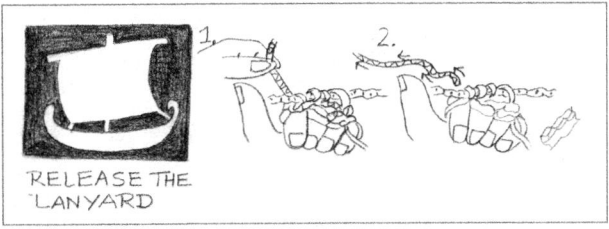

✳ You have secured the work.

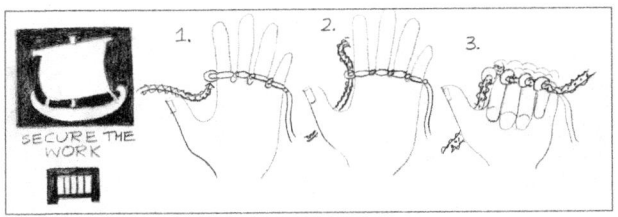

Now for the exciting part: Tug on the knot that is on the Thumbwise side of the lanyard until it is free of the work.

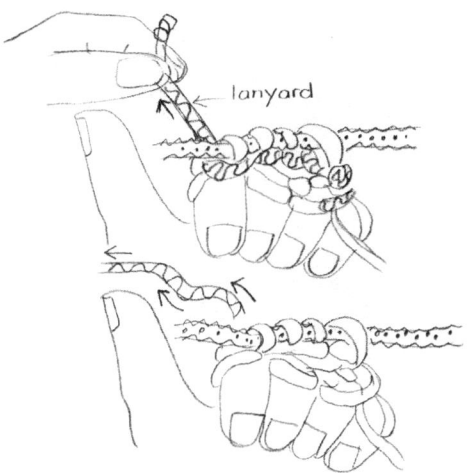

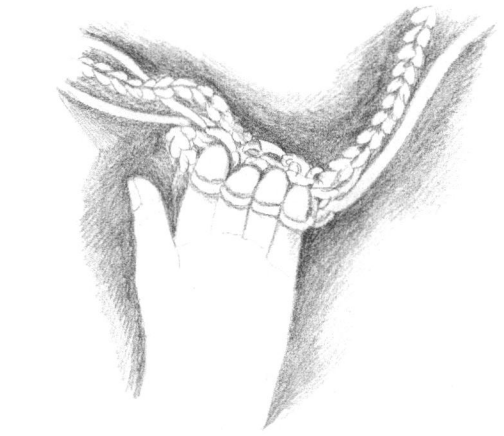

✳ You have completed the sequence for launching a spruce panel, Pinkywise.

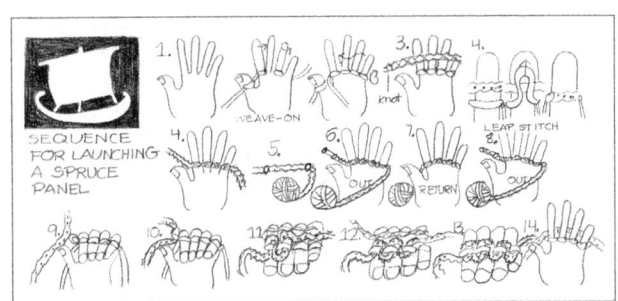

All of the real knitting is still secured on the mooring while the pilot weave-on rows fall away.

chapter ten

Knit rows

Continue to knit regular pylon rows with your working yarn until you have achieved the desired number of rows for the length of your project. For the practice project, knit 48 single rows of leapstitches.

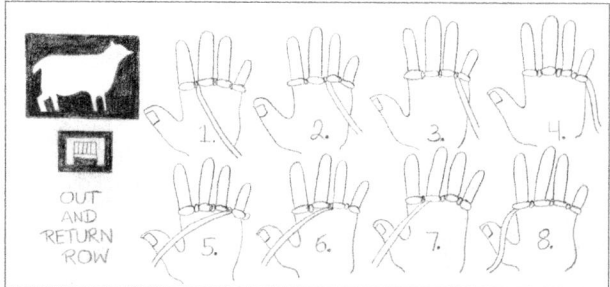

Purposeful aesthetics

You may wish to work in an optional color change introduced at the 5th and 40th rows. A lighter shade of the color you are working with will accentuate the opening in the treasure sack. Color indications such as these improve the appearance and simultaneously render the knitted object more user-friendly.

Even and odd numbers of rows

Note: The number of rows for this technique must be even so that the leed ends up back on the side it started at.

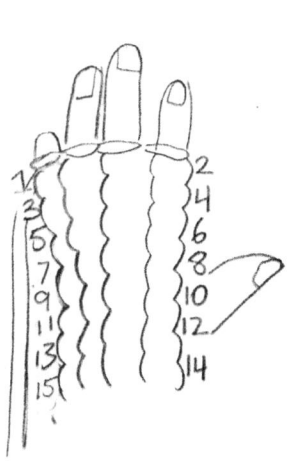

The work started on an out row, so for this column of knitted fabric all out rows are odd-numbered, and all return rows are even-numbered. This is another indicator to tell you whether you have counted the number of your rows properly.

Shore up the panel

Your knitting ends on a return row with the leed coming from the yarn-ring on Pointer. Knit a final out-and-return row as a border to attach onto mooring #2. You have finished the border on a return row.

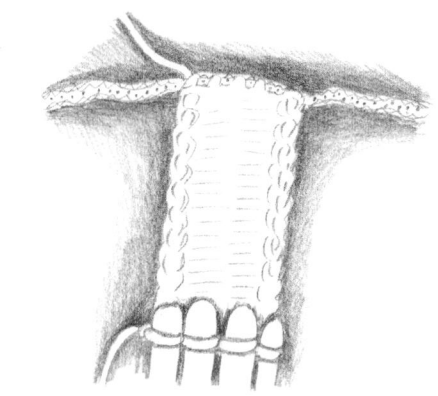

Secure end row to mooring frame

Lay mooring #2 along your Finger Palm Crease just above the yarn-rings in preparation for securing the work onto it.

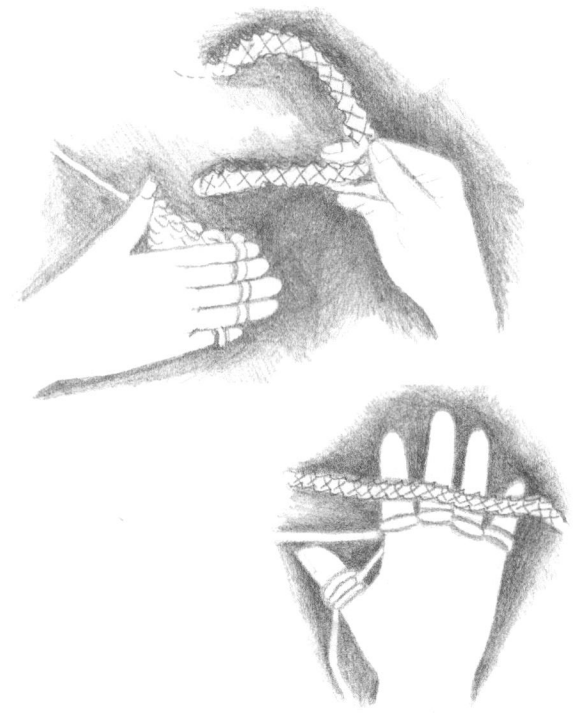

Spruce

Leapstitch over mooring

Leapstitch the yarn-ring on Pointer up and over the mooring to create a mooring ring.

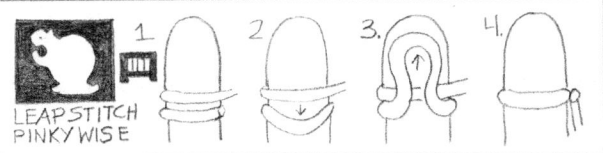

Pull out mooring end

Pull out the Thumb-most side of the mooring until it comes free of the work on that side only leaving a yarn-ring around the mooring. This yarn-ring has now become a mooring ring.

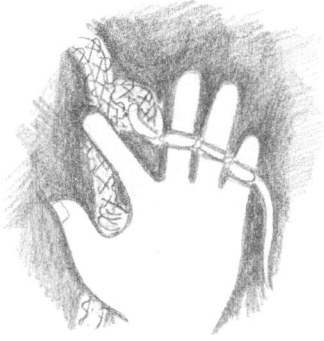

✳ You have shored up a ring onto the mooring frame, creating a mooring ring.

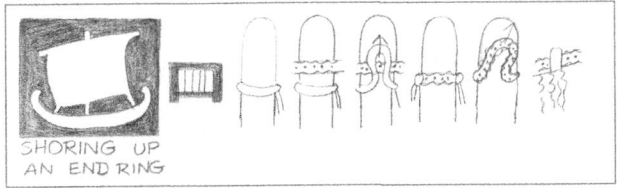

Transfer the remaining yarn-rings on Middler, Ringa, and Pinky onto the mooring in the same way.

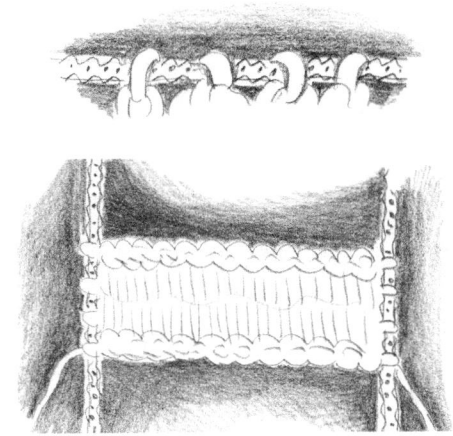

✳ You have shored up the end row of an entire column of spruce knit fabric.

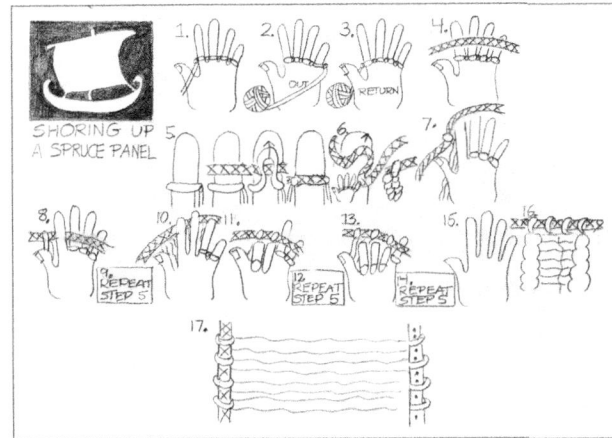

At this point you have the choice to cast-off, add more strips, or work some barehand embroidery into your strip of fabric.

Adding another panel

To add a knitted panel, bring the leed back to the start side of the work where mooring number 1 is. Leaving a length of leed between columns, hold your Loom Hand in front of mooring #1 and begin the sequence again, starting with casting on the pilot slalom style. Leapstitch a single row over the lanyard (see p. 169). When it is time to work with the leed, hold your Loom Hand in front of mooring #1, just Shuttlewise of the previous panel, and bring the leed up. Leave a stretch of it lying diagonally across the panel to where you will begin your first out row.

chapter ten

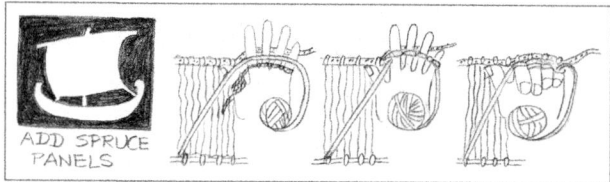

Add more panels

Repeat the steps for creating the previous panel. Create as many columns as you wish in the same number of rows. For the practice project we will knit three columns in total.

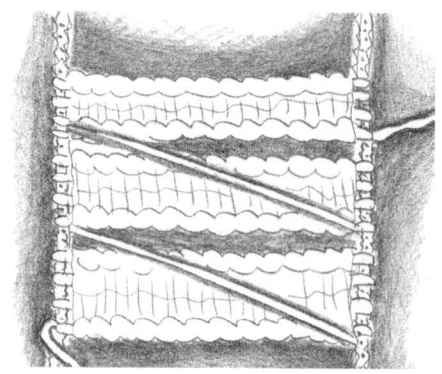

* This completes the spruce sequence for spruce-knit columns.

Keywords Reminder
for knitting spruce panels

- Prepare your yarn tools and lay them out.
- Launch spruce panel.
- Cast-on slalom style using the pilot. With the tug knot at the Thumb gap, lay the lanyard and do a single row of leapstitches. Take up the project yarn and knit an out-and-return row for the border row, followed by another out row. Secure the four yarn-rings of the start row onto mooring #1.
- Knit rows
- Knit an even number of rows of the desired length for your project. Knit an additional out-and-return row for the border row.
- Shore up panel.
- Shore up the end row of yarn-rings onto mooring #2. Double-check the number of rows you have before knitting another panel.

- Add a panel.
- Bring the leed back to the mooring you started on and launch a new column, knit the same number of rows and shore it up in the same way as previously. Continue to add columns of knitted fabric to your mooring in the same way, until you have the desired number of columns.

Prepare for Stitching

Before you stretch out the work in preparation for stitching, measure and cut your stitching-yarn so that it is three times the length of the seam you will be stitching and double it over for crisscross stitching. Once the knitted fabric is conditioned and stretched out, it will appear much longer than the final piece will be. Stitching the work brings it back to its original un-stretched length.

Preparing mooring frame

Tie the two ends of mooring #1 off on each other. Best to use a bow knot as it is easiest to undo. Do the same with mooring #2. Each mooring now forms a triangle shape.

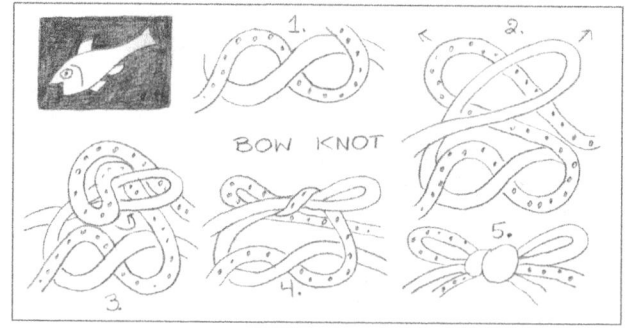

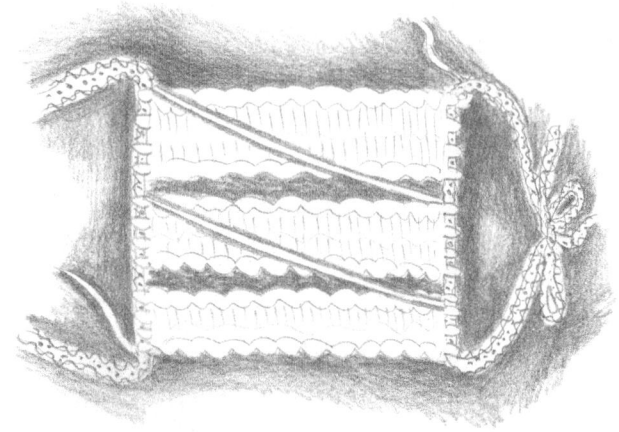

Autonomous workspace

One ergonomic option is to place one mooring triangle around your feet and the other around your waist. Adjust the lengths of the mooring triangles for good tension to create a workspace wherever you might be.

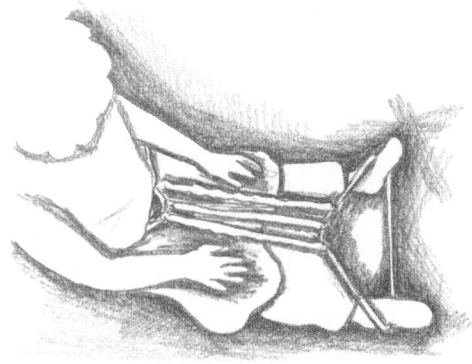

Any good surface will do

The other option is to lay the work across a flattish surface and string a piece of scrap yarn through the tips of the two mooring triangles to make a workspace out of almost any surface such as your lap or a bench, desk or table. The work should be just taut enough to give you the necessary tension needed for the stitching process. Experiment to find the best tension for you.

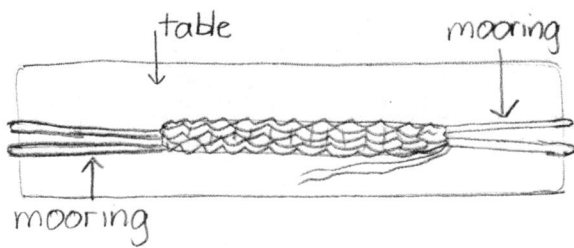

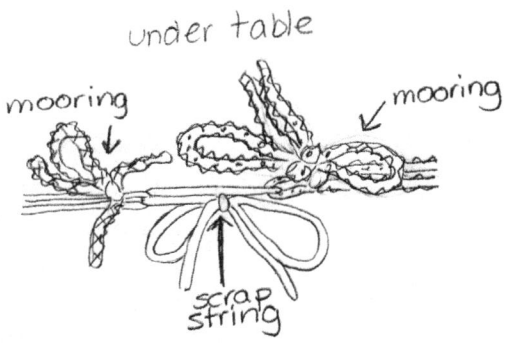

Barehand sewing tips

The stitching can be accomplished with one long unbroken strand of yarn if you "shrink-down" the stitching-yarn. This approach eliminates or greatly reduces the need for "re-threading" the stitching-yarn as you go.

Stitching techniques were introduced in a step-by-step format in *Bare Hand Knitting* Book I.

Here are a few reminders:

Prepare the seams

For all stitching techniques, remember to line up the selvages so that the matching pairs of start and finish stitches are aligned. You can check this by counting rows. Double-check that the two selvages to be stitched together have the same number of rows by recounting the number of fish lips on either side of the seam. Condition corresponding pairs of fish-lip stitches along the seams you are about to join.

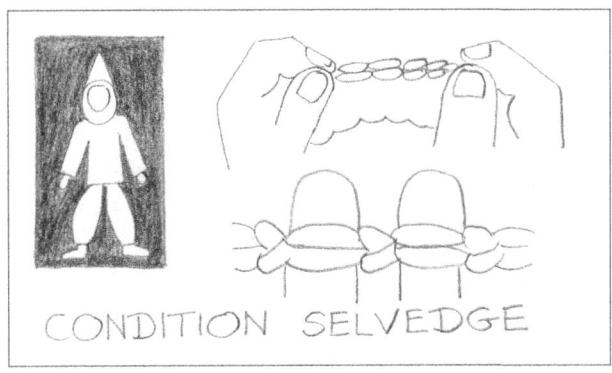

chapter ten

Remember your lockstitches

Two basic stitches

Secure the first and last stitch of every seam with a *lockstitch* (pull the thread through twice).

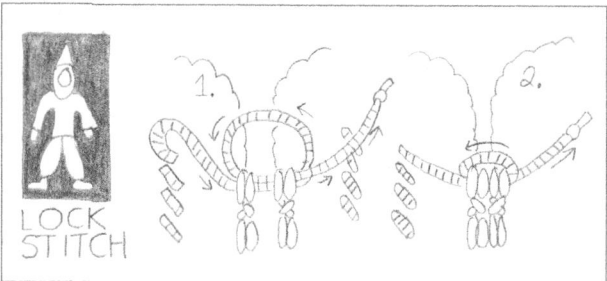

It is possible to use whip-stitching or crisscross stitches as called for in this practice project. For any type of stitching you will tie a tug knot at the ends of the stitching thread. A tug knot, or tugger for short, is used in the place of a needle.

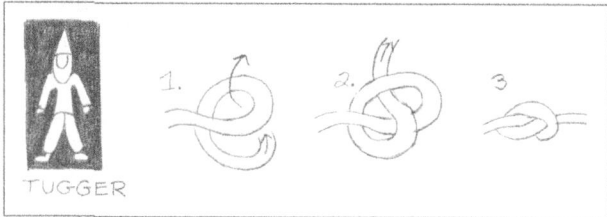

Use the *tugger* now to draw the stitching-yarn through the work. (This action is great for the development of the opposition pinch of Thumb and Pointer.)

Whip-stitching

The whip-stitch is a common stitch and its barehand component was introduced in a step-by-step fashion in *Bare Hand Knitting* Book I, Chapter 7.

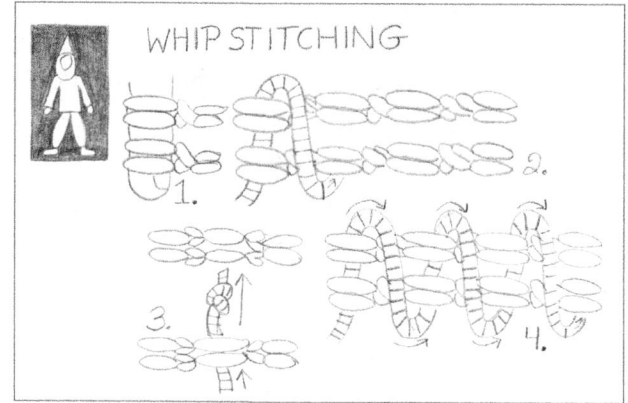

Crisscross stitching

The crisscross pattern for sewing your seam uses two alternating tug knots.

Note: Should you stitch a project with an opening in the seam (for example for a neck hole), be sure to work lockstitches on either side of the opening.

Joining seams as you knit

At the end of this chapter you will learn a method of connecting two selvages without any stitching at all, called grafting.

Dealing with the danglers

Before you begin stitching, cut the sections of diagonal-lying danglers between columns of knitted fabric.

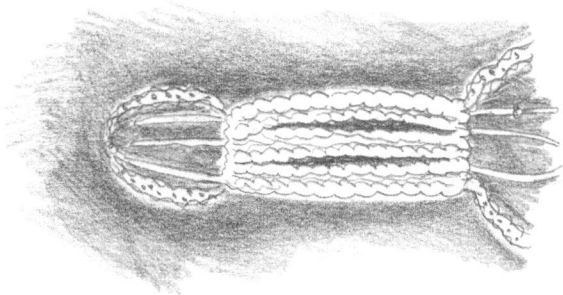

Tuck away loose ends

One at a time, tuck away the danglers and tails. To do this, place a tug knot into each and feed it under the five neighboring yarn-rings along the mooring of its column. Working through the fifth yarn-ring helps bridge the gap between strips of fabric. Then push them away to the underside of your work to have them out of the way for stitching.

Begin this process of tucking away the danglers from the mooring rings at the Loom side of the top edge of the work and work your way around until they are all tucked away.

Sewing Your Viking Pouch

This project calls for crisscross stitching, which makes for a snugger seam.

Prepare the stitching-yarn

For crisscross stitching, bend the panel at the midpoint and measure out your stitching-yarn and fold it in half so that each side is three times the length of the seam to be stitched. Shrink-down both ends of the stitching-yarn to about a yard from the tip and secure with a tell-tail.

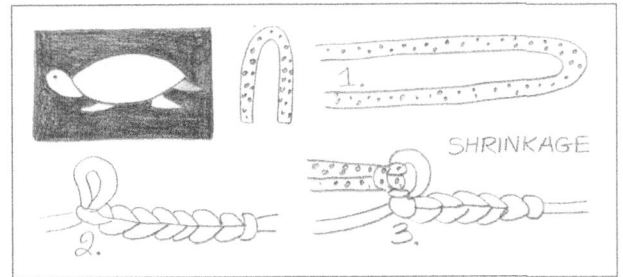

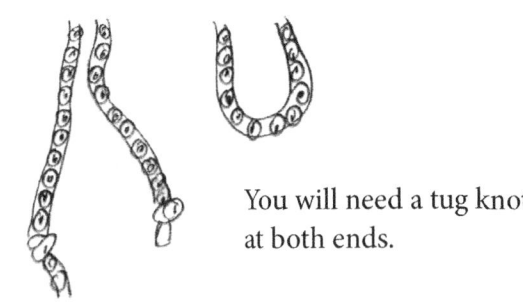

You will need a tug knot at both ends.

Begin stitching

Open with lockstitch

Begin at the top of each seam. Pull the stitching-yarn through the fishlips at the top of the seam and pull through to the midpoint of the stitching-yarn. Secure the first stitch by pulling it through a second time, making it an opening lockstitch.

chapter ten

Alternate tuggers for a crisscross seam
Work under the pairs of lips of the selvage. (You can optionally just stitch under the single inner lip of both fishlips along the selvage for a thinner seam).

Alternate tuggers for each stitch as you pull the stitching-yarn through the parallel selvages of the seam in a crisscross pattern.

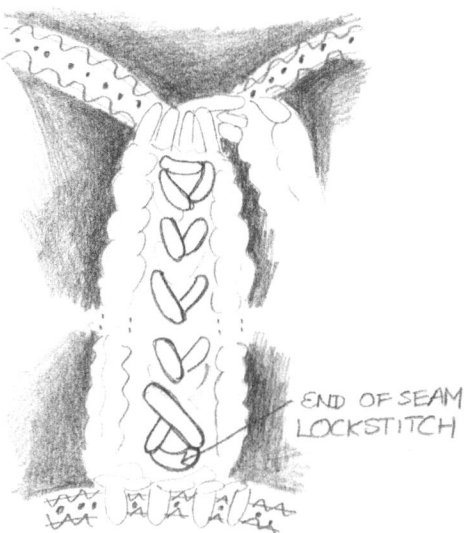

Tending to the tensions
Be mindful of the tension of your stitching and deslack as you go, but do not pull too tight. The seam should have snug and even tension in each crossed stitch.

Close with lockstitch
When you reach the end of the seam, draw the stitching-yarn through twice for a closing lockstitch.

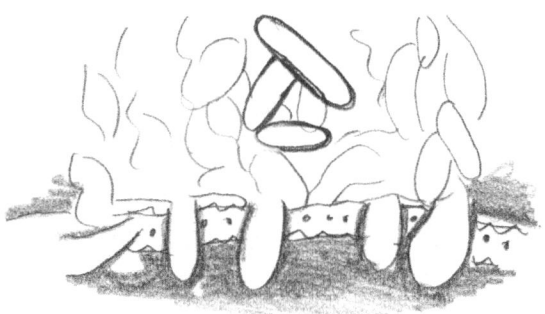

Transition to next seam
Draw the two stitching-yarn ends through the four yarn-rings of the column, along the mooring workwise, and flip the work to stitch down the next seam.

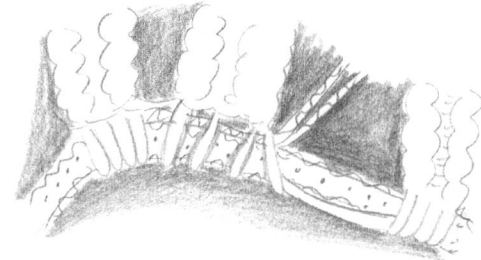

Rotate and repeat
Flip the work around and stitch up the next seam in the same way.

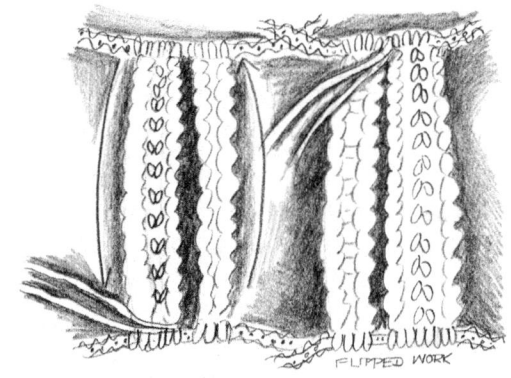

Continue stitching up the seams and rotating the work as you go until all of the panels are stitched together.

Hide the ends
Bring the danglers back to the ripple side of the kitted fabric. Weave the danglers into the seams and tie them off, except for the last dangler. Leave one free dangler for securing the last leapfrog stitch of the top edge later.

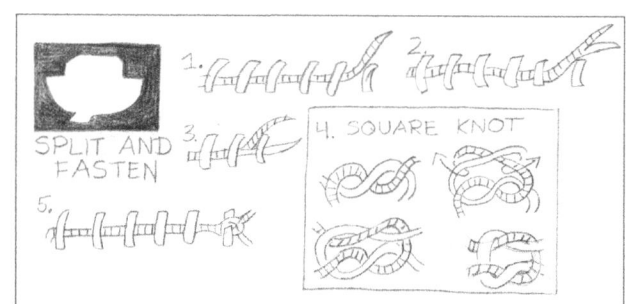

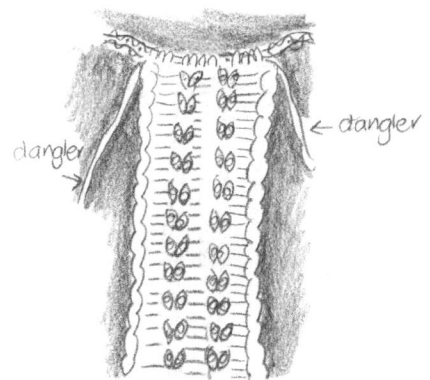

Prepare for stitching the sides

Once you have stitched up the seams, do not cut the remaining length of the stitching-yarns as you will use them to sew up one side of the pouch.

Fold work

Bring the bottom mooring frame up, laying it against the top mooring frame, creating a fold midway through the work. The work is now inside-out—ripple stitches on the outside—for the purpose of stitching up the sides.

Stitch up first side

Beginning with the side you ended on, and using the dangler as your stitching-yarn, stitch down the seam side-to-side. When you reach the end of the seam, do a lockstitch, cut the stitching-yarn, and tie off.

Stitch up second side with new yarn

Use a new doubled-over stitching-yarn to work crisscross stitches up the last side. This yarn will not need to be longer than a yard, so there is no need to shrink it down.

Finish the top rim with leapfrog stitches

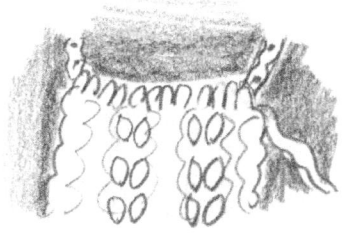

Finishing the top edge

The mooring must remain in place for this step, as it keeps the stitches even and helps with proper placement. Afterward, it will be removed.

Condition mooring rings

In preparation for stitching the top rim, adjust the tensions in the yarn-rings on the mooring frame so that they are even, not too tight or loose. Each ring should be just loose enough for your Pinky-tip to fit snugly between the loop and the mooring chain. (This way you will still be able to leapfrog the loops over one another.)

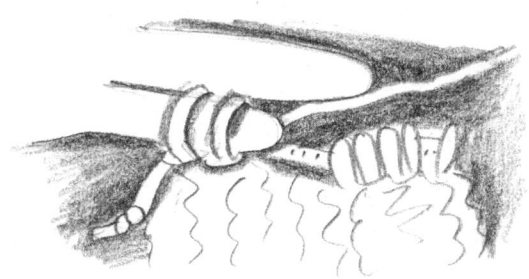

Start near the dangler

Since you will be working frog stitches in a complete circle, you will begin next to the corner stitch that has the free dangler or tail coming out of the neighboring stitch, just counter-topwise from it.

Leapstitch mooring rings

Pluck-up the top side of the first two yarn-rings above the mooring and place them onto your Loom Pinky.

Pull the first ring—the one nearest your Pinky-Notch—over the second ring—the one nearest your Pinky-Tip—and pull it off your Pinky and

181

repeat this action. These are called leapfrog stitches—or frog stitches, for short—because it is like playing leapfrog with the yarn-rings. Work your way in a complete circle right along the top rim of the mooring and tie-off using the dangler.

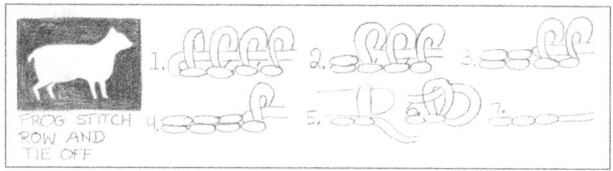

Secure the last ring

Continue working frog stitches until you have come to the last stitch near the loose dangler. Pull the loose dangler through the last stitch and through the back of the initial frog stitch, and tug until snug.

Finishing your treasure pouch

Weave-in and tie-off any last loose tails and danglers. Turn the purse right-side-out.

Finger knit the tie.

Knit a length of chain and weave it in-and-out of the fabric just under the top rim, to serve as a drawstring.

Fill your pouch with treasure and enjoy!

Variation

A purse with a shoulder strap can similarly be made using the same size of spruce-knit fabric: Just fold the fabric into three sections, to leave a flap overlapping and stitch up the two sides. Attach a stretchy strap by crisscross stitching the two ends of a length of knitted chain along the side seams.

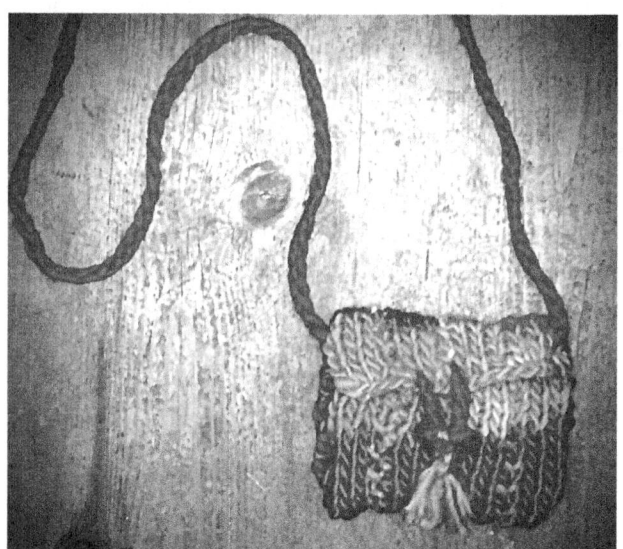

Setting your work aside mid-project

Now you know how to make a piece of knitted fabric as large as you like. If you are working on a spruce project and want to set the knitting aside to take a break, the most convenient place to pause is between knitted panels when both ends of the work are secured onto the mooring frame. At that point, tie the two ends of each length of mooring off on each other until you are ready to resume knitting.

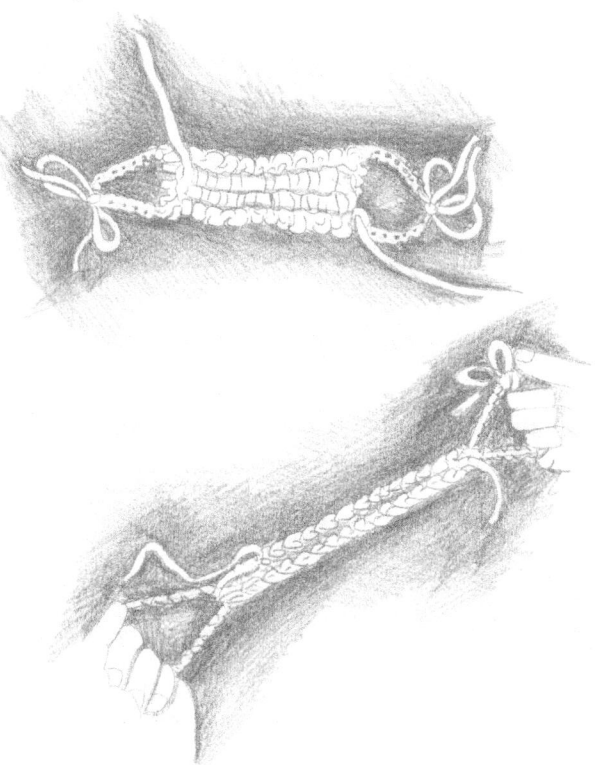

A single spruce knitted panel, made in the same way you knitted the first spruce panel will also be used as the foundation fabric for Barehand embroidery, as you will learn in the next chapter.

Variation: a single panel project

If you are knitting a single panel using the Spruce method, and do not wish to work any embroidery into it, you can at any point decide a project is complete and secure off the mooring rings using frog stitches.

At that point, you can remove the mooring by pulling it free of the work.

Grafting together spruce knit fabric

Rather than stitching the knitted columns together, you can also graft them together as you knit. Once you get the hang of grafting it opens the door to making large swathes of knitted fabric without needing to go back and stitch up the seam afterward.

There are a number of slightly different ways of grafting. We will just cover the basic extension graft here.

Begin with a spruce knit panel

Create the first panel of spruce knit fabric as instructed above.

chapter ten

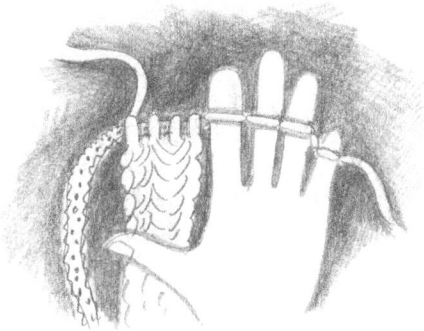

Launch the next panel
Also begin the next spruce panel as you normally would. Once the border row and the first actual out row are complete and you have secured the mooring rings, begin the next return row, but stop one digit short of completing it. In other words, do not work a Thumbwise leapstitch on Pointer upon the return of row #1.

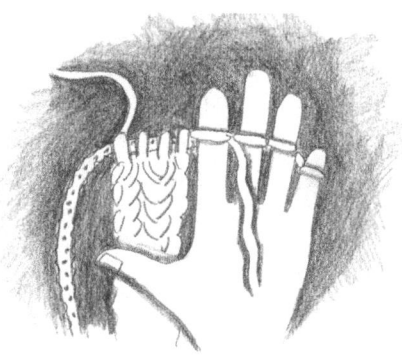

Hook and leap
Instead of completing the return row with a regular Thumbwise leapstitch, use your Pointer finger to hook up into the corresponding stitch along the parallel selvage of the previous panel of knitted fabric.

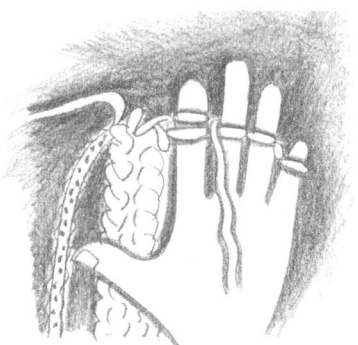

Do a leap-ring to bring the yarn-ring of the initial selvage over the upper yarn-ring that was already on Pointer.

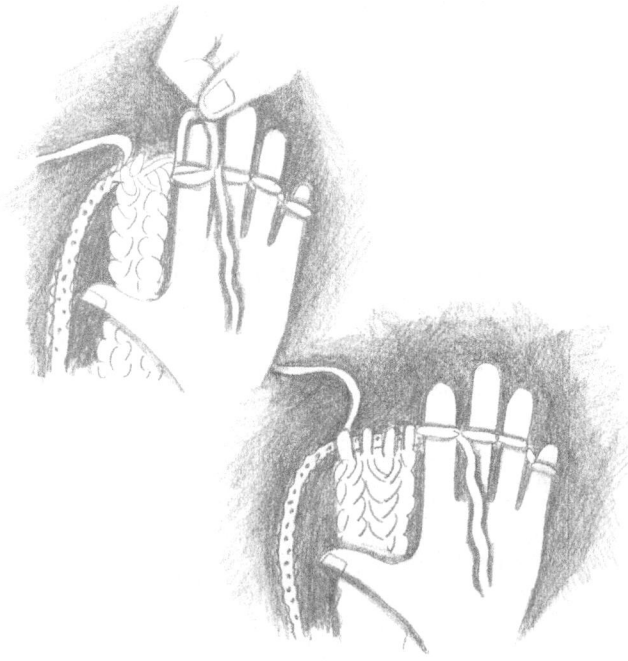

Finish out row
Now work a Thumbwise leapstitch on Pointer to complete the return row and follow it up with a Pinkywise leapstitch to initiate the next out row.

✻ You have grafted a row.

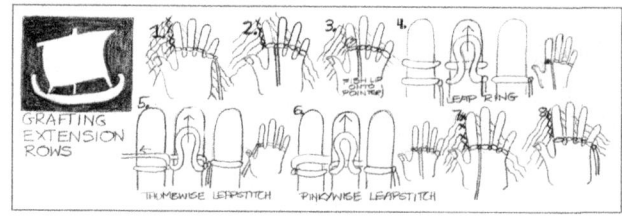

Graft-on and graftee
The previously completed panel is now the graftee panel as it will be receiving grafting stitches. The new active panel is the graft-on panel as it is applying the grafting stitches.

Continue grafting row as you knit
Complete your out-and-return row again, stopping short of Pointer on the return row and graft on again. Continue knitting graft-on rows until the number of graft-on rows matches the graftee rows and finally shore up the panel in the same way as you would for any spruce project.

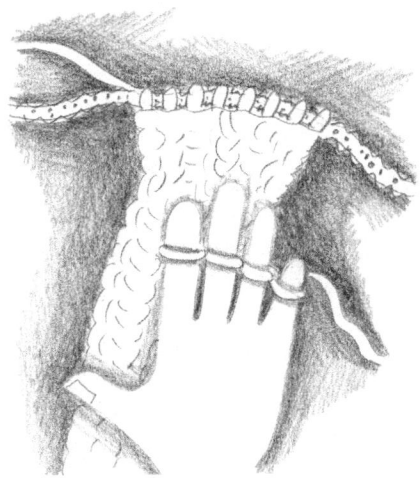

Grafting Variations

You learned to apply grafting while knitting extensions of regular spruce graft-on panels of a consistent width (four-digits) and of a consistent length. Grafting, however, can be applied when knitting with any barehand technique.

Here are some examples:
- In addition to grafting along one selvage of the knitting in progress, you can graft both sides simultaneously, creating a join between two graftee panels.
- In addition to grafting four-digit-wide panels, you can graft work of any width from a one-digit row to a 12-digit switchback row and beyond.
- You can even knit a graft-on tunnel!

Likewise, in addition to grafting a selvage with a consistent number of rows, you can graft increases (two into one) into the graftee panel. If you graft on increases back into the selvage parallel with the active panel, tapering out as you go, you can accomplish a spiral like you did in Chapter 9, only without any stitching.

Variations on that theme are a wonderful way of making all kinds of fun hats! (Apply the math from the diagram for increases on page 76 of Chapter 6 on finger crochet to help you achieve the desired geometric forms.) In other words, use your imagination and the sky's the limit!

Chapter Review

Vocabulary

pilot
lanyard
moorings
mooring ring
grafting

crisscross stitches
release lanyard
mooring frame
hook and leap

chapter eleven

Barehand Embroidery

chapter eleven

Decorative Stitching

Now for the fun part—you can decorate your barehand pieces with added embroidered designs without the use of a needle!

There are two types of embroidery stitches: *cling stitches* and *floater stitches*, which comprise interlocking loops in the same way that chain knitting does. Now, however, you will be chain-knitting through and onto a previously-finished piece of knitting called the foundation fabric. This can be any previously hand-knitted work, such as a scarf, a hat, a vest, a plain piece for a wall hanging, or simply a practice swatch to start with.

Embroidery rows run in lines that can be straight and parallel to the rows of the underlying fabric, or at a right angle, diagonal, zigzag, or curved. Barehand embroidery can be used for borders or for adding a decorative inlay between connected panels, artistic embellishment, for decorative structural reinforcement or for simply adding your initials to your creation.

Generally speaking, the stitching progresses in a Shuttlewise direction, working from left to right since it is the direction we read and write in. But working in the opposite direction is always possible, especially if one is left-handed.

Rhyme for embroidery

*Out against the garden shed, the honeysuckle vine
Climbs up along a trellis to reach the warm
    sunshine.
Where the honeysuckle reaches across an empty
    space,
A new leaf grows to gather sunshine at that place.
Where the frame it crosses, it clings and does not
    slip;
And then it sends out flowers for the hummingbirds
    to sip.*

    – H. Akin

Creating a crown with décor

Materials

You will need your collection of "yarn props" for creating the spruce foundation fabric as learned in the previous chapter.

For this project the mooring will end up acting as the tie for the crown, so choose the color and thickness accordingly. Alternatively, you can pull a different length of yarn through the mooring rings when you are nearly done, just before finishing the ends with frog stitches.

For foundation fabric: Half a skein of bulky yarn

For stitching: You will want at least three different colors of bulky yarn for stitching. The stitching-yarns should be the same thickness as that used for the foundation fabric, as this will help maintain the correct tension. Having the stitching-yarn in a ball also helps keep the right tension, so it is good to start with more than you will use, so you always have a ball to work with.

Creating the foundation fabric

Using the Spruce method, knit a strip on one hand that is just long enough to fit around the head of the intended wearer without stretching. The length of the fabric will vary a lot during the different stages of this project, but only when all of the embroidery has been inlaid will it resume its original, pre-stretched length.

When each side of the fabric has been secured-off onto the mooring, leave it in place there.

Barehand Embroidery

Set-up

Each length of mooring bears the mooring rings for one end of the foundation fabric.

Tie the two ends of each mooring off onto each other and use the scrap ties to secure the foundation fabric around a flat working surface such as your lap or a desk, so that the fabric is slightly stretched with the field stitches uppermost.

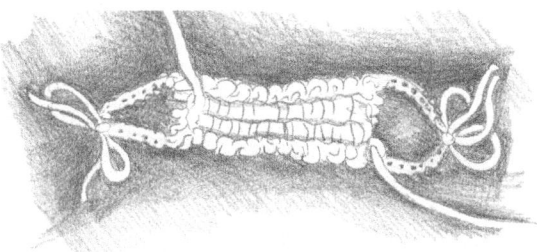

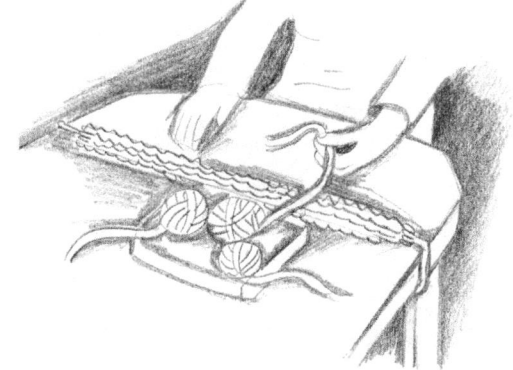

Begin stitching

Select a ball of stitching-yarn in the color you would like for your border, seat yourself comfortably and place the ball to your Loom side.

Examine your foundation fabric. If you use your fingers to spread out some stitches, you can see that it looks like a series of ladders laid side-by-side, with the "rungs" of the ladders arranged one after the other, and with "spaces" in between the rungs.

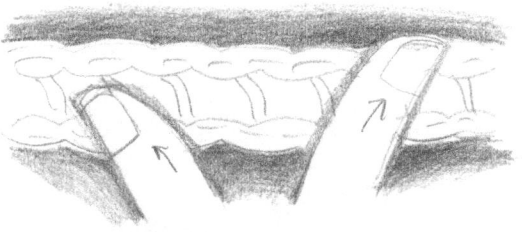

Two types of stitches

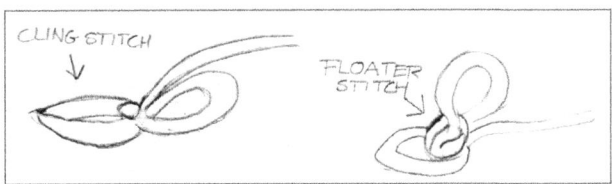

Corn rows consist of two types of stitches: *cling stitches* and *floater stitches*. The cling stitches cling or grab onto each successive rung of the foundation fabric, while floater stitches float between those that cling to the foundation fabric. The floater stitches are like those used in barehand crochet. They act as a link between the series of cling stitches in the spaces between the rungs

Make a tail-tugger slipknot in the end of your yarn. Check to make sure the slipknot tightens by pulling on the tail.

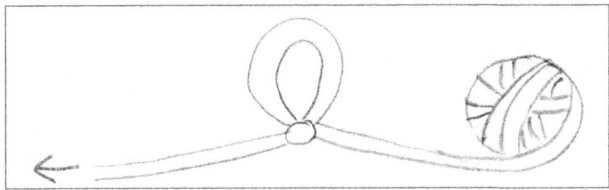

Plant the initial stitch

Starting a few rows in from the corner, you will first stitch along the upper border row of stitches (the selvage) of the foundation fabric.

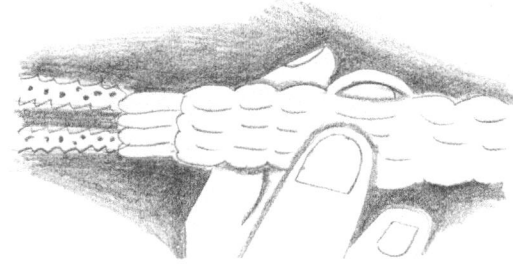

Push up half of the loop

Slip the loop of the slipknot about halfway through a fish-lip stitch that is two or three stitches away from the upper Loom-side corner of your foundation fabric. (Keep in mind these instructions will generally have you working Shuttlewise.)

chapter eleven

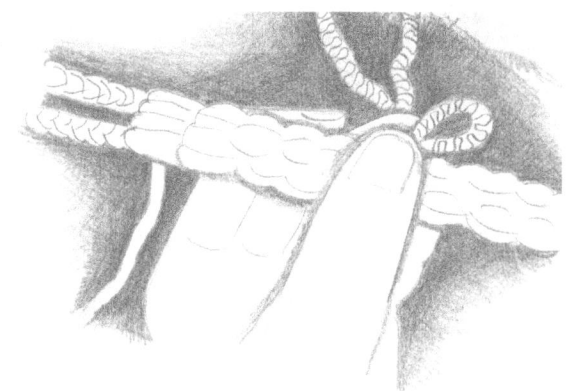

Lay top of slipknot over next fishlip

With your Loom Thumb, flatten the slipknot loop over the adjacent space, Shuttlewise, in preparation for bringing the leed up through. You may find it helpful to poke your Thumb-tip into the space a little to open it up.

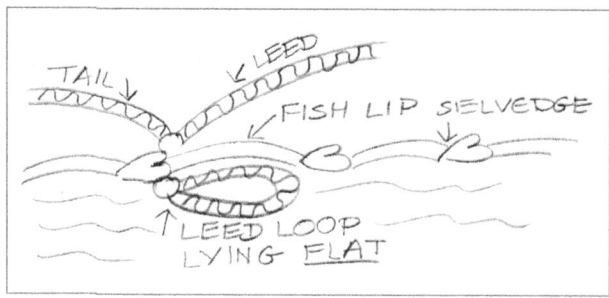

Pinch up bight

With your Loom Pointer, push a bight of the leed up through the newly opened space, then use your Shuttle bird-pinch to pluck the bight in a loop up through the space and through the slipknot loop.

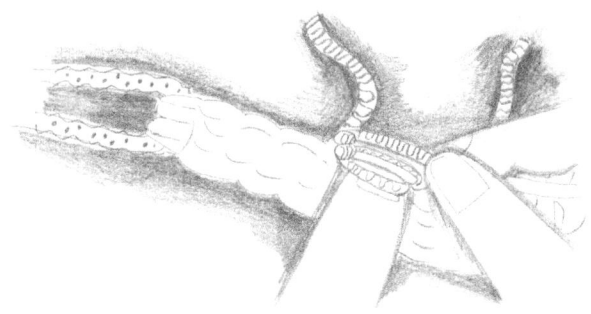

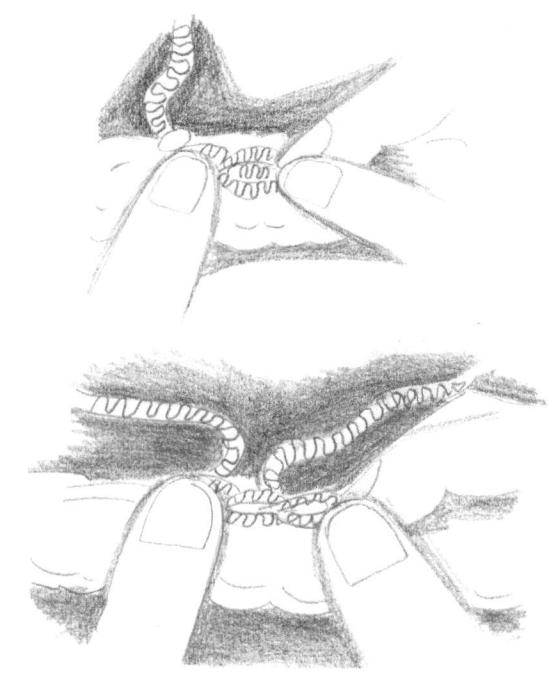

✶ You have planted the initial stitch for a closed-circuit row of embroidery inlay.

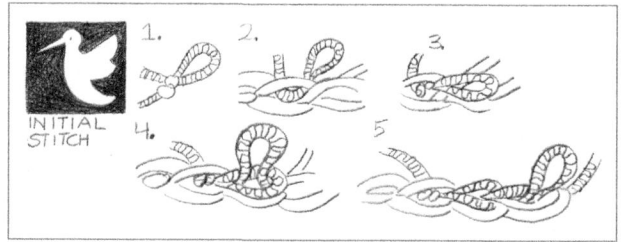

Do not pull on the tail

You may be tempted to tug on the tail of the slipknot to snug up the base of the planted stitch, but do not close it up all the way, as you will later be securing the last stitch of your border through that first loop. That is how you will close the circuit row.

Floater Stitch

Now do a floater stitch: Lay the leed loop flat across the same space its base occupies and pull another bight of leed up through it.

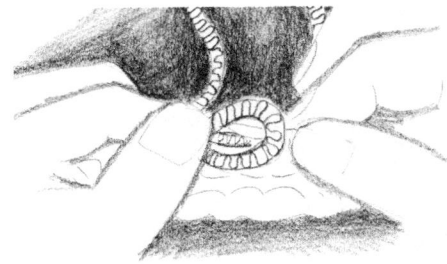

Pull again.

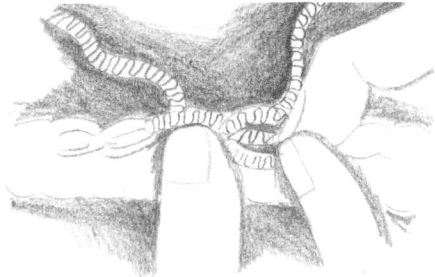

Pull loop through bight.

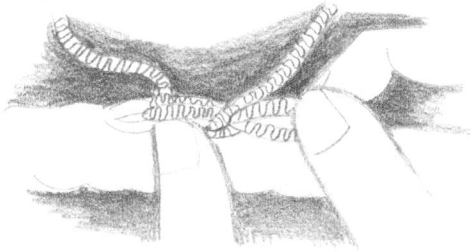

Completed floater.

As you can see a new stitch, a floater stitch, is formed by repeating the stitching-action through the very same hole as the previous stitch was worked through.

✳ You have now completed your first *floater stitch*.

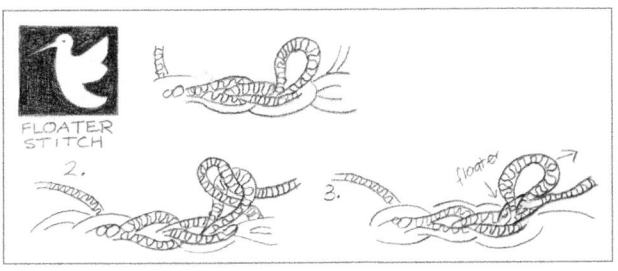

Adjusting the tensions of your inlay

Snug up previous loop
If you now tug on the Loom-side of your new bight loop, the previous loop will tighten around the base.

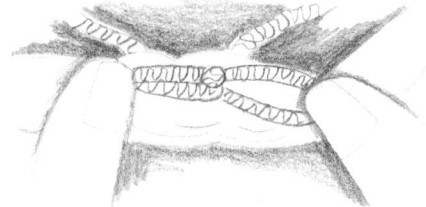

Shrink your leed loop as needed
If you need to reduce the size of the leed loop, draw it in gently by the leed.

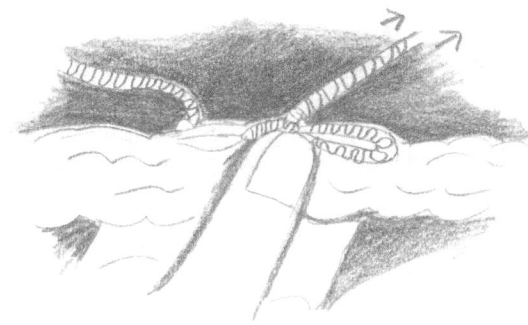

Snug up row as you go
You can work some of the slack out of loose stitches by tugging at the Loom-side of the new loop to snug up the previous stitch.

Cling Stitch

Lay the active loop down past the neighboring fishtail and over the next fish-lip stitch, along the selvage.

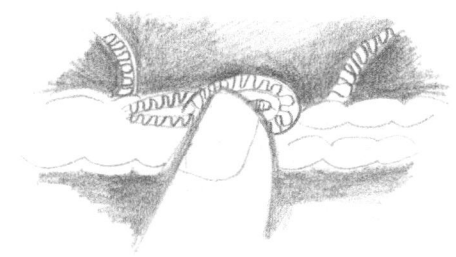

chapter eleven

Pinch another bight of stitching-yarn up through it. tugging till the stitch is snug. Cling stitches are formed when the stitching loop reaches up and is laid over the next hole over, then stitched up-through.

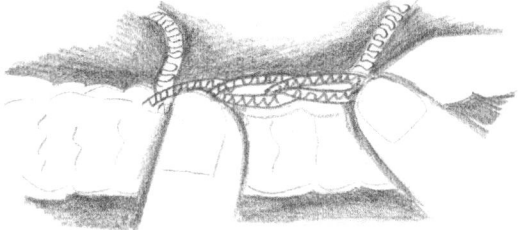

✸ You have worked a *cling stitch*.

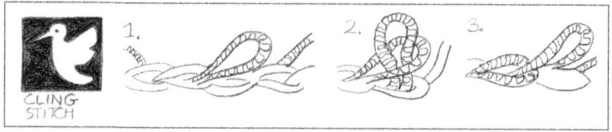

Continue Stitching

Continue alternating cling stitches and floater stitches along the border of the foundation fabric until you reach the end of the panel.

Cling stitches and floater stitches

Notice that for this pattern, the cling stitches are worked down into fishlips only where they cling to the foundation fabric, and the intermediary floater stitches are each pulled up through the same fishlip hole and worked through just the leed loop itself. This gives the stitching enough reach to skip over the fishtails along the selvage without bunching-up the fabric.

Round corners with increases

When you come to the corners of the foundation fabric, you can go round the bend by adding three extra floater stitches at each corner, on either side of the vertical row of four cling stitches along the short side.

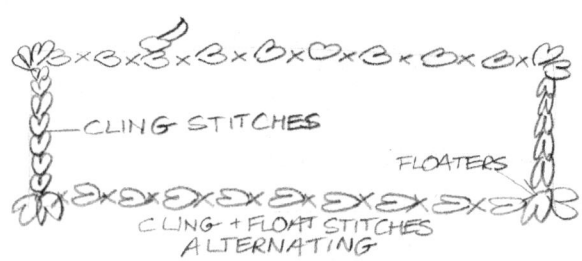

When you reach the corner of the panel, you will work a series of three or four repeat stitches just inward of the yarn mooring rings at the corner of your piece. Then continue along the vertical edge along the mooring rings until you reach the bottom corner on the Loomward side of your work.

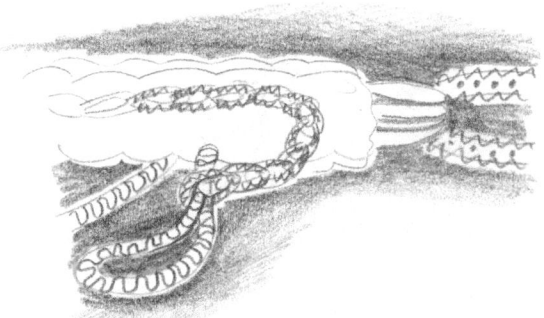

Rotate the work and continue

Once your stitching has rounded the bend, rotate the foundation fabric 180 degrees so that you can continue your stitching movements in the same direction as you embroider the opposite border. Then round the next bend and rotate the foundation fabric again.

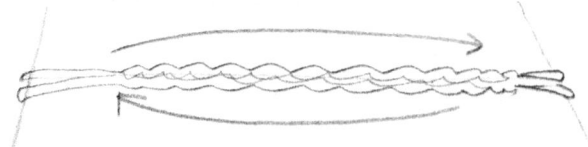

Complete the border

Complete your border by placing the last few alternating stitches along the original selvage until you reach the initial planted stitch.

Close the circuit

Align the base side of the initial planted loop under the pair of fishlips along the selvage. Cut the leed, to leave about a 6-inch dangler. Bring the leed loop over the initial pair of fishlips and push it down through the middle fishlip and down through the planted stitch to the underside of the selvage and bring the tail and dangler through the submerged loop. Tie them off with each other with a square knot.

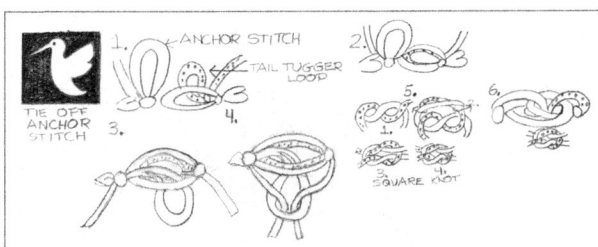

✳ You have submerged the last loop down through the initial planted stitch and have secured off the last loop.

Castle Stitch

At this point, you will do decorative embroidery only in the middle of your panel, on the same side, the field stitch side, rather than along the edge. Here you are no longer working with clearly delineated fishlips and fishtail stitches as are found along the selvage of the foundation fabric. You have only horizontal and vertical rows of field stitches. For the castle pattern we will only place floater stitches to create increases at the corners of the embroidery inlay and do consecutive cling-stiches to make the straight rows.

Switch yarn colors

Without rotating the foundation fabric, pick up a new yarn color—or keep the same color if you like—and start stitching the crenelated, or "castle-top," pattern at the bottom corner of the Loom-side of the piece, as shown.

Initiate stitch

Push a bight of the stitching-yarn up through the foundation-fabric from the underside.

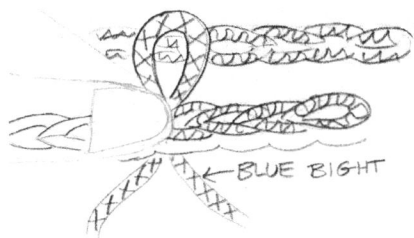

Lay loop workwise

Lay an opened loop over the next hole over in the foundation-fabric and pull another bight of the stitching-yarn up through the first hole. Snug up the first loop a bit by pulling at the top side of the leed loop.

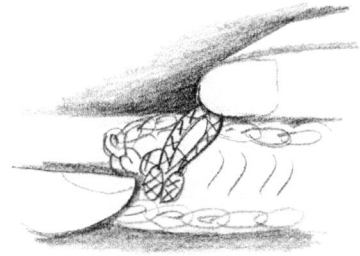

✳ You have worked an emerging polystitch.

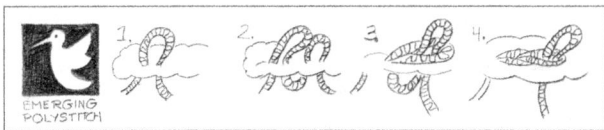

Work a straight horizontal row of four cling stitches—including the initial emerging stitch—Shuttlewise.

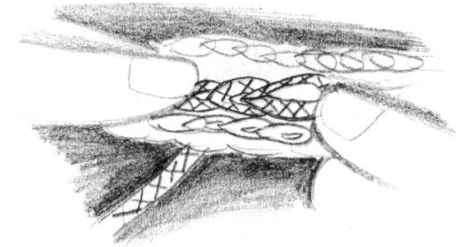

Round the corner with increases

Work two floater stitches to round the corner. (This creates an increase.)

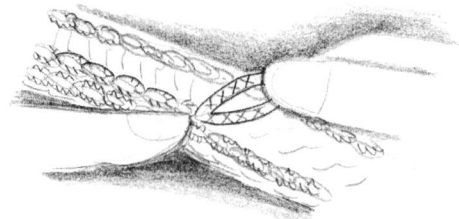

Work straight rows

Work a straight vertical row of four cling stitches across the fabric away from you. Work two floater stitches to round the next corner.

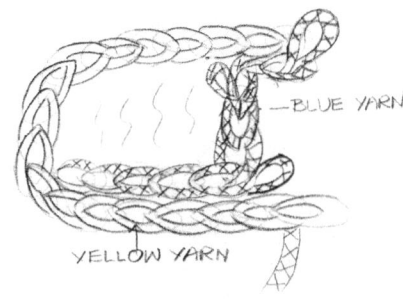

Horizontal row to corner, vertical row to corner

Embroider four horizontal stitches, followed by two floater stitches, for rounding the third corner. Do four vertical stitches, followed by two floater stitches, for rounding the fourth corner of the castle-top pattern.

∗ You have completed one open square for a castle pattern.

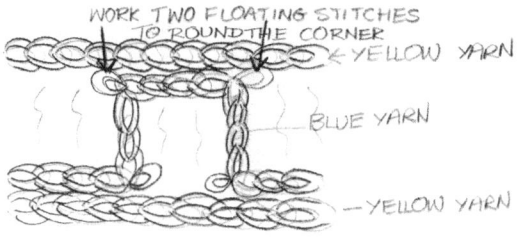

Continue to stitch the castle-top pattern until you have reached the Loom side of your piece.

Submerge the leed loop

Gently open up the leed loop a bit and push it down through the foundation-fabric to the underside.

Cut leed and tie off

Cut the leed and tie off the last stitch by pulling the dangler through the submerged loop to secure your work.

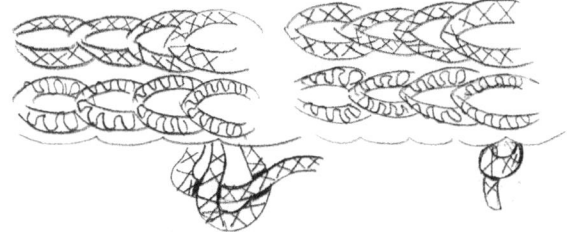

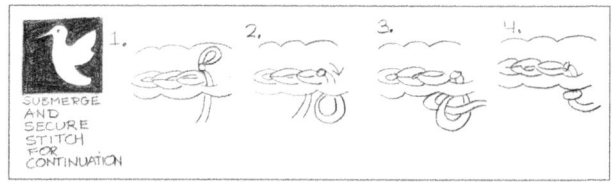

Re-emerging stitches

Choose another color of yarn and work on creating your next design pattern. The objective is to have the stitching-yarn within each square of the castle-top design disappear as it travels between squares. To accomplish this, it is neither desirable nor necessary to cut the stitching-yarn in-between sections of inlay. When you want the stitching-yarn to disappear from view for a distance, you submerge the stitching-loop and secure it off on the underside of the fabric.

Prepare stitching-yarn for re-emerging pattern

For this you will want to use shrunk-down yarn. The other option is to roll a tight little ball of stitching-yarn, just about the size of a walnut, which can be pushed through the leed loop to secure it off.

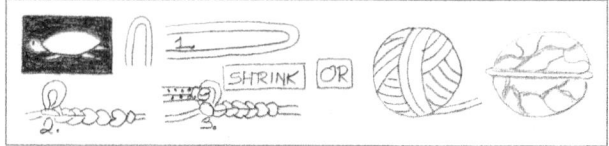

Uncut, the leed will then run under the fabric and re-emerge in the next square-over, where the pattern repeats itself. Keep doing the same until each of the lower castle-top squares are decorated.

Measure stitching-yarn

Measure out 4 yards of stitching-yarn, then chain it down to shrink it. Have a tell-tail handy. Place the tell-tail on the last stitch, about a foot from the dangler. Begin working with the end of the chain that has the tell-tail.

Begin stitching

For this project, begin at the lower Loom side of the open corner of the first square of the castle top pattern.

Work an emerging polystitch.

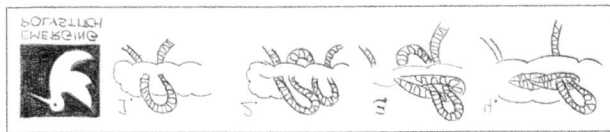

Work a series of stitches to create the design you want. Stitches can be inlaid foundation-fabric horizontally, vertically or diagonally.

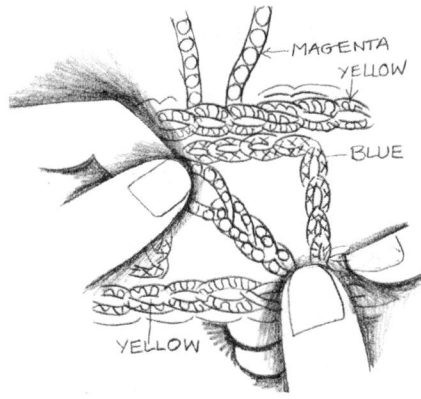

Push stitching-yarn through leed loop

Stretch the leed loop a bit to open it up and push it through to the underside of the foundation-fabric through the next opening, workwise.

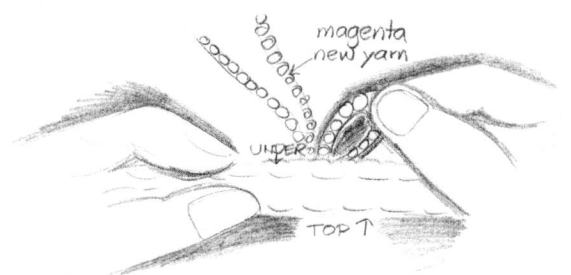

Push the entire shrunk-down chain of stitching-yarn, or the walnut-sized ball of yarn, through the loop on the underside of the foundation-fabric, securing-off that section without cutting the stitching-yarn.

✱ You have submerged the leed loop to the underside of the foundation fabric and secured-off the stitching-yarn unbroken, for continued stitching.

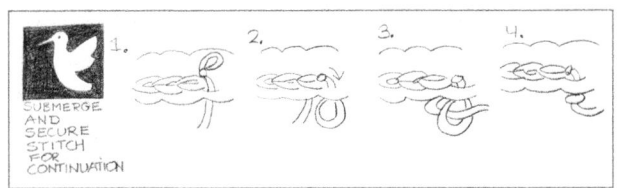

Bring the uncut stitching-yarn along the underside of the foundation fabric to where you want the stitching to re-emerge on the face of the embroidery work. There, poke a bight of the leed up through to the top side of the fabric.

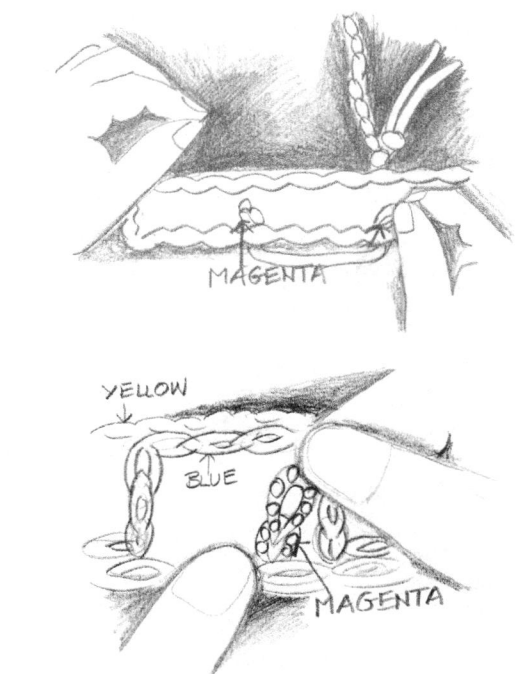

✱ You have created a re-emerging stitch pattern.

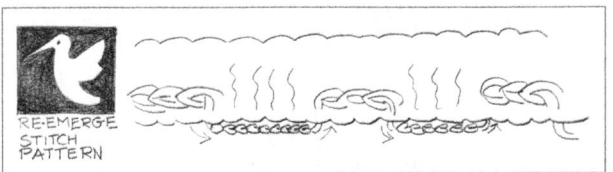

chapter eleven

Continue working stitches

Continue working in this way, laying the leed against the underside of the foundation-fabric to the point where it is to emerge, and push another bight of it up through for an emerging cling stitch.

Noticing surface tensions

You may have noticed how your stitching slightly broadens the surface of the fabric around it. In order to spread this broadening effect out evenly, you can add another row of re-emerging stitching across the top of the crown to balance the wheat-design you just completed across the bottom. Once the inner sections of the lower squares of the castle-top have been filled in with a decorative pattern, use the same stitch-sequence to add yet another pattern, or the same one in a different color, to the top inner sections of the squares of the castle-top design.

Create any pattern using the same number of stitches.

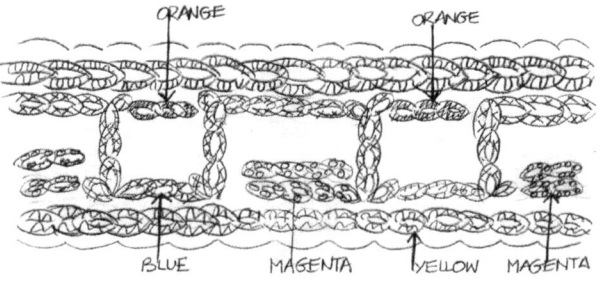

Tying-off

Finish-off by submerging the leed loop, and tie-off. Weave the dangler back into your piece.

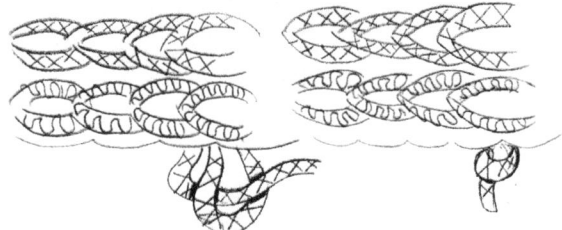

Finishing the ends

Leapfrog the four stitches of the start end and finish end of the work. Use the mooring to tie the crown at the back of the head.

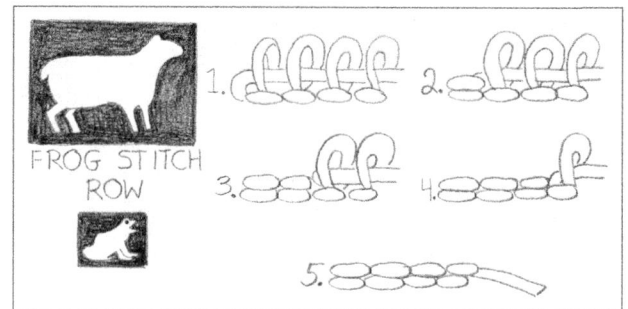

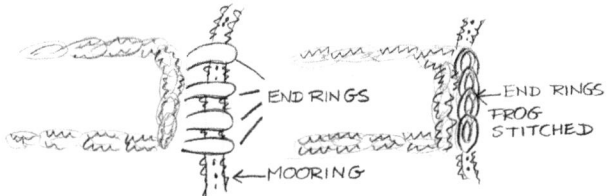

Option for securing a crown end to end

If the crown is a perfect fit, you have the option of stitching the two ends together. This can be accomplished with the tail and dangler. Place tug knots near the tips of each. Use either the tail or the dangler to do the stitching and tie them off on each other before weaving in and tying off the ends. This way of securing off a crown was introduced in *Bare Hand Knitting*, Book I.

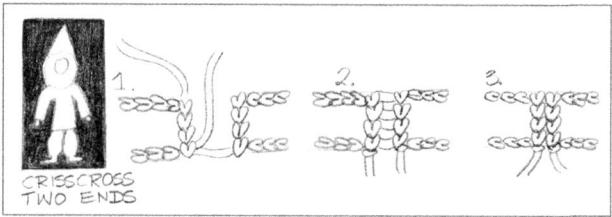

196

Embroider away!

Enjoy coming up with your own embroidery patterns and projects. The number of floater stitches and cling stitches you choose for your designs will vary, depending on the thickness of the yarn you are stitching relative to the foundation fabric yarn. In general, when doing embroidery, use your best judgment as to how many floater stitches you will need to place between cling stitches, so as not to bunch up your piece—unless bunching is a desired effect. In some instances, you may want to embroider with a length of previously knitted chain that is thick, yet flexible.

Chapter Review for "Barehand Embroidery"

Plant a stitch: Create a tail-tugger slipknot. With the leed below the foundation fabric, bring half of the t.t. slipknot up through the foundation fabric so that its front half hangs over a stitch. Bring a bight of the leed up through the slipknot and tug it to secure another slipknot into the foundation fabric, securing embroidery stitching row in place.

Border row: Work a row of stitches along the edges of the selvages into fishlips only, alternating floater stitches with cling stitches.

Floater stitch: Work a free-floating chain stitch through the active loop.

Cling stitch: Let the active loop hang over a stitch in the foundation fabric and work the leed up through the active loop, attaching it to the foundation fabric.

Emerging stitch: Create a bight in the leed and feed it up through any stitch of the foundation fabric. Proceed to work a cling stitch up through the overhanging loop, attaching it to the foundation fabric.

Castle pattern: Four cling stitches in a straight vertical line moving away from you, followed by two floater stitches with which to round the corner, followed by four cling stitches in a straight horizontal line followed by two floater stitches with which to round the corner, a straight vertical line moving back toward you. Repeat the above steps for a castle wall pattern.

Submerge leed loop: Push the active loop down to the underside of the foundation fabric.

Re-emerging stitch pattern: Work a series of embroidery stitches into the foundation fabric. Submerge a stitch and push the end of the leed through the submerged stitch to secure the active loop. Bring the leed along the underside of the fabric to where you want it to re-emerge and work an emerging stitch. Repeat this pattern for a re-emerging pattern.

Looking Ahead

You now have the techniques you need for creating many wonderful useful and beautiful projects! By combining the techniques covered in this volume you can create large blankets, a small gnome, a mobile of planets orbiting the sun or even a five-fingered glove. The possibilities are limitless and in your hands every minute of the day!

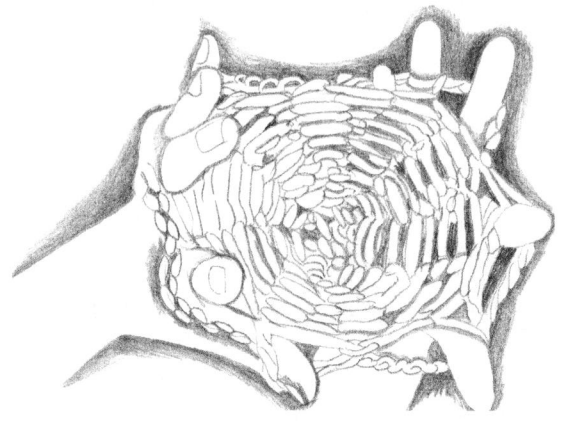

Countless additional techniques that have also been developed by the author are well within reach! Included among these are the tube, bilateral techniques, barehand nuno felting, and social knitting. The latter is a wonderful activity wherein students sit in a circle creating fabrics while simultaneously enhancing the social fabric of the group through the work itself. To receive information about instructions and projects for these and other methods, news on workshops or events, or to inquire,

Email the author at:
barehandcrafting@gmail.com

Find a variety of all-inclusive crafting kits at:
BareHandCrafting.com

To be added to Bare Hand Knitting's earth friendly snail mail, just drop a line with your contact information to the author at:

Aleshanee Akin
dba Bare Hand Crafting
PO Box 223
Wilton, NH 03086 USA

Acknowledgments

The story of how I arrived at this art form was related in the foreword to the first volume of *Bare Hand Knitting*. As the story has continued to unfold, every step of the way I continue to be astounded by the goodness of the people in my life and humbled by the faith and support that has come both from without and within, spurring me on. *Barehand Crafting* is the second book in a series that has taken over a decade to develop, write, and see come to life through its amazing illustrations. The book you now hold in your hands is not simply the result of a lengthy, extended project: It has been interwoven through the social fabric of the communities where I have lived.

Revelations sometimes occurred in mysterious and unpredictable ways, but often arose organically from the work itself. Substantiating evidence of transformation through this form of handcrafting was discernable through observations of my students at work in a classroom setting. Superb ideas arose from suggestions made by my own wonderful children and I derived much from the countless interesting conversations on this topic with my brilliant dad.

My three children, Daniella, Alessandro, and Abby, never gave up on my vision for this publication—which, early on, I did not realize would occupy our lives for most of their childhoods. I am grateful for the truly wonderful human beings that they have become, and I count them as true blessings.

Special thanks goes out to Brown Sheep Company for sponsoring my projects with, beyond compare, the best barehand-knitting-friendly yarn to be obtained for classroom use (unless you learn to spin yarn yourself from Chapter 2!) A great deal of appreciation goes out to The Research Institute for Waldorf Education and Waldorf Publications for the priceless gift of believing in this project and in me—even when the chips were down. My first illustrator gave up, and my original manuscript was plagiarized by a mass-producing publisher.

There are no words adequate for thanking Elizabeth Auer, the amazing woman who stands behind the over 1500 hand-drawn illustrations in the Bare Hand Knitting series. (There are even more if we count those that were cut during the final editing process!) A gifted artist and illustrator, she stands simultaneously as the organizational entity behind this mammoth volume of work. If beauty can save the world, a significant contribution has been made through the skilled hands and life-work of this very fine artist! – Aleshanee Akin

About the Author

Aleshanee Akin was born in San Francisco and grew up in California and Hawaii. As a child she attended the Waldorf school on Maui. This childhood experience sparked her lifelong interest in handwork and knitting with her hands.

Aleshanee has an unusual biography. As a youngster she was a youth ambassador and an advocate for world peace. She spent her teenage years traveling in Russia where she met with world leaders to promote world peace. She married in Russia and lived there, teaching in one of the first Russian Waldorf schools. Her first published book, *Nine Months and a Lifetime* (St. Petersberg, 1999, 2006), grew out of her life as a mother and a writer there.

Aleshanee earned her MEd and Waldorf Teaching Certification from Antioch University New England. She also has a LifeWays Early Childhood Certification. She has been a teacher at Waldorf schools in Hawaii, California, and New Hampshire. Her inventive techniques of knitting without tools rose from her own lifelong interest in knitting and her daughter's need for therapeutic activity during a convalescence. Currently she continues to develop and teach bare hand knitting techniques, as well as other arts and crafts.

About the Illustrator

Elizabeth Auer, MEd, lives with her husband Arthur in a little house in the big woods of the Monadnock region in southern New Hampshire. She is the author and illustrator of *Learning about the World through Drawing*, a manual for Waldorf teachers, and *Creative Pathways*, a collection of hands-on activities and projects with children ages 6–14. Most recently she has edited and illustrated a compendium of essays about how to work with children with special needs, *Helping Children on Their Way*.

With a background in design and illustration, Elizabeth has also illustrated several books including Arthur's *Learning about the World through Modeling*, a children's book *Dance of the Elves*, the Stella Natura Biodynamic Agricultural Calendar, the *Waldorf Community Cookbook*, and *Bare Hand Knitting* Book I.

Having graduated her Waldorf class in 2011, Elizabeth currently works as an adjunct faculty member at Antioch University New England and as a freelance artist. She teaches workshops in the arts and is a consultant to Waldorf and teachers in other settings. The joys and benefits of integrating arts into academic learning are reflected in her artistic skill, wit and sensitivity in illustrating the journey of knitting without tools.

Made in the USA
Middletown, DE
11 March 2023